Helion & Company Limited
Unit 8 Amherst Business Centre
Budbrooke Road
Warwick
CV34 5WE
England
Tel. 01926 499 619
Email: info@helion.co.uk
Website: www.helion.co.uk
Twitter: @helionbooks
Visit our blog http://blog.helion.co.uk/

Designed & typeset by Farr out Publications, Wokingham, Berkshire
Cover design by Paul Hewitt, Battlefield Design (www.battlefield-design.co.uk)

ISBN 978-1-804512-05-0

British Library Cataloguing-in-Publication Data
A catalogue record for this book is available from the British Library

We always welcome receiving book proposals from prospective authors.

CONTENTS

Note: In order to simplify the use of this book, all names, locations and geographic designations are as provided in *The Times World Atlas*, or other traditionally accepted major sources of reference, as of the time of described events.

Abbreviations

AA	anti-air; anti-aircraft
AAA	anti-aircraft artillery
AAMG	anti-aircraft machine gun
AB	*aeródromo-base* (airfield-base)
AD	air defence
AM	*aeródromo de manobra* (manoeuvre airfield)
AT	*aeródromo de trânsito* (transit airfield)
BA	*base aérea* (air base)
BCP	*Batalhão de Caçadores Páraquedistas* (Parachute Infantry Battalion)
CCAA	*Centro Conjunto de Apoio Aéreo* (Joint Air Support Centre)
CCEF	*Centro de Campanha de Exploração Fotográfica* (Campaign Centre for Photographic Exploration)
CCFAG	*Comando-Chefe das Forças Armadas da Guiné* (Commander-in-Chief of the Armed Forces of Guinea)
CCP	*Companhia de Caçadores Páraquedistas* (Parachute Infantry Company)
CECA	*Comissão para o Estudo das Campanhas de África* (Commission for the Study of the African Campaigns)
CEMFA	*Chefe do Estado-Maior da Força Aérea* (Air Force Chief of Staff)
CEMGFA	*Chefe do Estado-Maior-General das Forças Armadas* (Chief of the Armed Forces General Staff)
COIN	counterinsurgency
CTIG	*Comando Territorial Independente da Guiné* (Guinea Independent Territorial Command)
CZACVG	*Comando da Zona Aérea de Cabo Verde e Guiné* (Cape Verde and Guinea Air Zone Commander)
DAA	*Destacamento de Apoio Aéreo* (Air Support Detachment)
DShK	*Degtyaryova-ShpaginaKrupnokaliberny* (Degtyaryov-Shpagin large-calibre)
EMFA	*Estado-Maior da Força Aérea* (Air Force General Staff)
EMFGA	*Estado-Maior-General das Forças Armadas* (Armed Forces General Staff)
EP	*Exército Nacional Popular* (People's Army)
FAC	Forward Air Control; Forward Air Controller
FAG	*Force Aérienne de Guineé* (Republic of Guinea Air Force)
FAL	*Forças Armadas Locais* (Local Armed Forces)
FAP	*Força Aérea Portuguesa* (Portuguese Air Force)
FARP	*Forças Armadas Revolucionárias do Povo* (People's Revolutionary Armed Forces)
FFAR	folding-fin aerial rockets
FLNG	*Front de Libération Nationale de Guinée* (Guinea National Liberation Front)
GP	*Guerrilha Popular* (People's Guerrilla)
GP	general purpose
IVO	in the vicinity of
JPRS	Joint Publications Research Service
LOC	Line of communications
MDN	*Ministro da Defesa Nacional* (Minister of National Defence)
MEDEVAC	medical evacuation
MiG	*Mikoyan i Gurevich* (Mikoyan and Gurevich)
MP	*Milícia Popular* (People's Militia)
NATO	North Atlantic Treaty Organisation
NFI	no further information
N/R	not reported
OAU	Organisation of African Unity
PAIGC	*Partido Africano da Independência da Guiné e Cabo Verde* (African Party for the Independence of Guinea and Cape Verde)
PCP	*Partido Comunista Português* (Portuguese Communist Party)
PCV	*Posto de Comando Volante* (airborne command post)
POW	prisoner of war
RA	*Região Aérea* (Air Region)
RPG	rocket-propelled grenade
SADN	*Secretário Adjunto da Defesa Nacional*
SAM	surface-to-air missile
SCAA	*Secção Conjunta de Apoio Aéreo* (Joint Air Support Section)
SEA	*Secretário de Estado da Aeronáutica* (Secretary of State for Aeronautics)
SGDN	*Secretário-Geral da Defesa Nacional* (Secretary General of National Defence)
SITREP	situation report
STOL	short take off and landing
TAGP	*Transportes Aéreos da Guiné Portuguesa* (Portuguese Guinea Air Transport)
TAP	*Transportes Aéreos Portugueses* (Portuguese Air Transport)
U/I	unidentified
UAT	*Union Aéromaritime du Transport*
U.N.	United Nations
unk	unknown
USAF	United States Air Force
ZA	*zona de acção* (zone of action)
ZACVG	*Zona Aérea de Cabo Verde e Guiné* (Cape Verde and Guinea Air Zone)
ZICC	*Zona de Intervenção do Comando-Chefe* (Commander-in-Chief Intervention Zone)
ZLIFA	*Zona de Livre Intervenção da Força Aérea* (Air Force Free Intervention Zone)

Military Ranks and Positions

Portuguese military ranks broadly conformed to the American and British systems, on which the NATO table of ranks was based. Officer ranks were divided into the junior (company grade), senior (field grade), and flag (general or admiral) tiers, and enlisted personnel occupied either junior or senior enlisted ranks, the latter including non-commissioned officers.

Table 1: Air Force Officer Ranks[1]

Portugal	NATO	USAF equivalent	RAF equivalent
Alferes	OF-1	2nd Lieutenant	Pilot Officer
Tenente		1st Lieutenant	Flying Officer
Capitão	OF-2	Captain	Flight Lieutenant
Major	OF-3	Major	Squadron Leader
Tenente Coronel	OF-4	Lieutenant Colonel	Wing Commander
Coronel	OF-5	Colonel	Group Captain
none	OF-6	Brigadier General	Air Commodore
Brigadeiro	OF-7	Major General	Air Vice Marshal
General	OF-8	Lieutenant General	Air Marshal
General (4-star)	OF-9	General	Air Chief Marshal
Marechal	OF-10	General of the Air Force	Marshal of the RAF
NATO grades OF-1 through OF-2 = Junior (or Company Grade) Officer NATO grades OF-3 through OF-5 = Senior (or Field Grade) Officer NATO grades OF6 through OF-10 = Flag (or General) Officer			

Table 2: Air Force Senior Enlisted/Non-commissioned Officer Ranks

Portugal	NATO	USAF equivalent	RAF equivalent
Primeiro-Cabo	OR-4	Senior Airman	Corporal
Segundo-Sargento; Furriel	OR-5	Staff Sergeant	none
Primeiro-Sargento	OR-6	Technical Sergeant	Sergeant
Sargento-Adjudante	OR-7	Master Sergeant	Flight Sergeant; Chief Technician
Sargento-Chefe	OR-8	Senior Master Sergeant	none
Sargento-Mor	OR-9	Chief Master Sergeant	Warrant officer

1
An 'Uncomfortable' Command

'The Command entrusted to me was not 'comfortable'. It was necessary to start by reforming attitudes of mind, fighting against vicious routines, and creating as efficient a war machine as possible with the means available.' (*Coronel* José Krus Abecasis, Portuguese air commander in Guinea, 1965–67)[1]

By mid–1966 the war for Portuguese Guinea was well into its fourth year, and not going Lisbon's way. Despite the steady build-up of Portuguese forces following the outbreak of rebellion in January 1963, insurgents of the *Partido Africano da Independência da Guiné e Cabo Verde* (PAIGC – African Party for the Independence of Cape Verde and Guinea) posed an increasingly grave challenge to Portuguese colonial rule.[2] Highly motivated, ably led, and increasingly well-armed, by the summer of 1966 the PAIGC had recovered from losses incurred during Portugal's early counter-offensives and embarked on a sustained campaign of military harassment, economic disruption, and ongoing popular mobilisation.[3] 'The enemy continues to make the greatest efforts to enlarge the area affected by his action,' observed Portugal's provincial governor and military commander[4] *Brigadeiro* Arnaldo Schultz[5] in a July situation report. 'He does not appear to lack resources in terms of weapons and ammunition, and there are no signs his manpower has been significantly reduced.'[6] During the previous two years PAIGC activity had steadily intensified in every sector, but especially in southern Guinea where 'the enemy [was] most strongly rooted,'[7] and by its own accounting the PAIGC by then occupied and controlled 50 percent of the entire province.[8]

The small, inhospitable, resource-poor *Provincia Ultramarina da Guiné* (Overseas Province of Guinea)[9] was considered the least valuable remnant of Portugal's 500-year-old colonial legacy, which also included the far more lucrative and populous territories of Angola and Mozambique. Indeed, since the abolition of the Atlantic slave trade Guinea had become a net liability on the Portuguese treasury, of value to only a handful of corporations that wrung a modicum of profit from the cultivation of groundnuts and palm kernels.[10] But despite the territory's anaemic economic potential and negligible European population, the worsening situation there presented the most serious military threat to continued Portuguese rule throughout its overseas empire. As one senior officer informed *Brigadeiro* Schultz in August 1966, 'if it is true that the Overseas War cannot be won in Guinea, it can, on the other hand, be lost completely there.'[11]

To quell the expanding insurgency, Portugal had flooded the province with military manpower. Troop strength more than doubled between 1963 and 1966, growing from 9,650 personnel to 20,801, including larger contingents of special forces such as commandos, paratroops, and marine infantry (*fuzileiros*).[12] Portuguese surface

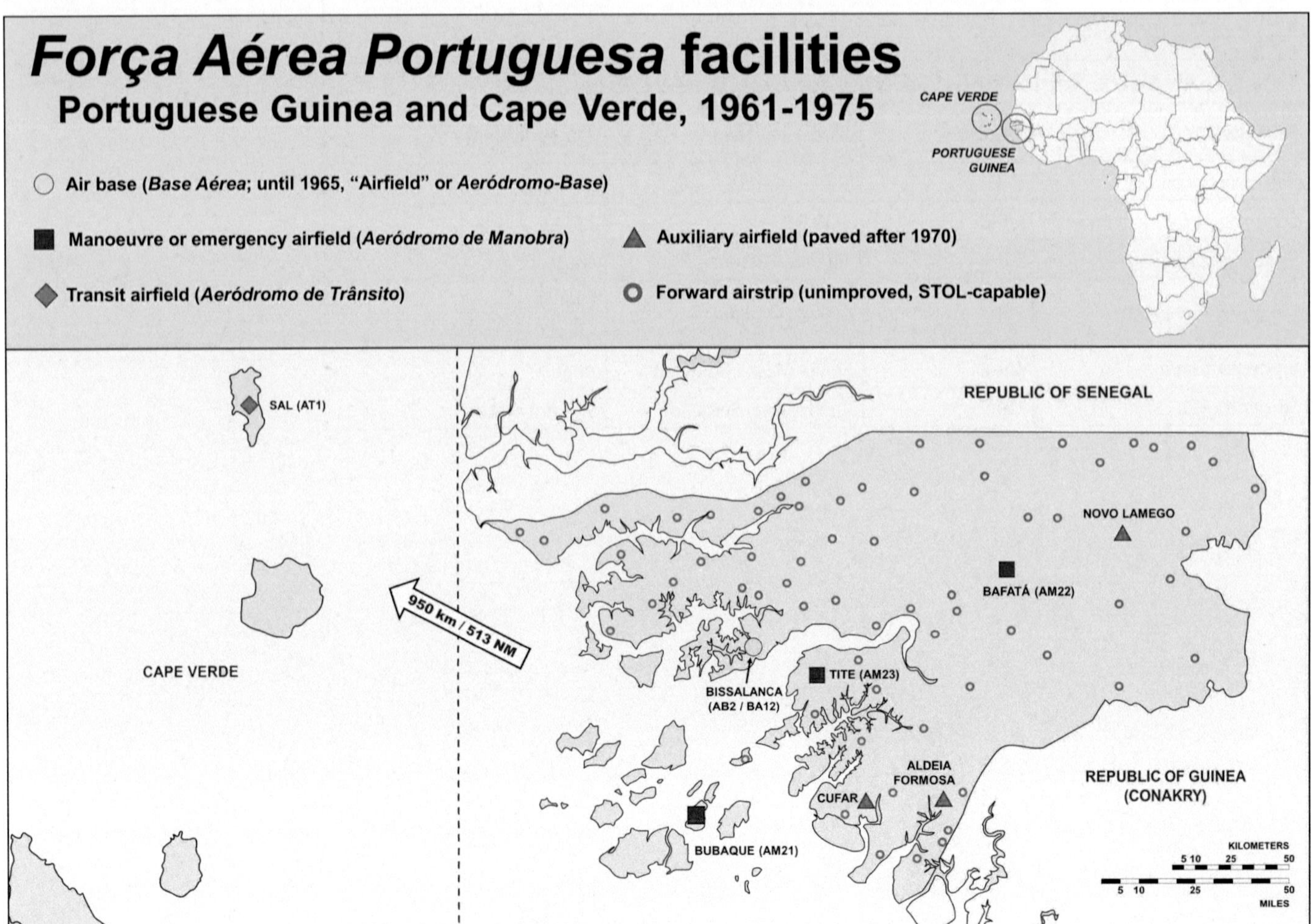

FAP installations, Guinea-Cape Verde theatre 1961–1975. (Matthew M. Hurley)

A unit of the PAIGC armed forces crossing one of the Savannas in southern Guinea. (Familia Cristiana Archive)

forces in Guinea, however, suffered from chronic shortfalls in training, equipment, and morale compared to their allegedly 'irregular' opponents, who were 'perfectly adapted to the terrain and life in the bush, well-trained in this type of warfare,' and under 'competent operational direction,' according to an August 1966 assessment by Portugal's Deputy Secretary for National Defence,[13]

Brigadeiro Arnaldo Schultz, Governor, and commander of the Portuguese forces in Guinea from 1964 to 1968. (José Matos Collection)

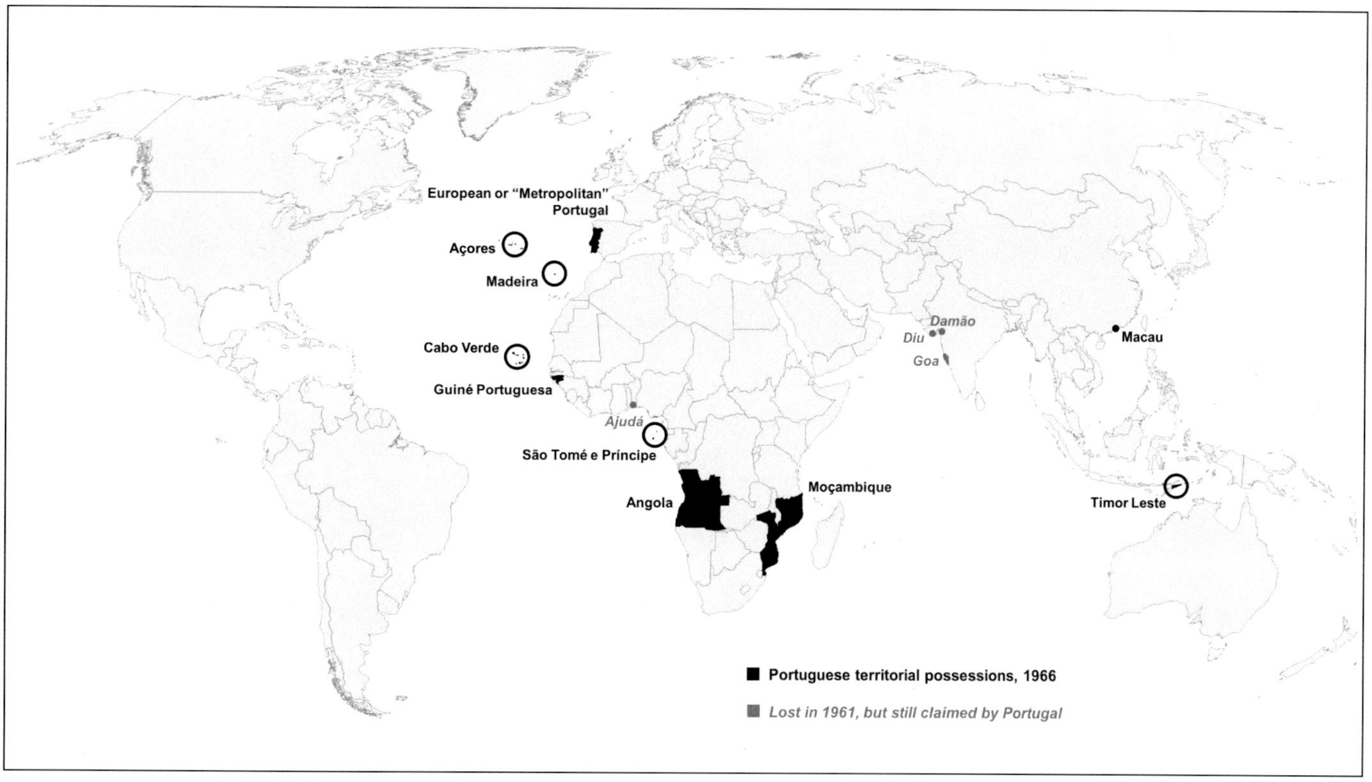

The Portuguese *Ultramar*, 1966. (Matthew M. Hurley)

Portuguese Army barracks in Guinea. The worsening military situation in the colony became a serious threat to the continuity of Portuguese rule throughout its overseas empire. (José Matos Collection)

Portuguese naval assets in Guinea. (Virgílio Teixeira Collection)

General Venâncio Deslandes. To correct this imbalance, Deslandes considered creating specialised artillery units or rearming naval vessels to provide supporting fires to ground forces, but ultimately concluded that 'the simplest and possibly quickest way to achieve this objective would be the reinforcement of air power.'[14]

By the raw numbers, that reinforcement had been underway since the war's beginning: from 1963 to 1966 military aircraft assigned to the province increased from 32 to 50 (see Appendix I).[15] However, the aggregate increase in numbers belied systemic shortfalls that hamstrung the *FAP*, the Portuguese Air Force, throughout the conflict. Chief among these were a chronic shortage of pilots and maintenance personnel, insufficient base facilities, and 'a general clamour for spare parts' and ordnance, according to *Coronel* José Duarte Krus Abecasis, commander of the FAP's *Zona Aérea de Cabo Verde e Guiné* (ZACVG, Cape Verde and Guinea Air Zone) until January 1967.[16] This last issue included a shortage of engines for the ZACVG's three Second World War-era C-47 Dakota transports, only one of which was reliably available for operations throughout 1966 due to maintenance difficulties. Mechanical failures and the scarcity of parts also limited Do-27 employment in Guinea, degrading the FAP's ability to supply Portuguese surface forces, and its serviceability rates were further depressed by a lack of qualified technicians and crew chiefs.[17] The maintenance quandary affected the entire FAP, which only avoided a service-wide stand-down in July 1966 with emergency funding.[18] Continued protests by senior Air Force officers and officials resulted in modest improvements

Deputy Secretary for National Defence, General Venâncio Deslandes, advocated strengthening Portuguese air power in Guinea in 1966. (National Defence Archive)

by Autumn 1967, but spot shortages, unfulfilled requirements, and 'excessive' delivery times continued to plague the FAP for the rest of the war.[19] As a result, according to Portuguese Secretary of State for Aeronautics, Fernando Alberto de Olivera, in 1968, 'the Air Force has not been able to regularly carry out all the support activities that by law are incumbent upon it alone.'[20]

Airfields and associated facilities likewise proved inadequate during the first phase of Portugal's war in Guinea. The FAP's main installation and ZACVG headquarters at Bissalanca had not even been designated a permanent air base (*Base Aérea*) until May 1965, two and a half years into the conflict; until then it had served as a second-tier *aeródromo-base*.[21] Even after its redesignation, Bissalanca's *Base Aérea* 12 (BA12) wanted for adequate personnel lodging and shelters to accommodate the new aircraft arriving throughout 1966.[22] The base's air defences, meanwhile, were deemed 'irrelevant' despite the handful of obsolescent 40mm and 12.7mm guns assigned to BA12's lone anti-aircraft platoon.[23]

Bissalanca's air defences were made up of a handful of 12.7mm and 40mm guns assigned to BA12's sole anti-aircraft platoon. (Historical Archive of the Air Force)

Filling the ranks of the growing FAP organisation in Guinea presented another daunting challenge. From 1966 to 1967 the ZACVG could call upon only 40 pilots to fill 52 aircrew positions – a significant improvement from the 50 percent manning levels available in 1963, but still leaving one in four cockpit seats vacant.[24] 'Given the intense activity in that theatre,' Schultz informed Defence Minister Manuel Gomes de Araújo in March 1967, 'the lack of pilots with which the Air Zone is struggling entails an appreciable burden for existing pilots.' Personnel shortfalls were

Aerial view of Air Base No.12 (BA12) in the mid–1960s. At that time, the T-6 was Portugal's main combat aircraft in Guinea. (José Nico Collection)

A Nord 2501D Noratlas in Portuguese Air Force service visiting Bristol (Lulsgate) Airport in 1969. This aircraft was the ex-West German air force Noratlas that Portugal had purchased from that country. This Noratlas belonged to *Esquadra 92 'Os Elefantes'*, based in Angola. (Chris England Collection)

An FAP C-47 Dakota ('Skytrain' in U.S. military service). In Guinea Portugal employed these venerable aircraft for air transport, photoreconnaissance, and night bombing operations. (Virgílio Teixeira Collection)

exacerbated by poor planning, ill-timed rotation schedules, and a 'petty reality' – a general unwillingness among pilots to volunteer for duty in Guinea, and a corresponding reluctance among their superiors to compel officers to serve in that 'hard and underpaid' assignment.[25]

Despite the increase in the number of aircraft assigned, the ZACVG consistently protested that it lacked the *right* aircraft. Senior Portuguese officers complained repeatedly about the ZACVG's 1) scarce helicopter lift potential, 2) lack of a fast attack platform, 3) inadequate intra-theatre airlift, and 4) anaemic medium bombing capability. The first shortfall – rotary-wing lift – had been largely addressed by the introduction of the French-produced Alouette III helicopter in late 1965; by March 1966, nine were assigned to the ZACVG, enabling commencement of the helicopter assault operations which featured prominently for the rest of the war.[26] With regard to fixed-wing airlift within the province, Portuguese forces faced a peculiar operational contradiction. Guinea's small size implied rapid surface movement: the territory occupied only 36,000 square kilometres, an area only slightly larger than Belgium. However, the prevalence of forest and marshland – combined with heavy seasonal rains, tidal floods, and long-term infrastructural neglect – compelled Portuguese forces to rely on aviation to satisfy transport requirements within the province.[27] By *Coronel* Abecasis' estimate, 'air transportation was the only option in 85 percent of the territory' when he took command of the ZACVG in June 1965.[28] Yet 'the existing availability [of airlift] falls short of the needs,' Portugal's army commander in Guinea protested in October 1966, meaning essential resupply operations 'cannot be done regularly, due to the lack of air transport capacity, without resorting to chartering civil aircraft.'[29] Indeed, the ZACVG routinely conscripted civilian planes of the *Transportes Aéreos da Guiné Portuguesa* (TAGP), but it found a more enduring solution in the purchase of French-built *Noratlas* transport aircraft. Those would not become available until 1971, however, forcing Portuguese forces to rely on the ZACVG's ragtag assortment of cast-off Second World War cargo craft and bush planes.[30]

Equally alarming from a utilisation perspective, the workhorse of the airlift fleet – the venerable C-47 Dakota – was given the additional (and resource-intensive) duty of supplementing ZACVG bombing operations. From 1965–66 the three Dakotas then stationed in Guinea, fitted with improvised weapons mounts and a rudimentary aiming sight, were employed as night bombers during major ZACVG operations such as December 1965's *Operação Resgate*.[31] Although the in-house modifications provided a modest boost to the ZACVG's bombing effort, the need for them underlined the scarcity of medium attack options available to the FAP in Guinea.[32] That shortfall became more apparent with the withdrawal of two P2V-5 Neptune maritime patrol aircraft from the ZACVG; those planes, also used as stopgap bombers, were grudgingly returned to mainland Portugal in 1966 following intense American diplomatic displeasure over their use in colonial combat over Africa.[33]

To restore this capability Lisbon sought to acquire a dedicated medium bomber as its African wars intensified. Between 1962 and 1964, Portugal negotiated the purchase of up to 25 English Electric

A FAP P2V-5 Neptune and F-86 Sabre at AT1, on the island of Sal in Cape Verde. (Touricas Collection)

A FAP B-26 Invader in Angola. Portugal clandestinely bought seven of these aircraft to serve in its African wars. (Historical Archive of the Air Force)

In the early 1960s, Portugal considered buying 25 English Electric Canberra B.2 medium jet bombers, but eventually gave up on the deal due to political and budgetary restrictions. (José Matos Collection)

Canberra B.2 medium jet bombers; however, the UK government declined the sale when Lisbon refused to guarantee the bombers would not be used in its colonial conflicts.[34] Rebuffed by its oldest ally, Portugal turned to its most important, the United States, to obtain 24 surplus Second World War-era B-26 Invader bombers. Washington, too, declined the deal because of its own restrictions on arms sales to Lisbon, leading the latter to seek a smaller number from a private American supplier through 'irregular' channels.[35] Seven B-26s were delivered to Portugal before the operation was disrupted by U.S. authorities in 1965,[36] but only two would ever see action in Guinea, and that only during a three-month combat evaluation in 1971.[37]

Portugal's inability to acquire medium bombers compelled the ZACVG to rely on tactical fighters and light attack aircraft for its entire offensive effort, and of all the FAP's deficiencies in Guinea the lack of a fast jet attack platform was the most acute as 1966

The North American T-6 Texan was the workhorse of the Portuguese forces in Guinea, performing a variety of attack and fire support roles. (José Nico Collection)

Two FAP F-86F Sabres on the island of Sal in Cape Verde. Due to strong American pressure Portugal was forced to withdraw these fighters from Guinea, and they returned to their original base in Monte Real. (Touricas Collection)

Following their 1964 withdrawal from Guinea, Portuguese F-86s would never fly again in the skies of Africa. (Touricas Collection)

began. At the war's start three years earlier, Portugal's theatre air command could employ up to eight each F-86F Sabre jet fighters and T-6 Texan piston-engine, armed trainers to fulfil the various attack and fire support roles, but by 1964 Portugal had succumbed to intense American pressure to withdraw the F-86s. This left the slow, antiquated T-6 as the sole tactical attack asset in the ZACVG's inventory, a fact that worried Brigadeiro Schultz considerably. Portugal's military commander in Guinea understood the importance of airpower to his strategy – particularly the FAP's ability to provide fire support to surface forces – and he agreed with his air commanders that the T-6s alone were insufficient to the task.[38] The 1930s origin aircraft were designed and built as trainers, not warplanes, and they lacked the armour plating, self-sealing fuel tanks, and redundant systems characteristic of dedicated combat aircraft.[39] By 1964 the ZACVG's T-6s had already proven 'increasingly vulnerable in the face of the constant improvement of the enemy's anti-aircraft resources,' as Schultz had complained to Defence Minister Gomes de Araújo.[40] Portuguese pilots also complained that the T-6's machine guns frequently jammed due to age and wear, while the enemy – aware of the noisy aircraft's slow speed and approximate transit time to any point in the province – knew when to break contact before their arrival at the scene of an attack.[41] By the Autumn of 1966 the ageing trainer's utility was largely limited to pre-planned escort missions supporting ground columns and river traffic, although that was an increasingly essential task given the PAIGC's preference for ambushes and hit-and-run attacks.[42]

Fiat Aviazione G.91-R4 light strike fighters in flight over Germany. The R4 variant was originally produced for Greece and Turkey; the aircraft were ultimately sold to Portugal after those nations retracted their purchase agreement. (José Matos Collection)

To resolve the gap in offensive capacity, the FAP sought to acquire 65 second-hand Canadian-built F-86 variants for service in Guinea. The West German *Luftwaffe* had recently withdrawn its Canadair CL-13 Sabre Mk.6 fighters in favour of the F-104, and the jets' Canadian manufacture presumably shielded them from American sanctions. Nonetheless, Washington adamantly lobbied to prevent their use in Portuguese Africa; this pressure, along with Canada's own reluctance to facilitate Lisbon's imperial ambitions, ultimately persuaded Ottawa to veto the sale.[43] They did so despite Portuguese assurances that the aircraft were 'to be used on Portuguese territory and strictly and exclusively in defensive missions of this same territory,'[44] and even though FAP pilots and maintenance personnel had already been dispatched to West Germany for training on them.[45]

José Fernandes Nico, one of the Portuguese pilots who took the five-week G.91 training course at Militärflugplatz, Leipheim, West Germany. (José Nico Collection)

As an alternative, in 1965 the Portuguese Defence Ministry proposed designating 10 FAP F-86Fs as 'reinforcement aircraft', ready to deploy to Guinea if required by local conditions. These fighters, permanently assigned to BA5-Monte Real on the Portuguese mainland, could be dispatched to Bissalanca within 48–72 hours.[46] Lisbon, however, proved unwilling to further anger the U.S. by redeploying American-built combat aircraft to Africa. Less than two years earlier, in December 1963, Washington had even threatened to suspend all aircraft and equipment deliveries to Portugal over the participation of F-86s in Guinea.[47] Consequently, the FAP again turned to the Federal Republic of Germany to remedy its attack fighter deficit. As part of a *quid pro quo* arrangement with Bonn, Lisbon had traded the use of the FAP's *Base Aérea* No.11 (BA11) at Beja to the *Luftwaffe* for an infusion of additional aircraft, including North American T-6 armed trainers, Dornier Do-27 short take off and landing (STOL) utility aircraft, and most critically, 40 new Fiat Aviazione G.91-R4 light strike fighters produced under licence in West Germany.[48] The latter aircraft, originally intended for Greece and Turkey, had been rejected by those nations in favour of American designs, and so were offered to Portugal at an 'advantageous price' agreed to on 8 October 1965.[49] As part of the procurement effort, named Project Feierabend, nine FAP pilots and a contingent of maintenance personnel undertook a five-week training course at Leipheim, Germany, prior to the arrival of the first eight G.91s in Portugal that December.[50] At the end of March 1966 the first four disassembled aircraft arrived in Guinea by sea,[51] and on 6 May *Tenente Coronel* Hugo Damásio flight tested the first 'Fiat' from BA12. By mid-summer a total of seven G.91s had been assembled and flown at the Bissalanca air base, with an eighth completed that November.[52]

The first group of G.91 pilots assigned to *Esquadra* 121, BA12-Bissalanca. From left to right: *Tenente Coronel* Hugo Damásio (G.O. 1201 commander), *Alferes* Luís António, *Tenente* Egídio Lopes (*Esquadra* 121 commander), *Capitão* Costa Pereira (G.O. 1201 operations officer), Sargento-Adjudante Mota Cardoso, Furriel Ary Meca. (Egídio Lopes Collection)

Powered by a Bristol Siddeley 'Orpheus' Mk 803-D11 turbojet produced under licence in Italy, the G.91 could reach speeds of up to 600 knots (Mach 0.88) at sea level. (Historical Archive of the Air Force)

The G.91 promised to fulfil most of the FAP's requirements for an attack jet in Guinea. Designed to fulfil NATO specifications for a lightweight strike fighter, the 'Fiat' could operate in austere environments with a minimum of servicing and turnaround time, and the FAP appreciated the G.91's ease of maintenance and ability to operate from short, rough airstrips. Given the air defence environment for which it had originally been intended, the aircraft's cockpit was enclosed on three sides by steel plating and an armoured glass windscreen, while vital aircraft sections including the seven split fuel tanks were also protected by armour.[53] The G.91's flight characteristics and aerodynamic stability rendered it an excellent gun platform, and it carried three Vinten F.95-MK3 70mm cameras in the nose to collect vertical and oblique imagery of suspected PAIGC targets, including cross-border staging bases and anti-aircraft positions in Senegal or the Republic of Guinea.[54]

The G.91 also offered something the lumbering, droning T-6s could not: tactical surprise. Powered by a Bristol Siddeley 'Orpheus' Mk 803-D11 turbojet produced under licence in Italy, the G.91 could reach speeds of up to 600 knots (Mach 0.88) at sea level, putting nearly any point in the province at risk of air attack within 15 minutes of take off.[55] At low altitudes the new jet fighter proved 'silent on approach and terrifying in attack,' returning a valuable psychological weapon to Portugal's aerial arsenal.[56] The G.91's airshow-calibre performance during demonstration flights at Bissalanca reinforced that impression, prompting *Brigadeiro* Schultz to express his 'certainty' that the aircraft would decide the war in Portugal's favour.[57]

Schultz' exuberance overlooked the aircraft's shortcomings, however. Most significant was the G.91s limited range and tactical endurance, and Portuguese pilots had to develop a series of operational workarounds to compensate. These included high altitude routes to and from target areas, potentially giving advance warning to enemy forces; carriage of external fuel, for a corresponding reduction in ordnance; and strict limits on the amount of time spent in actual combat, often restricting pilots to a single bomb or strafing run on the objective.[58] On its longest-duration profile (high altitude ingress and egress, two external fuel tanks, guns only) the G.91 could reach any point in Guinea, but with a mere 10 minutes on station to prosecute a target. The most aggressive mission profile – low-level throughout, with maximum ordnance and 15 minutes on station – could strike targets out to only 80NM, however.[59] Furthermore, as a dedicated low-altitude

A G.91 from *Esquadra* 121 during the reception flights at BA12 in May 1966. (Historical Archive of the Air Force)

strike fighter the G.91 handled poorly above 15,000 feet, an acute disadvantage against determined air-to-air opposition, and even as an air-to-ground platform its loadout was lighter than that of the F-86F it was meant to replace.[60] Pilots were also dissatisfied with the G.91-R4's four .50in (12.7mm) nose-mounted machine guns, preferring the heavier punch of the twin 30mm DEFA cannons carried on *Luftwaffe* G.91-R3 models.[61]

Portugal's G.91 fleet was also affected by the supply and maintenance difficulties afflicting the FAP at large. In this case the problem originated with the initial agreement, which contracted Germany to provide replacement parts for the first thousand hours of flight – enough to cover just six weeks of combat operations. 'The use of a new type of plane such as the Fiat implied a much higher stock of spare parts,' the ZACVG complained to the FAP staff in June 1966, alluding to the G.91's novelty and complexity compared to other types then serving in Guinea.[62] It would take at least six months to make the 'necessary adjustments,' given the thousands of new items introduced into the supply chain.[63] Defence Minister de Araújo also protested Germany's failure to perform contracted maintenance and supply the agreed stocks, due in part to competing requirements in support of the *Luftwaffe's* own G.91 fleet.[64] By March 1967 the situation had become so dire that the ZACVG was forced to cannibalise one of its aircraft, FAP 5406, for parts to keep the other seven in flyable condition.[65]

Consequently, insufficient inventories of several systems and replacement items curtailed early FAP G.91 operations in Guinea. Portugal had received just 10 replacement Orpheus engines for the

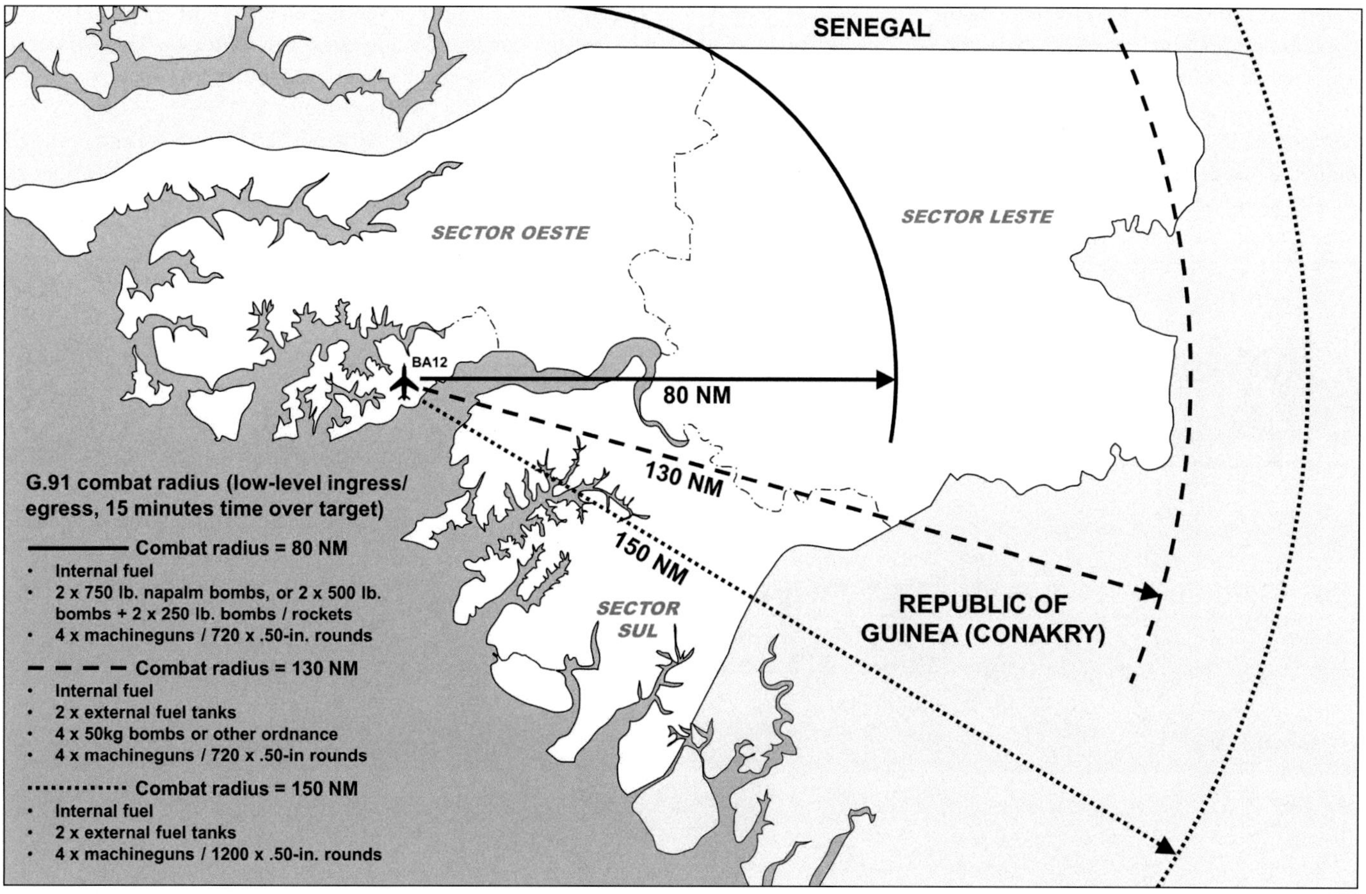

G.91 combat radii in Guinea. (Matthew M. Hurley based on SGDN/1REP, 'Planeamento de Operação do Fiat G-91,' 20 November 1967, SGDN/1REP/105/0345/003, ADN.)

G.91 operations were restricted by numerous technical and logistical issues during the type's first months of service in Guinea. (Historical Archive of Air Force)

40 G.91s received under Project Feierabend, for example, but the FAP's request for additional power plants took several months to resolve, leaving some aircraft grounded while awaiting them.[66] Want of Martin-Baker Mk4 ejection seat components also limited initial operations, and by the time the 'new' G.91s first flew in Guinea they had already exceeded the inspection deadlines for their ejection seats.[67] Other unforeseen operational and logistical challenges – including premature tyre wear, braking chute shortages, depletion of engine starter cartridges, and unexpectedly high fuel consumption – further impeded the ZACVG's early attempts to fully utilise the G.91.[68] In his initial report on G.91 activities in Guinea, the FAP's chief of operations there concluded that 'the ability of the G.91 to intervene in the initial phase of operations had been profoundly influenced and restricted' by these problems.[69]

The most pressing shortfall, however, was a persistent lack of armament and delivery systems for the new aircraft. Nominally, the G.91 packed a respectable offensive punch: for close support missions the light attack fighters operated in pairs, each armed with four .50in. machine guns and eight 2.75in. folding-fin aerial rockets (FFAR), along with external fuel tanks to extend nominal endurance up to 1 hour 20 minutes. For tougher targets, the G.91 could carry six 100lb or 50kg general purpose bombs; two 500lb GP bombs or 200kg fragmentation bombs, and four 50kg GP bombs; or two larger weapons, either 750lb GP/napalm bombs or 300kg/350 litre napalm canisters.[70] However, low quantities of available bombs 'virtually restricted the aircrafts' operations to strafing' through at least March 1967,[71] and at one point G.91 crews were prohibited from using 200kg bombs in order to preserve the few available 'for more serious emergencies,' according to retired FAP *General* and Guinea veteran José Nico.[72] Underwing racks for 50kg bombs were completely absent until the first pair arrived in July 1966, with an additional eight delivered that October. The G.91s were also unable to mount rocket attacks until launchers became available after 25 October.[73] Although additional armament and delivery systems dribbled into Bissalanca's armoury during the following year, Guinea-based G.91s could only mount single-bomb attacks until early 1968, when the ZACVG finally received enough ordnance to arm individual G.91s with multiple 200kg and 50kg bombs.[74]

These complications combined to severely restrict initial G.91 employment in Guinea, such that BA12-Bissalanca could only sortie a daily average of two to three combat-ready jets through October 1967.[75] But even in such meagre numbers, the new fighter-bomber's debut returned a vital offensive component to Portuguese forces and provided the ZACVG a viable means of attacking the insurgents' most fortified and best-defended positions. As a result, G.91s would play a pre-eminent role in every major ZACVG operation for the remainder of the war. Highly prized by the Portuguese and despised by its independence-minded foes, the 'Fiats' allowed the former to strike almost at will throughout the territory – even as the PAIGC's

A sampling of the munitions carried by the Fiat G.91-R4. (Egídio Lopes Collection)

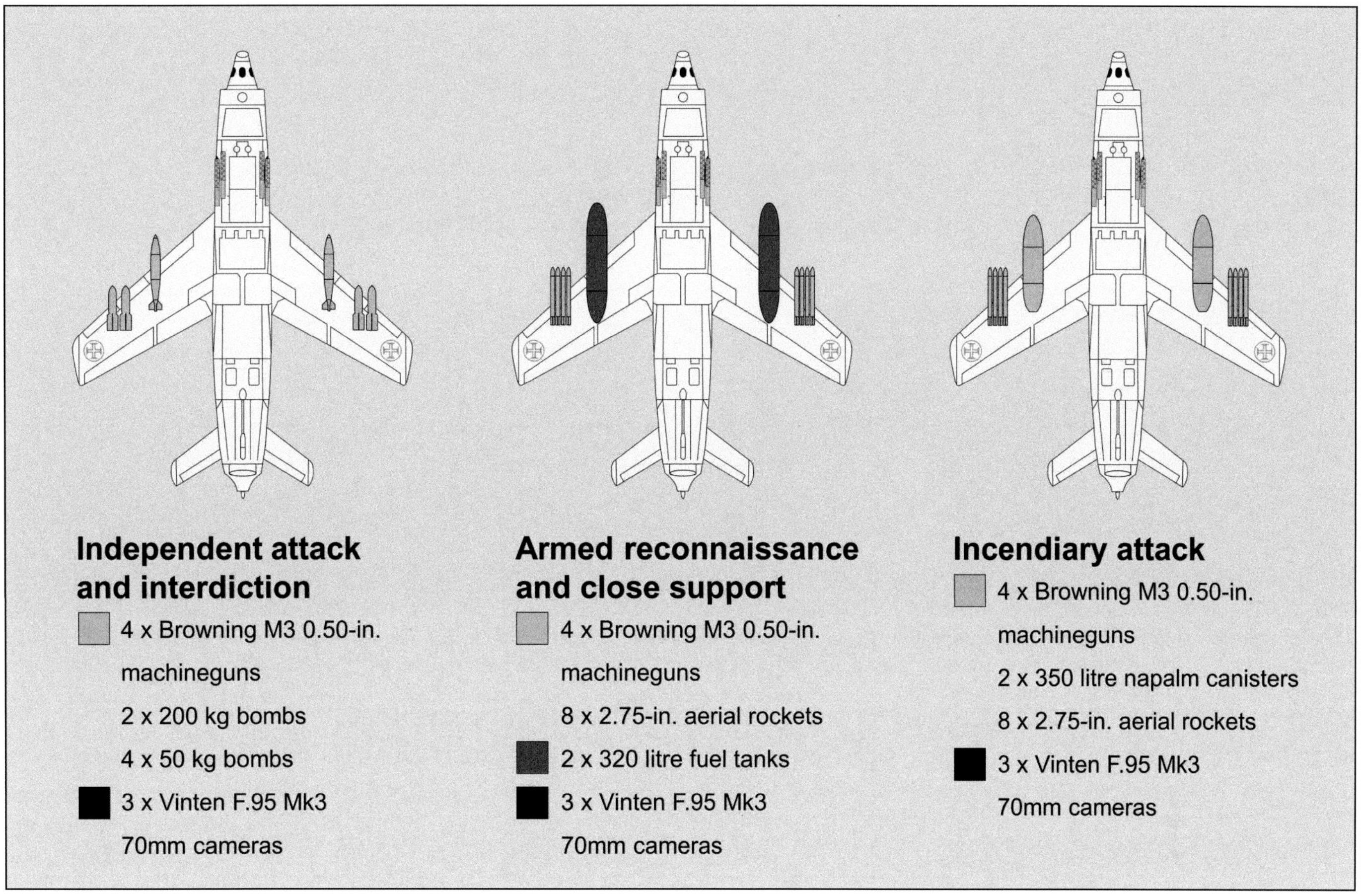

G.91 combat loads. (Matthew M. Hurley based on EMFA/3REP, 'Relatório da missão à Alemanha relativa ao Projecto Feierbend,' 11 March 1966, CMLA/025/0057/019, ADN.)

militants refined their methods, improved their mobility, and established credible anti-aircraft defences in their strongholds.

Though the G.91 revitalised ZACVG strike operations, the real revolution in Portugal's air war for Guinea accompanied the arrival of the first Alouette III helicopters in November 1965.[76] The new craft were immediately pressed into service performing the same liaison and medical evacuation duties as the trio of older Alouette II helicopters already operating in the country, but the Alouette III was a significant improvement over its predecessor, with a more powerful engine and 50 percent greater carrying capacity.[77] For combat transport, each of these helicopters could carry five soldiers and their individual equipment (four in the rear seat and one facing backwards from the front, to the pilot's left). A sixth passenger could be carried in a centre-front seat, but this was normally left unoccupied to prevent inadvertent interference with the pilot or flight controls. Alternatively, the French-built helicopter could lift two stretcher patients and two medical attendants during evacuation missions.[78] The Alouette III, described by one Portuguese pilot as an 'extraordinarily sturdy aircraft and very easy to fly,' was also easy to maintain in austere field conditions and could absorb 'astonishing quantities of small arms fire.'[79]

The new helicopters allowed Portugal to initiate a limited air assault campaign, and on 6 March 1966 the ZACVG and *Comando Territorial Independente da Guiné* (CTIG)[83] executed *Operação Hermínia*, Portugal's first true heliborne assault operation in the province. At the start of the operation six Alouette IIIs lifted 30 Portuguese commandos on a 20 minute flight to raid guerrilla encampments in Jabadá, 15 miles east of the provincial capital, Bissau; the same helicopters returned the commandos to the Portuguese air base at Bissalanca following three hours in the objective area.[84] *Hermínia* was quickly followed by additional helicopter assault operations: on 10 March five Alouette IIIs transported paratroops to attack a PAIGC camp in Salancaur during *Operação Odete*, while on 14 March Alouette IIIss landed Portuguese commandos to block and encircle insurgent forces during *Operação Desforço*.[85]

Compared to contemporaneous helicopter operations in Southeast Asia especially, *Hermínia* and its immediate successors were brief, seemingly insignificant episodes. For example, on the same day as *Operação Hermínia* took place, American and allied forces concluded Operation Masher/White Wing, a massive 41-day airmobile campaign in South Vietnam's Binh Dinh Province. That operation involved a record-setting 74,385 helicopter sorties, lifting the equivalent of 78 infantry battalions, 55 artillery batteries, and the

Table 3: Helicopter Capabilities (UH-1D included for comparison to contemporary American operations in South-East Asia)

	Alouette II[80]	Alouette III[81]	UH-1D Iroquois ('Huey')[82]
Maximum speed (kmh/kt)	175 / 95	220 / 118	222 / 120
Cruising speed (kmh/kt)	170 / 92	195 / 105	203 / 110
Maximum range (km/NM)	530 / 329	540 / 335	507 / 274
Accommodation (equipped troops)	4	5–6	12
Accommodation (casualty stretchers)	2	2	6

A French detachment of Alouette II helicopters at Tizi Ouzou airfield in Algeria during the war for independence in the 50s. French forces used helicopters extensively in this type of warfare, providing the Portuguese a template on which to base their own heliborne operations. (Raymond Varoqui/Georges Petit/ECPAD)

A French T-6 Harvard, used in the Algerian war and later sold to Portugal. This aircraft was equipped with two 7.62mm machine guns on each wing, these were later replaced by two Browning 7.7mm guns. (EALA/ECPAD)

materiel necessary to sustain them through six weeks of intensive combat operations – 93,351 passengers and 9,701 tons of cargo in all.[86] Although *Hermínia* represented a much smaller effort, Portugal's platoon-sized *golpe de mão*[87] inaugurated a series of over three hundred heli-assault operations in Guinea alone, operations which came to symbolise the war to many of its participants. 'Perhaps the most important fleets in Africa were the helicopter units,' FAP General (and one time Chief of Staff) Rui Alberto Fidalgo Ferreira later recalled. 'Certainly the Alouette IIIs especially represented, for those who were there, the air effort in Africa.'[88]

The FAP had long understood and appreciated the value of vertical lift in combat operations, particularly against irregular opponents. Portuguese officers observing French counterinsurgency (COIN) operations in Algeria during the late 1950s had reported that 'the use of helicopters, in the particular case of subversive warfare, offers exceptional possibilities.'[89] This was especially true of helicopter assault operations, which granted COIN forces surprise and superior mobility when combating an elusive opponent operating in otherwise inaccessible terrain. These factors prompted the SGDN (Secretary General for National Defence), General Deslandes, to recommend the development and employment of heliborne 'intervention forces' in Guinea as early as 1963. Despite the FAP receiving its first examples of the type that same year, however, the Alouette III did not appear in the restive province until November 1965, when an initial complement of six was dispatched to Bissalanca – the core of a fleet eventually peaking at 21 helicopters.[90]

The timing proved fortunate, as the ZACVG's G.91s entered service shortly after its first Alouette IIIs; together, the two new types made a limited air assault campaign possible. 'This was one of the missions where timing and precision were most needed,' observed Portuguese military historian Luís Alves de Fraga. 'With the synchronisation of [bombardment and helicopter landing] actions, the greatest surprise effect was sought, which is why Fiats were used.'[91] As retired FAP *General* and Guinea veteran António Bispo elaborated:

> Heli-transport operations were, in aerial terms, an authentic spectacle of aeronautic demonstration, worthy of the Paris Air Show. With a high degree of synchronisation, the disembarkation was preceded by an attack by Fiat [G.91] and/or T-6 aircraft, in a manner in which the last bomb to fall comes immediately before the first man exits. Thus, it was sought to keep the enemy paralysed, guaranteeing protection to the attacker.[92]

Additional protection was often necessary, however, as the Portuguese soon discovered. FAP aircrews and passengers found the helicopters to be tempting targets for enemy fire, especially during the landing and disembarkation phases of a heliborne operation – 'the moment of greatest vulnerability for our forces,' Bispo recalled.[93] On 30 March 1966, for example, one Portuguese helicopter had been immobilised by enemy fire during *Operação Narceja*.[94] The ZACVG consequently sought a means of providing embedded overwatch and fire support during airmobile missions. Initially, individuals armed with hunting shotguns were placed aboard some helicopters to provide rudimentary suppressive fire; later, embarked troops would direct their personal weapons at sources of enemy resistance while hovering or landing. Neither expedient proved sufficient, however, leading the FAP to seek a more effective solution. Early trials involving a tripod-mounted MG42 7.62mm calibre machine gun were quickly abandoned because of the weapon's difficult handling and irregular fire trajectory. Subsequent efforts to mount a .50in. Browning M3 machine gun in the Alouette III's side door were likewise halted due to the weapon's size, weight, and the excessive vibrations experienced when firing it.[95] Alternatively, the FAP developed and tested axially mounted weapons, including .50in. machine guns and rocket launchers adapted from T-6 armament.[96]

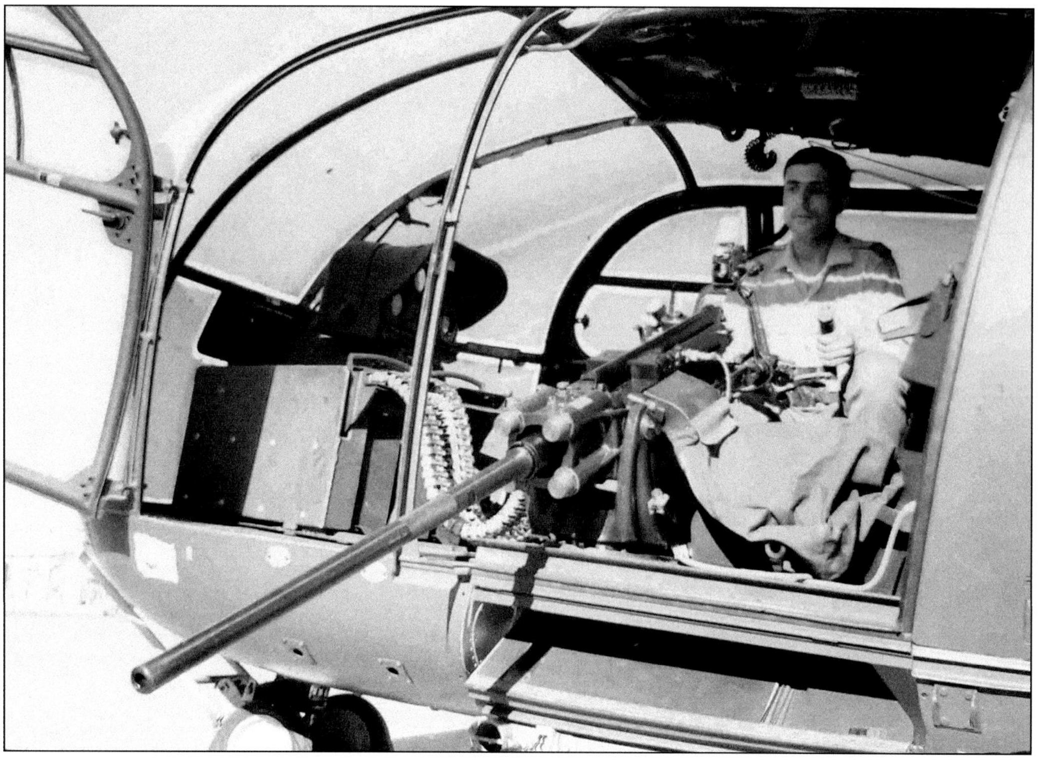

The Matra MG151 20mm cannon installed on the side door of the Alouette III. (Costa Neves Collection)

Another view of the side-mounted 20mm cannon on the Alouette III. (Serrano Rosa Collection)

The FAP ultimately found its answer in a successful French programme to install swivelling door-mounted cannon on the Alouette III.[97] In 1965–66 the FAP tested the Matra MG151 20mm cannon in a similar arrangement at its Alcochete firing range, in Portugal, having received a quantity of the weapons from post-war French stocks. The Portuguese found the results satisfactory, and by December 1966 the first MG151 cannons arrived at Bissalanca. The pairing of these weapons with the Alouette III resulted in the *helicanhão*, or 'heli-cannon', although aircrews and the forces they supported more commonly referred to the improvised gunship as *lobo mau* (bad wolf).[98] Fed by two 200-round ammunition belts and firing 700 rounds of high-explosive or incendiary rounds per minute, the *helicanhão* proved 'a weapon of extraordinary effectiveness,' as Guinea veteran *General* José Brochado de Miranda recounted, 'preventing the movement of the enemy while the transport helicopters disembarked the troops.'[99] Although the cannon and its ammunition reduced the Alouette III's carrying capacity by displacing one of the passenger seats, later analyses characterised *helicanhão* employment as 'decisive' during the most delicate phases of helicopter assault operations.[100]

The Alouette III line at BA12, Bissalanca. All Guinea-based helicopters were assigned to *Esquadra 122*. (Alberto Cruz Collection)

The G.91s (the '*Tigres*') were integrated into *Esquadra 121* along with the T-6s and Do-27s. (Alberto Cruz Collection)

Three of the first pilots assigned to *Esquadra 121*. Left to right: *Sargento-Adjudante* Mota Cardoso, *Tenente* Egídio Lopes, and *Alferes* Luís António. (Egídio Lopes Collection)

The growing fleet of Alouette III helicopters also performed the support missions previously undertaken by the Alouette II: light transport, observation, liaison, and most crucially, medical evacuation. 'Rapid evacuation of wounded in combat is critical to the troops,' FAP *General* Alfredo Cruz explained. In all three African theatres of Portugal's colonial war, 'Thousands of lives were saved by the selfless efforts of hundreds of pilots and crew, taking high risks and often under enemy fire, putting their lives in danger to save others.'[101] ZACVG Alouette IIIs flew more than 1,000 casualty evacuation sorties in 1967 and 1968, representing 37 percent of all TEVS (*transporte de evacuações sanitárias*) operations flown during this period, with the rest conducted primarily by Do-27s.[102] However, only the Alouette IIIs could retrieve wounded personnel from active combat zones or areas inaccessible to fixed-wing aircraft – 'from trails, from forests, from everywhere and whenever needed,' as *General* Cruz recalled.[103]

Integration of the Alouette IIIs and G.91s coincided with fundamental organisational changes at *Base Aérea* 12 in Bissalanca, the FAP's primary facility in Guinea and ZACVG headquarters. Formerly known as *Aeródromo-Base* 2, continued expansion since 1961 resulted in Bissalanca's redesignation as a main operating base in May 1965.[104] The FAP's operational flying unit there, the *Esquadra Operacional*, also saw significant organisational growth, becoming *Grupo Operacional* 1201 (G.O. 1201). Three squadrons made up the aviation element of the operational group:

- *Esquadra 121,* responsible for attack, fire support, and airborne command and control, flying G.91s (the '*Tigres*'), T-6s ('*Roncos*'), and Do-27s ('*Cafeteiras*')
- *Esquadra 122*, incorporating all helicopters – both unarmed transports (the '*Canibais*') and gunships ('*Lobo Mau*')
- *Esquadra 123,* performing airlift, observation, and liaison under the legend '*Tudo Alcança*.' The squadron flew C-47 Dakotas.[105]

BA12 was home to three FAP squadrons supporting Portuguese operations in Guinea. (Virgílio Teixeira Collection)

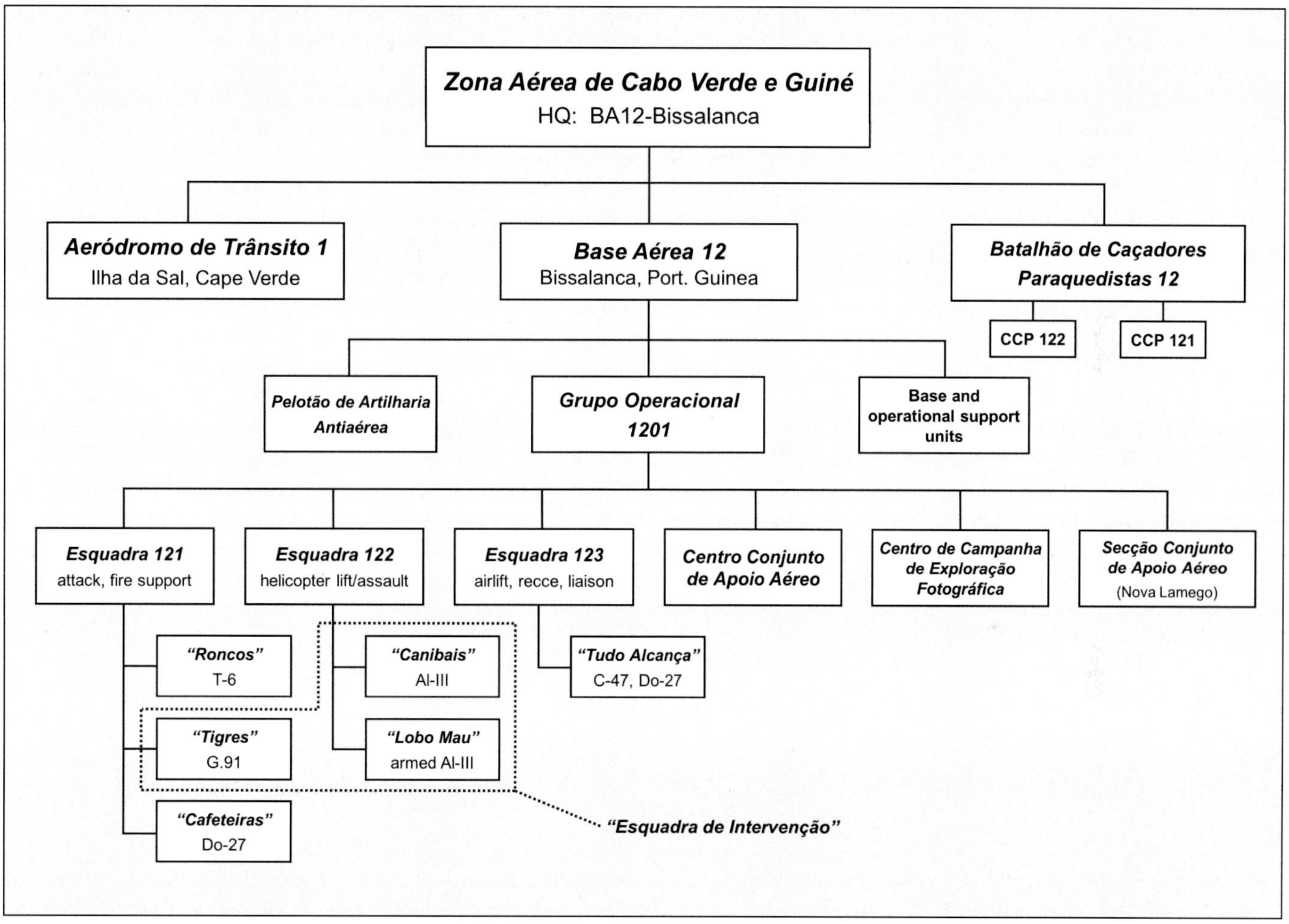

ZACVG organisation, November 1966. (Matthew M. Hurley based on CZACVG, 'Organogramos,' October 1968, AFHA; CZACVG, 'Operação 'Barracuda', Directiva No. 01/67,' 3 February 1967, ADN; Fraga, *A Força Aérea na Guerra em África;* Lopes and José Costa, *Os Aviões da Cruz de Cristo;* Lopes, 'Portugal's Ginas.')

G.91s and Alouette IIIs were often grouped into informal *esquadras de intervenção*, or intervention squadrons. These were typically activated to carry out and support airmobile operations, which began to increase in frequency during the same period.[106]

To adequately man these airmobile operations the FAP deployed additional paratroops, then under Air Force control, into Guinea. A single platoon of paratroops had been dispatched to the province in 1963, and this contingent grew over the following years – first to company size, then to a full battalion, *Batalhão de Caçadores Páraquedistas* 12 (BCP12). Established on 20 October 1966, by July 1970 BCP12 had grown to three companies (*companhias de caçadores páraquedistas*) designated CCP121, 122, and 123.[107] Actual parachute operations were rare despite the unit classification, however, and throughout the paratroops' tenure in Guinea the helicopter remained their 'main vehicle for vertical assault.'[108]

Crucial though these reinforcements were, developments in command, control, and intelligence raised the 'pillars of the whole system,' according to then ZACVG commander *Coronel* Abecasis.[109] One change was perhaps the most fundamental, affecting the top tier of Portugal's military aviation establishment in Guinea: the merger of the ZACVG and BA12 commands at Bissalanca. Previously invested in two different officers, the split command arrangement had created personal and operational frictions which the FAP leadership had been unable to resolve. *Coronel* Abecasis especially blasted 'The incompetence of successive Zone commanders without any past service at the flight, squadron, or operations group level,' who inevitably tried to hide their incompetence through constant meddling in unit affairs more properly left to subordinate officers. 'Victims of a mixture of vanity and spite,' he concluded, such commanders 'were the origin of unease and the source of superfluous problems.'[110] Upon Bissalanca's redesignation as BA12 in May 1965, the ZACVG's functions were wholly combined with the base command, placing Abecasis in charge of both when he assumed command the following month.[111]

Among Abecasis' first actions as ZACVG and BA12 commander was to establish the *Centro Conjunto de Apoio Aéreo* (CCAA, Joint Air Support Centre) as a dedicated control authority for tactical air operations in support of surface forces. Located at Bissalanca and given the aspirational call sign *Marte* (Mars, after the Ancient Greek God of War), the CCAA was responsible for prioritising incoming requests for air support, tasking aircraft to satisfy approved requests, and managing the necessary communications links – areas that had long been targeted for improvement.[112] 'This organisation was essential to responsibly plan, programme and profit from the use of air resources,' FAP historian Luís Alves de Fraga later concluded. 'With the creation of the CCAA, the difficulties of communication between the land forces and aircraft were overcome.'[113] A satellite *Secção Conjunto de Apoio Aéreo* (SCAA) was also established at Nova Lamego to streamline operations in *Sector Leste*, the eastern part of the province furthest from Bissalanca.[114]

Linking the CCAA and supported forces, specially-equipped planes – usually Do-27 STOL utility aircraft – served as airborne command posts, or *Postos de Comando Volante* (PCV). Flying over or near the battle area, PCV aircraft provided a tactical overview of the air-ground environment as well as a communications link between land units and supporting aerial assets, either through the CCAA/SCAA or with aircraft directly. Additionally, the overall commander of a given operation typically flew aboard the PCV to maintain real-time situational awareness and provide on-scene assessments of tactical requirements and priorities.[115] PCV aircraft carried radio sets employed by both air and surface forces, permanently set to the immediate air support request frequencies of 49.0 and 51.0 MHz; the CCAA likewise monitored those channels during operations. Despite incompatibilities between available terrestrial and airborne radio equipment, Portuguese forces managed a satisfactory level of tactical communications through these arrangements, ensuring fire support, emergency resupply, or medical evacuation could be provided within 20 minutes in most circumstances.[116]

To improve intelligence support during mission planning and damage assessment, *Coronel* Abecasis also directed the creation of a *Centro de Campanha de Exploração Fotográfica* (CCEF, Campaign Centre for Photographic Exploration), established at BA12-Bissalanca in Autumn 1966.[117] Despite the variety of photographic gear employed during ZACVG reconnaissance missions – from hand-held cameras carried aboard light aircraft to the built-in photoreconnaissance capabilities of the G.91 – the CCEF quickly developed 'a remarkable capacity' to interpret spot imagery, analyse photographic trends, and produce detailed mosaic displays of planned objectives.[118]

By the end of 1966, then, and despite the many challenges yet to be overcome, the FAP had installed a 50 aircraft fleet into a fully developed air base, supplemented by multiple auxiliary fields, and supported by a more efficient command and control structure and an improved intelligence apparatus. With proper planning and resource management, the FAP's Guinea contingent could project air power throughout the province in all relevant roles – to include the deployment of the air force's own 'infantry', the paratroops of BCP 12. The G.91 and Alouette III in particular improved the ZACVG's ability to harry its opponents anywhere in the province, directly threatening the PAIGC's military strategy and ultimate viability as a national liberation organisation. In many measurable respects, it appeared that the highest levels of the Portuguese government and armed forces were, after nearly four years, finally getting serious about the air war in Guinea.

2
'They couldn't stop our struggle'

> The colonialist criminals used jet planes, modern helicopters, cluster bombs, napalm and phosphorus bombs, [but] they couldn't stop our struggle. They managed, however, to make our people's hatred of Portuguese colonial domination even greater. (Amílcar Cabral, 2 January 1968)[1]

The PAIGC, like its Portuguese enemy, also experienced a period of growth and reorganisation. By 1966 the nationalist movement had evolved into a widespread insurgency that credibly threatened imperial control over much of the territory, but still retained the military structure adopted at the party's 1964 congress. That structure incorporated the *Exército Popular* (EP, People's Army), the *Guerrilha Popular* (GP, regional part-time guerrilla units), and the *Milícia Popular* (MP, local defensive militia).[2] Together, these elements comprised the *Forças Armadas Revolucionárias do Povo* (FARP, Revolutionary People's Armed Forces). In November 1966 the PAIGC and FARP were again restructured, this time through the establishment of a War Council at the highest levels of party leadership and the removal of the *Milícia* from the FARP's chain of command. Through the *Conselho da Guerra* the FARP directed the EP and GP at the front, region, and sector levels, while the MP was now subordinate to the *Bureau Político* (Political Bureau) through a similar geographical hierarchy. The *Bureau Político* retained oversight of the FARP and subordinate structures through political commissars, who also exercised operational authority through a deputy command arrangement.[3]

The PAIGC's 'regular' military component, the EP, numbered approximately 3,000 full-time combatants operating within Portuguese Guinea or occupying cross-border sanctuaries for training, recuperation, or resupply. These forces were typically organised in *grupos* of 22 to 24 personnel, usually combined and employed as *bi-grupos* of twice that size. When reinforced for missions requiring heavy equipment or specialist personnel, *bi-grupos* could number as many as 66 combatants. The irregular units of the GP added another 6,000 fighters to the PAIGC's military manpower pool, generally relegated to defensive duties but available

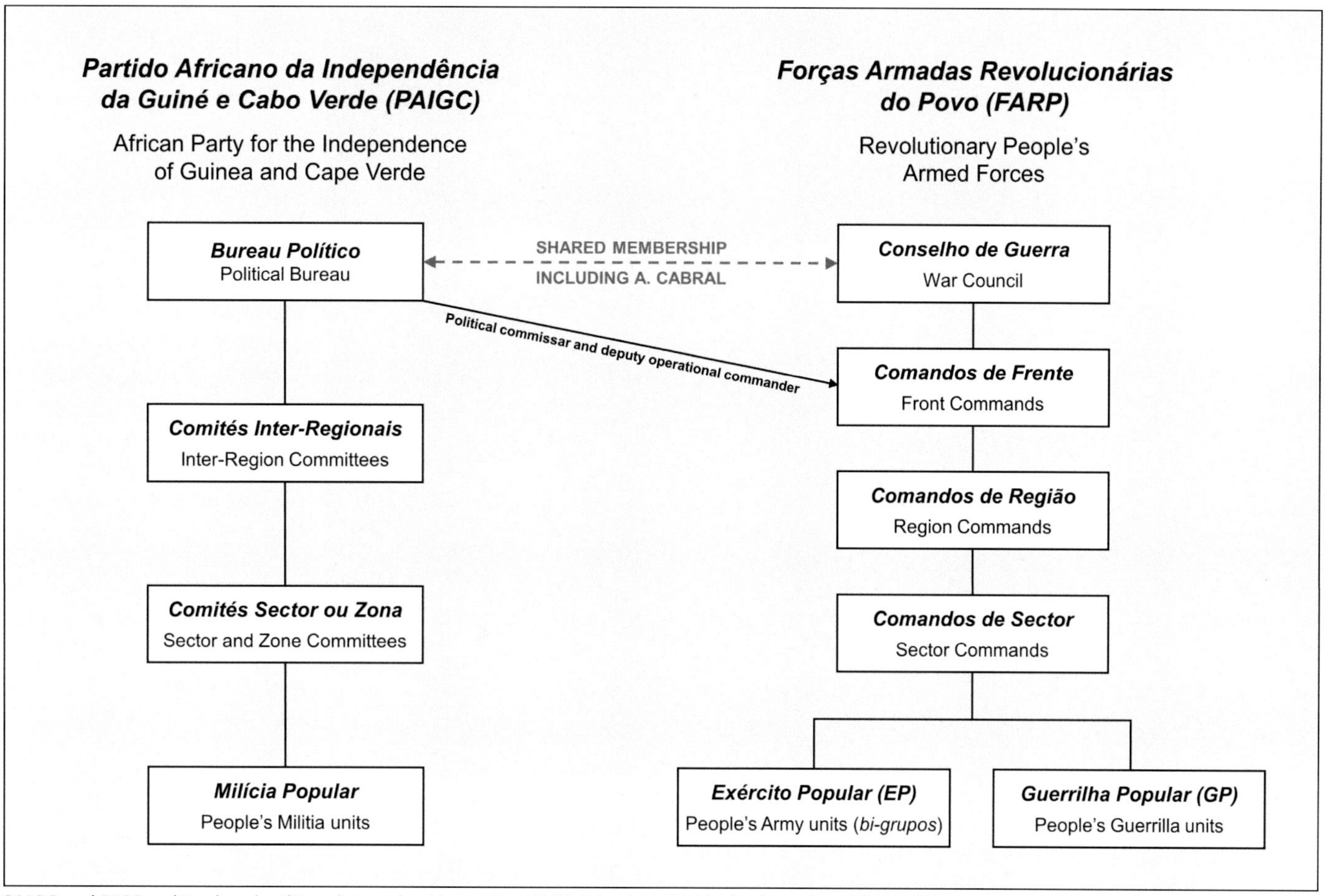

PAIGC and FARP political and military hierarchy, November 1966. (Matthew M. Hurley based on COMCHEFE Guiné, 'SUPINTREP no. 35,' Anexo H, SGDN/2REP/088/0364/024, ADN.)

A EP unit on patrol. Comprising the 'regular' military component of the PAIGC, the EP fielded some 3,000 full-time combatants by 1966. (Reg Lancaster/Express Hulton Archive/Getty Images)

to reinforce large-scale operations when required.[4] In all, Portuguese forces in Guinea faced up to 9,000 armed opponents, excluding local militias, who were increasingly well-trained, well-organised, and better equipped with each passing year.[5]

In the party's military plan for 1966–67, PAIGC General Secretary and chief strategist, Amílcar Cabral, announced that these forces would 'intensify, develop and extend the fight across the country' to 'force the enemy to fight on all sides.'[6] To facilitate the aim of spreading rebellion, the PAIGC established three *Inter-Região* (Inter-Regions, the three were North, South, and East) divided into 13 regions and 32 zones or sectors. Each *Inter-Região* hosted at least one EP *bi-grupo* and 250 guerrillas, with additional units assigned at the regional or 'front' level. Each sector was also assigned artillery (recoilless cannon and mortar), sapper, and/or anti-aircraft machine gun units as required by tactical conditions or pending operations.[7]

Cabral's strategic intentions quickly became apparent to Portuguese commanders. Major areas of concern to the colonial military authorities in 1966 included the Oio zone of northwest Guinea; the central Xime-Xitole region; the southern littoral; and the PAIGC's three central 'base areas' at Morés, Injassane, and Cafal.[8] They also expressed alarm over the party's ability to infiltrate personnel and material from outside the province, characterising the frontiers as 'completely open to the enemy's entry and exit.'[9] This enabled the insurgents to launch a

A member of the PAIGC's popular militia standing guard at an insurgent outpost near Cacine. (UPI)

'great intensification of military operations' in the late spring and summer of 1966, focused on disrupting lines of communications (LOCs) and harassing Portuguese forces in the western and southern regions especially.[10] On southern Guinea's troublesome Quitafine Peninsula, increased anti-aircraft defences complicated the ZACVG's efforts to relieve beleaguered outposts or pacify restive areas, leading the Portuguese Army's Chief of Staff to voice his concerns that some garrisons ran the risk of being overrun.[11] Throughout Guinea overall, the average monthly number of armed PAIGC activities had nearly trebled since the war's beginning, peaking at 293 incidents and attacks in May 1966. The accelerating pace and widening extent of insurgent activity was further reflected in the increasing casualties inflicted on Portuguese forces, which grew from 258 dead and wounded in 1963 to 1,226 during 1966.[12]

The war's geographic expansion gave the PAIGC a pretext to declare increasingly large swaths of territory as *zonas libertadas* (liberated zones),[13] where the nationalist party purportedly dominated and governed through rudimentary political, economic, and public service structures 'in general if not complete security from enemy action on the ground.'[14] By 1966, the PAIGC claimed the liberation of more than half the territory, a statistic vehemently disputed by Portuguese authorities but difficult to refute.[15] These *zonas libertadas* represented an essential component of the PAIGC's broader strategy, proclaimed and publicised to showcase the movement's military progress, administrative ability, and political legitimacy. As Amílcar Cabral asserted, 'In our liberated regions we now have all the makings of a state. Our people have a political, economic and cultural life, and the people rule the people.'[16] Visible demonstrations to that effect not only attracted the gratitude and support of a neglected populace, but also encouraged the backing of foreign benefactors – and the goodwill of both audiences was critical to the PAIGC's long-term success.[17]

Amílcar Cabral, the PAIGC's charismatic General Secretary, fought against Portuguese colonialism and for the independence of Guinea and Cape Verde. (Ben Martin/Getty Images)

The only way Portugal could conclusively disprove the PAIGC's claims of territorial dominion was through military occupation or, at the very least, by maintaining some degree of periodic military presence. However, by 1966 Portuguese forces had adopted a predominantly 'positional' strategy, fortifying existing garrisons in major towns and along key LOCs while restricting surface movement elsewhere for fear of ambush or mines.[18] The remaining Portuguese-held areas were the most densely populated, and as Portuguese Army Chief of Staff, General Luís da Câmara Pina, explained during an April visit to Guinea, 'For us it is important at this time to guarantee the safety of the populations… That's why we employ our forces in more static missions, in protection operations.'[19] A visiting British journalist put a less positive spin on the situation, writing that Portuguese ground forces in Guinea

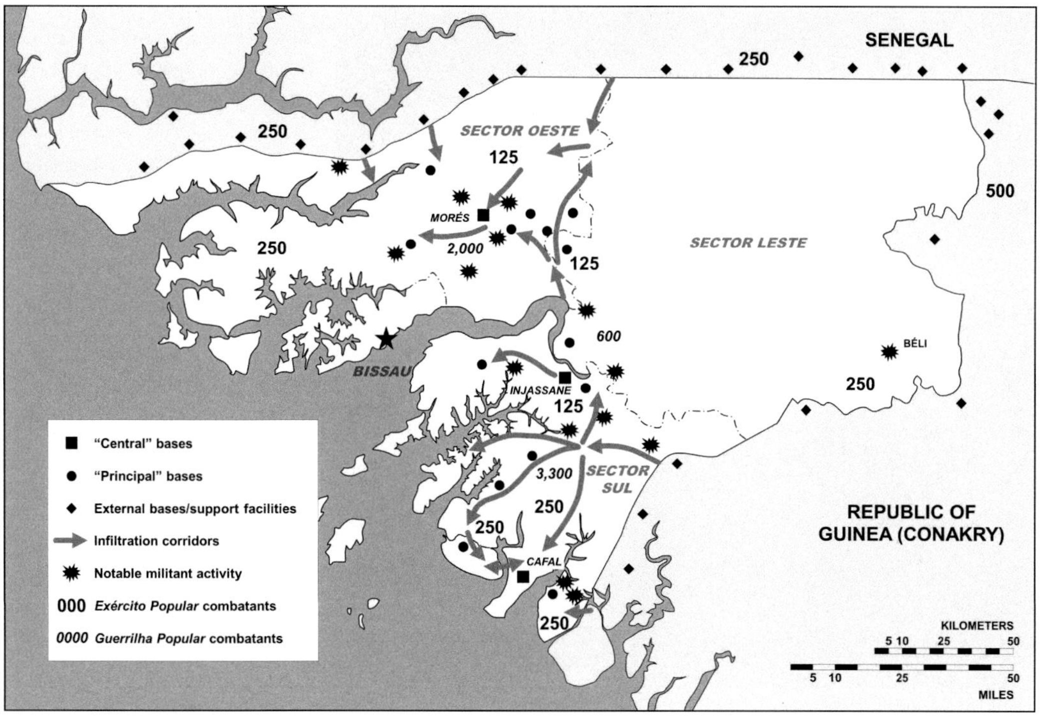

PAIGC/FARP deployment and activity, May 1966 – February 1967. (Matthew M. Hurley based on CECA, *Resenha Histórico-Militar das Campanhas de África*, 6-II-I, p. 431; SGDN, 'Visita do Ministro da Defesa Nacional à Guiné – 12 a 20 Fev 67,' February 1967, SGDN/1REPCUBAN/092/0309/015, ADN.)

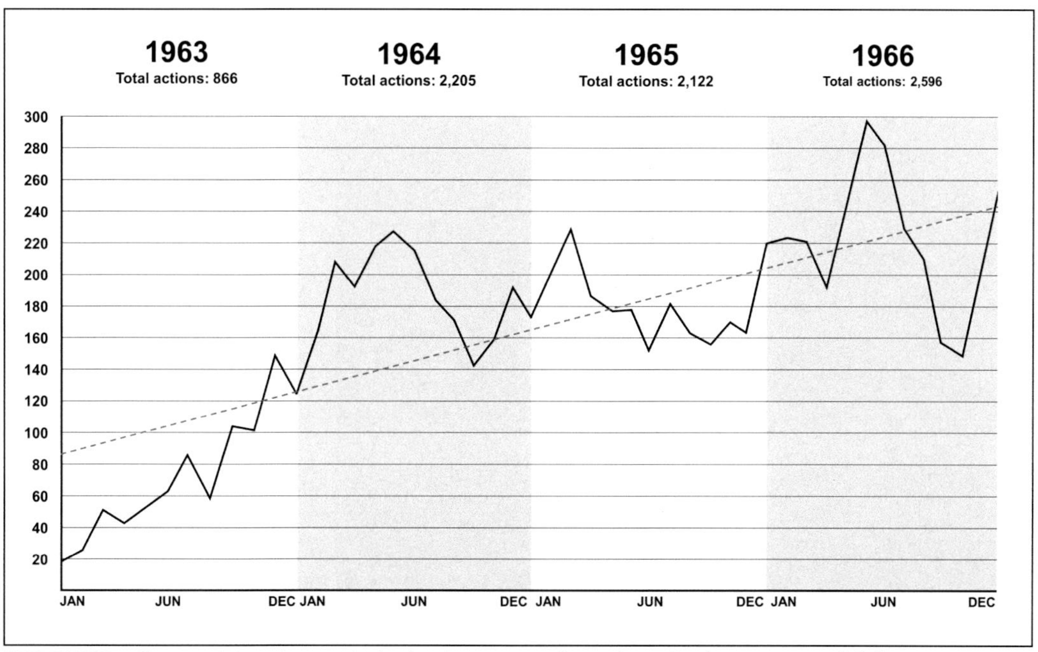

PAIGC/FARP military activity, 1963–1966 (rocket/mortar attacks, raids, ambushes, mines, and defensive actions). (Matthew M. Hurley based on CTIG/2REP, 'SUPINTREP no. 12: O Inimigo em 1966,' SGDN/2REP/088/0363/009, ADN.)

were then 'besieged in some 60 fortified camps and towns.'[20] Though strategically sensible given Portugal's equipment and manpower limitations, the retrenchment limited Portuguese surface units to 'merely reacting to actions undertaken by the PAIGC,' leaving air and airmobile forces as the only practical means with which to rapidly project Portuguese power into rebel-dominated areas.[21]

The chief obstacle to those forces was the PAIGC's growing anti-aircraft capability, particularly in the *zonas libertadas*.[22] Cabral and other party leaders had vowed to defend and enlarge their pseudo-sovereign statelets at all costs,[23] and since the Portuguese had elected to attack them primarily from the air, the PAIGC's militants would have to resist them there. To this end the insurgents concentrated their air defence assets and activities in southern Guinea, where the PAIGC was most entrenched. From 1963–1965 nearly two-thirds of all reported anti-aircraft incidents took place in *Sector Sul* (Sector South),[24] and by the end of that period the air defence threat in southern Guinea had grown serious enough to warrant a three-day air offensive to neutralise anti-aircraft positions on the Cantanhez Peninsula (*Operação Resgate*, 17–20 December 1965).[25]

Operação Resgate was the ZACVG's first dedicated counter-air defences operation,[26] but it failed to permanently subdue PAIGC resistance to Portuguese air power in southern Guinea. Throughout the first half of 1966 the insurgents continued to expand and consolidate their presence there, notably on the Cantanhez and Quitafine peninsulas.[27] Quitafine's domination of coastal and river transport, its designation as a *zonas libertadas*, and its proximity to major insurgent corridors from the Republic of Guinea placed it at the top of the PAIGC's list of defensive priorities.[28] Cabral's militants there 'began to challenge [the FAP] with an arrogant boldness,' Abecasis recalled, while on the neighbouring Cantanhez Peninsula 'the anti-aircraft opposition was as violent as it had been in December 1965, before *Operação Resgate*,' resulting in damage to multiple Portuguese aircraft overflying the region.[29] PAIGC anti-aircraft deployments also threatened Portuguese air operations supporting the garrisons at Cacine and Cacoca, jeopardising Lisbon's military position in the peninsula and throughout the southern region generally.[30] In total, reported anti-aircraft fire increased from 103 incidents during 1965 to 110 in 1966, again with two-thirds of them occurring over southern Guinea.[31]

While accelerating the pace of anti-air activity, the PAIGC also improved its anti-aircraft arsenal. Initially reliant on individual small arms, by mid-1964 the insurgents had equipped themselves with 7.62mm and 12.7mm anti-aircraft machine guns (AAMGs).[32] Growing support from foreign benefactors in Africa and the Communist Bloc over the following years included the delivery of Soviet-designed 14.5mm ZPU-series anti-aircraft guns.[33] The single-barrelled ZPU-1, dual-barrelled ZPU-2, and quad-mounted

During 1966 Portuguese casualties in Guinea (killed and wounded) totalled 1,226, including both combat casualties and accidents. (José Matos Collection)

A PAIGC school in one of the party's so-called *zonas libertadas* in northern Guinea. The party consistently showcased images of normalcy and progress within areas purportedly under PAIGC governance. (Roel Coutinho Collection)

ZPU-4 all appeared in Guinea at various stages of the war after 1965, significantly extending the reach and potency of PAIGC air defence positions. But despite being wheeled, the ZPU family's size, weight, and manpower requirements largely limited its deployment to well-defined operating areas, connected by roadways or improved trails, within the PAIGC's southern 'liberated' strongholds.[34] As a result, the anti-aircraft menace in the south increased in terms of reach and sophistication with a corresponding increase in risk to FAP aircraft, despite an overall reduction in air defence activity throughout Guinea generally from 1966 to 1967 (see Table 4 and graph of reported incidents).[35]

The ZACVG launched a renewed series of counter-AD operations to mitigate the threat over southern Guinea, beginning with *Operação Estoque* in August 1966.[37] Intended to destroy or dismantle the enemy organisation on the insurgent dominated Quitafine Peninsula, *Estoque* was conceived as a 12-hour attack in two phases. During the first phase, commencing at 1900 on 9 August and lasting until midnight, C-47s modified as night bombers would attempt to neutralise PAIGC anti-aircraft emplacements. This was considered an essential precondition for the second stage, which consisted mainly of armed reconnaissance and interdiction missions against

Table 4: PAIGC Anti-Aircraft Weaponry, 1963–1970[36]

Type(s)	Calibre (mm)	Maximum Range (m)	Effective Range (m)	Anti-Air Range (m)	Reported in Guinea
SG-43, Type 53/57	7.62	3,500	1,000	800	1963
DShK	12.7	6,500	1,500	1,000	1964
ZPU-1, ZPU-2, ZPU-4	14.5	8,000	5,000	1,400	1965–67*
M1939, Type 55	37	9,500	3,500	3,000	1970
*Depending on source. Abecasis in *Bordo de Ataque* suggests ZPU-series weapons first appeared in 1965, but most other sources indicate 1967					

A family in the *zona libertadas* of Cubucaré, holding a spent napalm weapon delivered by Portuguese aircraft. (Mikko Pyhälä Collection)

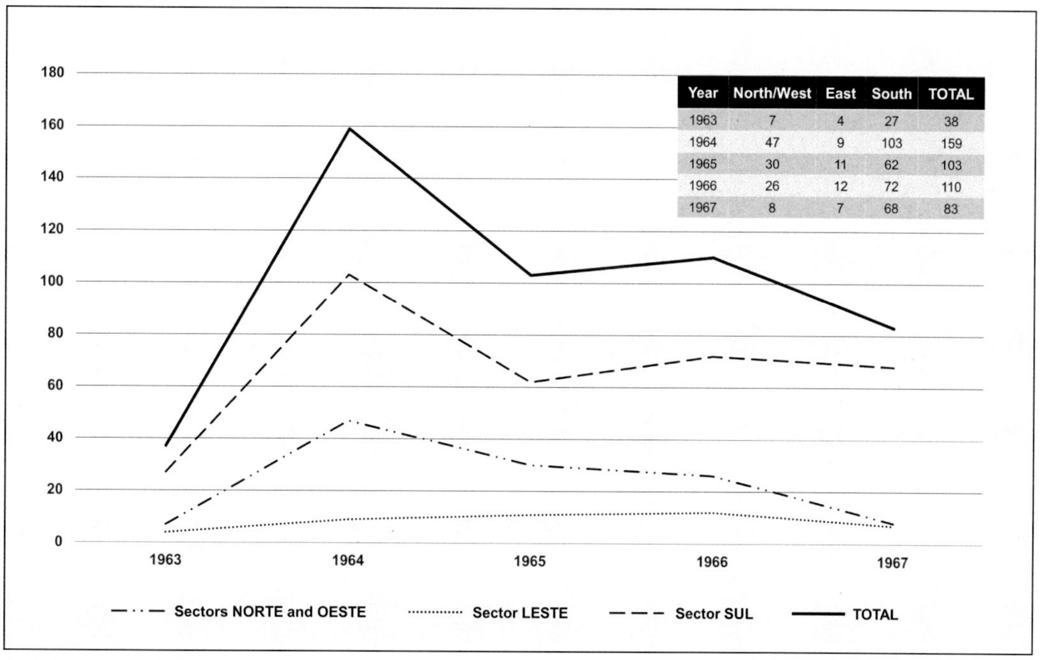

Year	North/West	East	South	TOTAL
1963	7	4	27	38
1964	47	9	103	159
1965	30	11	62	103
1966	26	12	72	110
1967	8	7	68	83

PAIGC anti-aircraft fire – reported incidents, 1963–1967. (Matthew M. Hurley based on COMCHEFE Guiné, 'SUPINTREP no. 35,' Anexo H, SGDN/2REP/088/0364/024, AND.)

supply and infiltration corridors from the Republic of Guinea.[38] In addition to FAP T-6s and the modified C-47s, newly arrived G.91s were to participate in their first major operation – and Abecasis intended to 'use them in force'.[39]

Quitafine was home to a significant civilian population, however, and both Schultz and his ZACVG commander recognised that indiscriminate bombing could result in unacceptable collateral carnage, drawing international condemnation and 'giving survivors a compelling reason to support the guerrillas.'[40] As with 1964's *Operação Tridente*, *Estoque* was preceded by leaflet drops on 7 August advising non-combatants to vacate the objective area. 'So the principle of surprise was sacrificed for humanitarian reasons,' Abecasis later complained.[41]

Two nights later Portuguese aircraft returned to drop ordnance, not leaflets. At 1930 the first of two C-47s approached the hamlet of Cassebeche, near the southern tip of the Quitafine Peninsula. Despite 5/8 cloud cover, the improvised bomber was able to locate and strike PAIGC anti-aircraft positions that revealed themselves with 'intense' fire.[42] The two C-47s successfully delivered 800lbs of ordnance and were shortly followed by the first G.91s, which also encountered fierce anti-aircraft fire over their targets at Cassebeche as well as nearby Cabonepo, Cassacá, and Camissorá.[43] One of the G.91s – FAP 5401, piloted by Tigres commander Tenente Egídio Lopes – returned from its mission with anti-aircraft hits to the right wing and one of its ailerons, the first time a G.91 had sustained combat damage over Guinea.[44]

Deteriorating weather conditions, including solid cloud cover down to 900 feet, forced a suspension of daytime operations on 10 August, but that night additional C-47 bombing raids took place against Cassebeche and the island of Canefaque, despite continued opposition. The following day G.91s attacked four of the remaining anti-aircraft sites, with two of them (FAP 5417 and, again, 5401) hit by ground fire. As a result, G.91 5417 was forced to make an emergency landing with severe engine damage at the Cufar auxiliary airfield.[45]

Estoque ended at 1300 on 12 August, concluding Portugal's second major counter-AD effort in Guinea. During the operation ZACVG aircraft flew 34 combat sorties and delivered 6,800lbs of bombs and incendiary grenades against PAIGC anti-aircraft gun emplacements, destroying at least one AAMG.[46] More importantly, the attacks caused 'great moral disorientation' among insurgent forces in the area, Abecasis later maintained; 'If we had not destroyed the enemy organisation in Quitafine, we had crippled it.'[47] That assessment proved premature, as the southern *zonas libertadas* and infiltration routes remained hotly contested for the rest of the war, but *Grupo Operacional* 1201 and the *Tigres* learned a number of enduring lessons regarding G.91 employment. *Estoque* had demonstrated the ineffectiveness of 2.75in rockets against gun

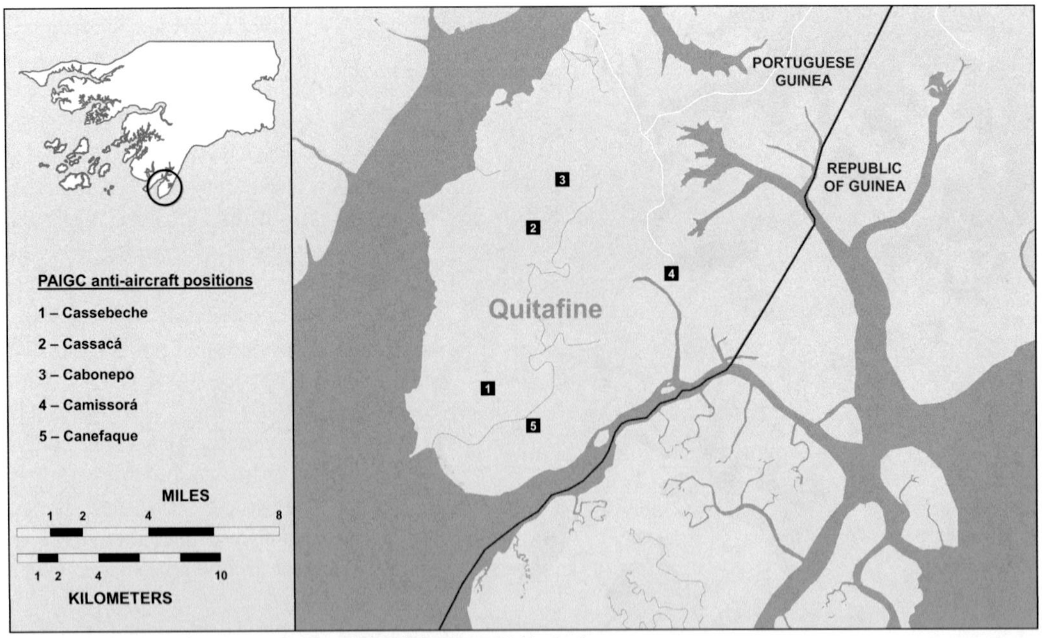

Operação Estoque objectives, August 1966. (Matthew M. Hurley)

2.75in rockets fired by FAP G.91s proved ineffective against gun emplacements during *Operação Estoque*. (José Nico Collection)

emplacements, for example, while the marginal results of bombing prompted G.91 crews to devise more accurate delivery profiles against point targets.[48]

Despite temporary setbacks in Quitafine, the PAIGC continued to challenge the FAP elsewhere in southern Guinea, next on the disputed island of Como. From late August to the beginning of November 1966 the insurgents staged a succession of major attacks against the Portuguese garrison at Cachil, 'the sole, final, and half-collapsed bastion of our forces on North Como Island,' according to Abecasis.[49] Nationalist forces had also intensified their anti-aircraft activity in the region, in one instance nearly downing a Portuguese Do-27 flying a daytime reconnaissance sortie. Fearing an all-out insurgent offensive to expel Portuguese troops from Como, *Brigadeiro* Schultz directed the ZACVG to plan a response to 'force the Enemy to change his attitude.'[50] To this end Abecasis and his staff devised *Operação Samurai*, which the ZACVG commander later described as 'the most daring Air Force operation to date in the Guinean theatre.'[51]

Samurai was conceived as an all air force operation conducted in two phases, with a company of the ZACVG's organic parachute battalion (BCP 12) serving as the ground component.[52] In the first phase Portuguese aircraft were to prosecute a three-day counter-AD effort, commencing on 13 November 1966 to take advantage of the new moon. G.O. 1201 committed virtually its entire fleet – eight G.91s, three C-47s, and all operational T-6s and Alouette IIIs – to this opening stage, intended to squash anti-aircraft resistance in the zone of operations.[53] *Resgate* and *Estoque* had revealed the need for precision when attacking these targets, so C-47s conducting the initial *Samurai* strikes were to deliver their ordnance from less than 4,000 feet, putting them 'at considerable risk.'[54] First phase targets also included PAIGC concentrations and encampments in the localities of Cauane, Cachide, Cassacá, and Caiar, as well as insurgent supply and infiltration routes.[55]

The second phase of *Operação Samurai* involved multiple helicopter lifts to deploy paratroops to their jumping-off points throughout the *zona de acção* (zone of action) followed by three days of additional airmobile and search-and-destroy operations on the island. An *Destacamento de Apoio Aéreo* (DAA, Air Support Detachment) was established at Cufar to assist the ground offensive, with additional coordination provided by the CCAA at Bissalanca and an SCAA operating from the forward command post in Catió. Aircraft on call to support the paratroops included a pair of G.91s on ground alert at Bissalanca, a pair of T-6s on 15-minute alert at Cufar, and a Do-27 and Alouette III forward deployed to Cufar for medical evacuation (MEDEVAC).[56] Throughout all phases of the operation, a Do-27 PCV flew continuously over the ZA, as did two additional T-6s and a single *helicanhão* on airborne alert. Portuguese aircraft were also tasked with nightly bombing operations in central Como and daytime interdiction operations elsewhere over the island for the duration of the campaign. Once the second phase had concluded, the Portuguese Army was expected to assume responsibility for reoccupying Como and eradicating any residual PAIGC presence.[57]

Samurai was preceded by a one-week reconnaissance effort beginning 4 November, covering especially the southern and western sectors of the island. G.91s flew low-level photo reconnaissance

Tigres commander *Tenente* Egídio Lopes. (Egídio Lopes Collection)

missions using their 70mm cameras to capture target and threat imagery of 'surprising clarity', according to Abecasis. Insurgent encampments at São Nicolau and Cauane received particular attention from the G.91s, while Do-27s 'flew exhaustively' to survey potential helicopter landing sites.[58] Hundreds of aerial photographs, including panoramic and stereoscopic imagery, were delivered to the newly-established Centro de Campanha de Exploração Fotográfica at Bissalanca for target identification and analysis in preparation for the coming air-ground offensive.[59] The preparatory reconnaissance effort drew praise from the ZACVG command for having produced intelligence information of 'extraordinary value', exceeding the commander's expectations.[60]

The counter-AD operation began at 2200 hours on 13 November, once again initiated by nighttime C-47 bombing raids against PAIGC air defence positions. Multiple anti-aircraft sites responded to the attack, especially around the insurgent base at Cauane, but the defensive fire 'did not reach the intensity we had seen in operations *Resgate* and *Estoque*,' Abecasis later reported. First over the objective area was C-47 no.6155, the first aircraft modified on Abecasis' initiative in 1965, carrying 15kg and 50kg bombs as well as tube-launched magnesium illumination grenades. Over the following three days G.91 and T-6 aircraft flew pre-planned and alerted attack missions over the island's coastal areas, while other T-6s carried out armed reconnaissance and interdiction raids throughout the ZA.[61] According to reports from Portuguese troops and PAIGC prisoners, the air action resulted in six militants killed and another 20 missing; the destruction of 'all military objectives' identified by reconnaissance; and 'great demoralisation as a result of the night bombing, [with] total insecurity in the area attacked.'[62]

The second phase of *Operação Samurai* was preceded by a rare C-47 airborne drop, when participating paratroops jumped onto the forward Portuguese airfield in Cufar for pre-operational staging on 16 November. At 0700 the following morning, multiple waves of five Alouette III helicopters transported the 97 participating paratroops to their first-day landing zones throughout southern

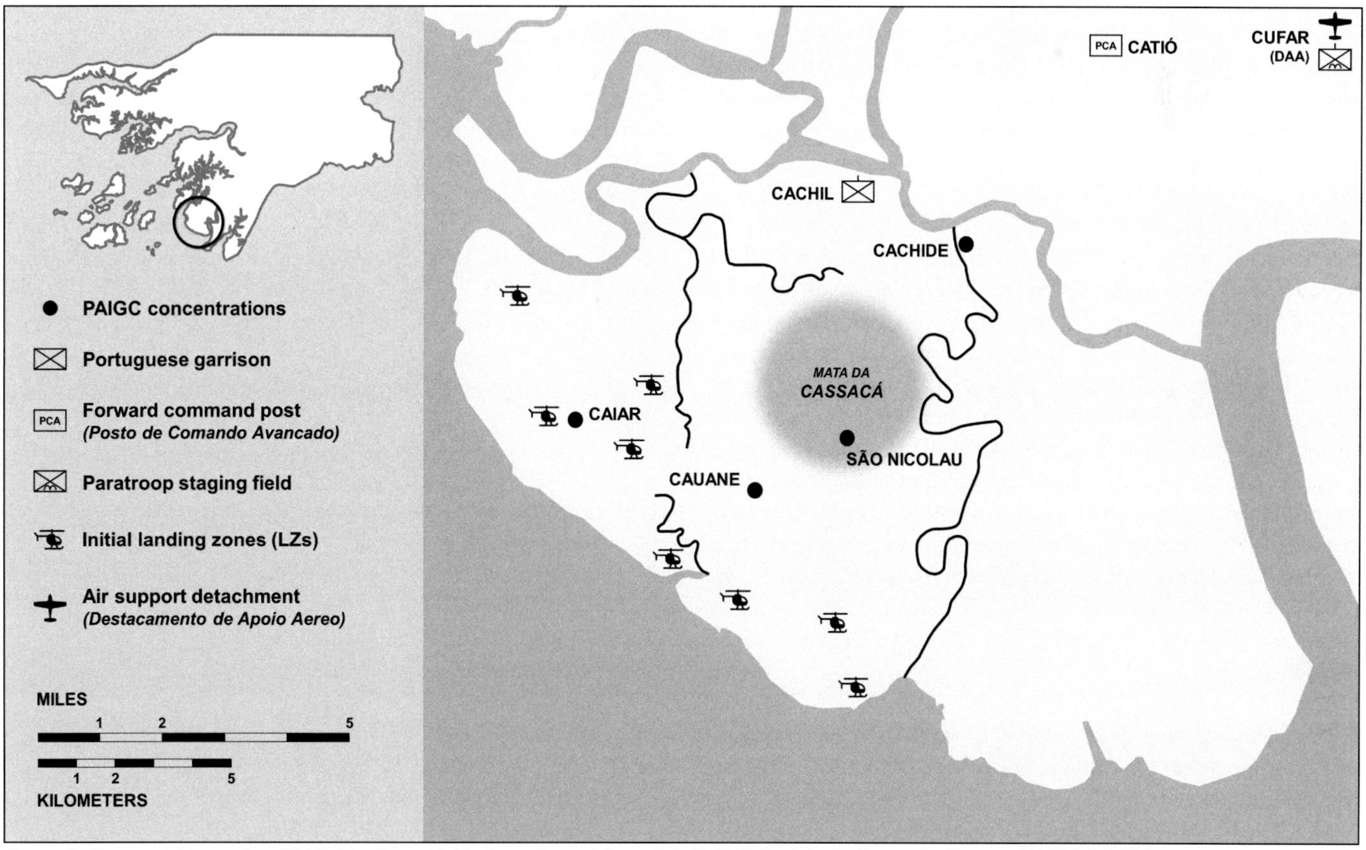

Operação Samurai, November 1966. (Matthew M. Hurley adapted from CZACVG, 'Relatório da Operação 'Samurai',' SGDN/1REP/105/0349/018, ADN.)

Table 5: *Operação Samurai* – ZACVG Sorties and Flight Hours[66]

	Night Attack	Day Attack	Transport	Photo Recon	Total	Hours
1st Phase 13–16 November 1967	7	54	16	5	82	140: 50
2nd Phase 17–19 November 1967	2	32	23	1	58	149: 25
TOTAL	9	86	39	6	140	290: 15

Table 6: *Operação Samurai* – Munitions Expended[67]

	50kg bombs	15kg bombs	Napalm canisters
1st Phase 13–16 November 1967	130	366	16
2nd Phase 17–19 November 1967	86	14	4
TOTAL	216	380	20

Como.[63] The vanguard element of páraquedistas soon encountered fierce opposition before the guerrilla stronghold of Caiar and called for fire support from alert aircraft. A pair each of T-6s and G.91s arrived almost simultaneously, deterring further resistance and permitting the assault force to continue its advance, although a Do-27 performing PCV duties was subjected to ineffective anti-aircraft fire during the episode. With continued air support, the paratroopers ultimately achieved all their assigned objectives while suffering no losses of their own.[64]

Enduring success on Como proved more elusive, however, as it had following *Operação Tridente* nearly three years earlier. In the short term, Como had again been pacified and attacks against the Cachil barracks halted, and the way appeared open for Portuguese forces to completely reoccupy the island. No such action was taken, however, and Como remained an insurgent stronghold for the remainder of the war, for while 'the enemy had been hit hard, there was no doubt that his combat capability was still intact,' Abecasis explained. Unwilling to accept open battle against superior air and ground forces, the insurgents had again retreated to the central forest to await the invasion's end and the inevitable Portuguese withdrawal that followed.[65]

A month after *Operação Samurai* the ZACVG and G.O. 1201 returned their focus to the Cantanhez Peninsula, site of *Operação Resgate* almost exactly a year earlier. Two intervening developments had drawn the attention of Portuguese commanders: first, the PAIGC's militants had restored their air defences in the region, again posing a credible threat to air operations there. Second, PAIGC forces had begun using the peninsula as a base to menace traffic on the strategically vital Cumbijã River – the sole surface link to the Portuguese Army garrison at Cufar – leading the navy to request FAP intervention. To suppress the renewed air defence threat and dislodge insurgent emplacements hazarding the river, the ZACVG launched *Operação Valquíria* (Operation Valkyrie) on 19 December, under the command of G.O. 1201 chief Tenente Coronel Hugo Damásio.[68]

The two-day air offensive followed the now-familiar template of nocturnal bombing raids followed by daytime interdiction and armed reconnaissance operations. Portuguese C-47s began attacking anti-aircraft positions and insurgent shelters on the night of 19–20 December while gathering additional target intelligence for follow-on strikes. These took place primarily during daylight hours on 20 and 21 December, comprising eight G.91 and twelve T-6 interdiction and armed reconnaissance missions.[69] A combined 25 C-47, G.91, and T-6 sorties delivered 5,930kg of ordnance in a confined area during the two-day operation, and at its conclusion indications of guerrilla activity had virtually ceased.[70] Nonetheless, *Operação Valquíria* left ZACVG commander Abecasis uneasy. Having personally survived 'raging' anti-aircraft fire during *Valquíria*'s opening night, he 'had occasion to admire the courage with which the anti-aircraft pieces in front of us were manned… The enemy was battered and died at his post,' displaying bravery 'unknown to the generality of the Portuguese military.' This presented a grave challenge to Portugal's cause, if his observations proved accurate: 'What would be this war's outcome if the psychological imbalance between the combatants was so shockingly in the enemy's favour?' the ZACVG commander wondered.[71]

To redress that imbalance, Abecasis recommended an all-out aerial offensive against Quitafine, where the PAIGC had re-established its dominance and resumed attacks against Portuguese outposts. Dubbed *Operação Apocalipse*, the proposal envisioned 'the most violent offensive within reach of our resources … *Operação Apocalipse* would mobilise our full potential and demolish Quitafine,' or so Abecasis hoped.[72] To his dismay, however, the initiative failed to garner any enthusiasm among his superiors or even his own staff of military aviators, given the growing risks of operating in the 'Quitafine Furnace'; in fact, one of his officers declared he would formally refuse to fly the mission. In the end *Apocalipse* ended up as 'nothing more than a mirage; the 'operation' that wasn't.'[73] Disappointed· *Coronel* Abecasis left Guinea when his assignment as ZACVG commander ended on 12 January 1967. He was replaced by *Coronel* Rui da Costa Cesário, an officer who shared his enthusiasm for heliborne 'intervention operations' and sharp, focused air attacks.[74]

3
'It was them or us'

> The most memorable missions I flew in Guinea were the missions against the anti-aircraft weapons. It was them or us. (*Tenente* Egídio Lopes, Esquadra 121 commander, 1966–67)[1]

In January 1967 *Brigadeiro* Schultz and his new air commander faced an increasingly uncertain strategic situation. 'Despite the blows suffered during the last two years, the [PAIGC's] political-military virulence has not diminished,' he had reported the previous December, drawing attention to the PAIGC's increased regional and international support, improved training and equipment, and more effective propaganda at all levels.[2] Schultz gave particular emphasis to 'a relatively new factor – the appearance of whites, especially Cubans, as instructors, advisers, or specialists.'[3] The participation of Eastern Bloc advisers had long been suspected,[4] but 1967 would see a dramatic escalation of foreign intervention on the PAIGC's behalf, spearheaded by self-proclaimed 'internationalists' from Fidel Castro's Cuba.

Cuban military involvement in Africa began with aid deliveries to Algerian rebels in 1960–1961, and over the next three years Cuban military advisory missions served in several sub-Saharan locales.[5] Havana's growing interest in Africa was reinforced by Ernesto 'Che' Guevara's seven-nation tour of the Continent from December 1964 to March 1965, which led to the first formal contacts between Cuba and the PAIGC.[6] By that time Castro's intelligence chief, Manuel Piñero, had already identified the Guinea insurgency as 'our strategic priority in Africa' given its early successes against an established, though declining, Western colonial power.[7] Castro agreed, and the first Cuban weapons for Amílcar Cabral's militants arrived in the port of Conakry on 14 May 1965, while the first PAIGC trainees travelled to Cuba for political and military instruction that same year.[8]

Additional arms and materiel sailed from Cuba in 1966, as did the first Cuban military specialists, who arrived on 1 May 1966.[9] Over the next eight years up to 500 Cuban 'volunteers' served as advisers, instructors, medical personnel, and combatants in the PAIGC's cause, according to Oscar Oramas, the former Cuban ambassador to the Republic of Guinea.[10] As many as 60 operated in Portuguese Guinea at any given time, with one 1967 insurgent dispatch listing 32 Cuban military and medical personnel active in the province – nine of them '*antiaéristas*', or anti-aircraft specialists.[11] As far as Amílcar Cabral was concerned, his 'Cuban comrades, whatever their specialty' were 'considered to be PAIGC militants for the entire duration of their collaboration' – collaboration which, he emphasised, 'could have decisive consequences for the progress of our struggle.'[12] The consequences were indeed decisive for the 17 Cubans that Oramas acknowledged were killed in Guinea, the first on 2 July 1967.[13] Additionally, at least one Cuban military officer, *Capitán* Pedro Rodriguez Peralta, was captured by Portuguese paratroops operating in the Guileje corridor on 18 November 1969.[14]

Other Eastern Bloc nations also provided arms, military training, and/or tactical and technical expertise to the PAIGC, particularly the Soviet Union and China, and to a lesser extent East Germany, Czechoslovakia, Romania, Bulgaria, North Korea, and North Vietnam.[15] In 1965 the USSR even constructed a training facility at Perevalnoe, on the Crimean Peninsula, specifically for members of the PAIGC and other African liberation movements. Instruction there focused on the use of artillery, mines and explosives, and air

Amílcar Cabral, Aristides Pereira, and Cuban ambassador Oscar Oramas meeting with Cuban 'internationalists' at Havana's Embassy in Conakry. (Casa Comum/Mário Soares Foundation)

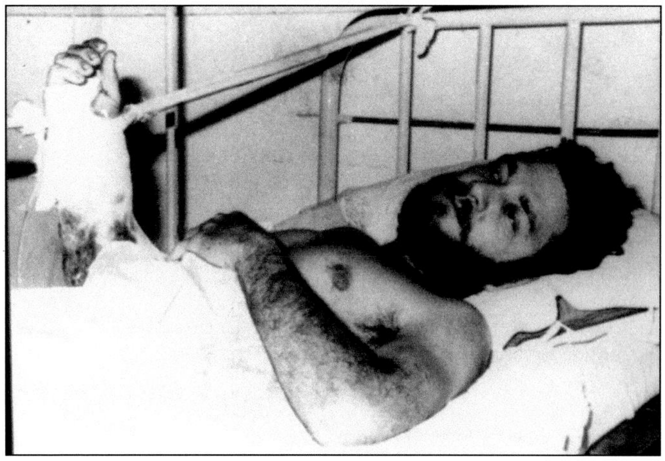

The first photo of Cuban *Capitán* Pedro Peraltain in his hospital bed, after his capture by Portuguese forces. Peralta was wounded in the right arm and evacuated to Bissau. (National Defence Archive)

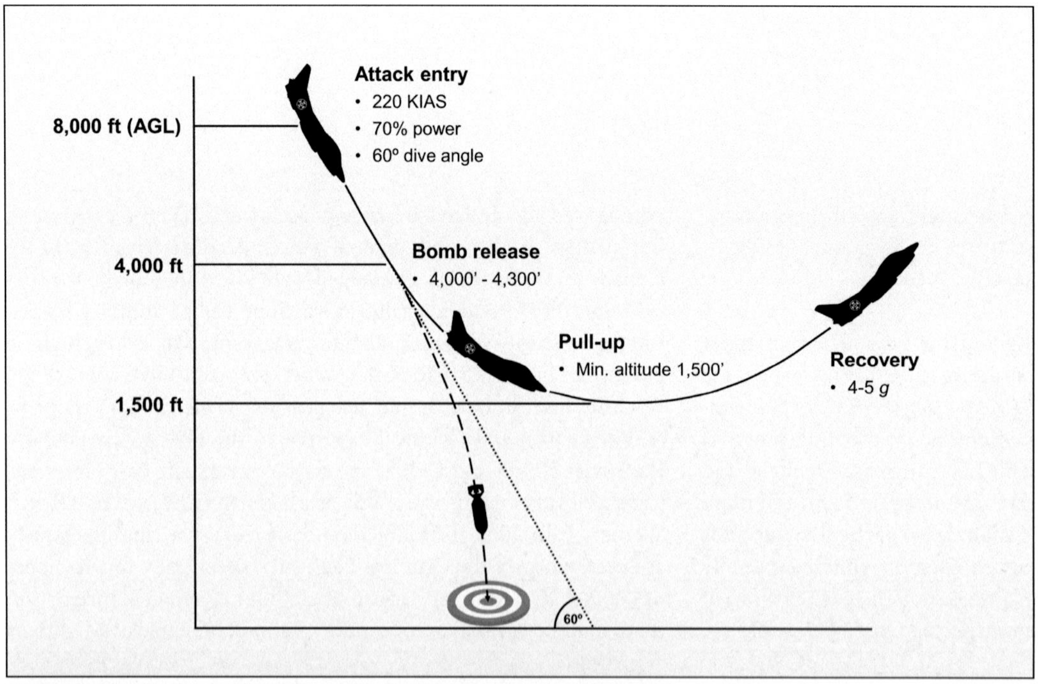

G.91 anti-aircraft site attack profile (50kg or 200kg bombs). (Matthew M. Hurley Adapted from Nico, *A Batalha do Quitafine*, p. 157.)

A ZPU-4 in the Cassebeche area, protected by a spiral *espaldão* (earth revetment). (National Defence Archive)

A DShK 12.7mm AAMG captured during *Operação Barracuda*. (National Defence Archive)

defence weapons, especially those 'designed to hit low-flying targets – Portuguese aircraft – at close range.'[16] By that time the OAU had decided 'to channel all its support to the party of Amílcar Cabral,' as did neighbouring Senegal, which under OAU pressure opened its territory to PAIGC bases and supply routes in 1966.[17]

The infusion of new equipment and expertise prompted tactical and organisational changes across the PAIGC, and its growing anti-aircraft corps was no exception. As Amílcar Cabral summarised in April, 'For a long time we fought enemy planes only with our light weapons, [but] we are gradually equipping our units and military bases with weapons suitable for anti-aircraft combat and combatants specialised in handling these weapons.'[18] Starting in mid–1966, then, Portuguese airmen began reporting a shift away from the guerrilla quality of early air defence efforts, which had been characterised by 'randomly dispersed weapons shrouded in vegetation.' In contrast, by 1967 insurgent air defence positions became more 'fortified and conventional,' with larger-calibre weapons deployed in circular or spiral *espaldões* (earth revetments) clustered in relatively open terrain. Although the new arrangement provided some protection against blast and shrapnel while giving PAIGC gunners the opportunity to rapidly concentrate fire in any direction, it also limited their mobility and rendered their positions far easier to detect.[19] From a strategic perspective, however, the transition to a more conventional area air defence posture supported the political aim of reinforcing PAIGC claims to *zonas libertadas* such as Como and Quitafine. 'While fire from the cover of vegetation aimed to cause attrition through anti-aircraft ambushes, the installation of a fixed anti-aircraft arrangement sought to prevent access to a portion of the airspace,' *General* Nico elaborated.[20]

Destroying the compact, better-shielded anti-aircraft guns required more accurate delivery profiles, but through hard combat experience Portuguese airmen soon developed effective methods against the offending weapons.[21] The optimum attack began with a 45 to 60 degree dive from 8,000 feet, the pilot releasing 50kg or 200kg fragmentation bombs at approximately 4,000 feet and then pulling out of the dive for egress. When carrying napalm, FAP G.91 pilots dropped them from 100 feet in level flight. Attacks originated from the direction of the sun whenever possible to delay visual detection and minimise reactive fire (ideally at approximately 0930 or 1500) – an approach that 'could be a help, but was not a guarantee,' according to onetime ZACVG commander General Manuel Diogo Neto.[22] No matter the time of day, the PAIGC's embryonic air defence network likely benefited from advance warning of attack, considering the intense insurgent interest in air operations at BA12 and their stepped-up information-gathering activities in the Bissau area more generally. Whatever the reason, anti-aircraft sites would often open fire immediately upon the initiation of an air raid from any quarter, despite the FAP's best efforts to achieve surprise.[23]

The FAP's new arsenal of aircraft, weapons, and tactics was first put to the test over the increasingly restive Quinara region. Shortly after new ZACVG commander *Coronel* Costa Cesário arrived in January 1967, stepped-up PAIGC activity in Quinara – directly across the

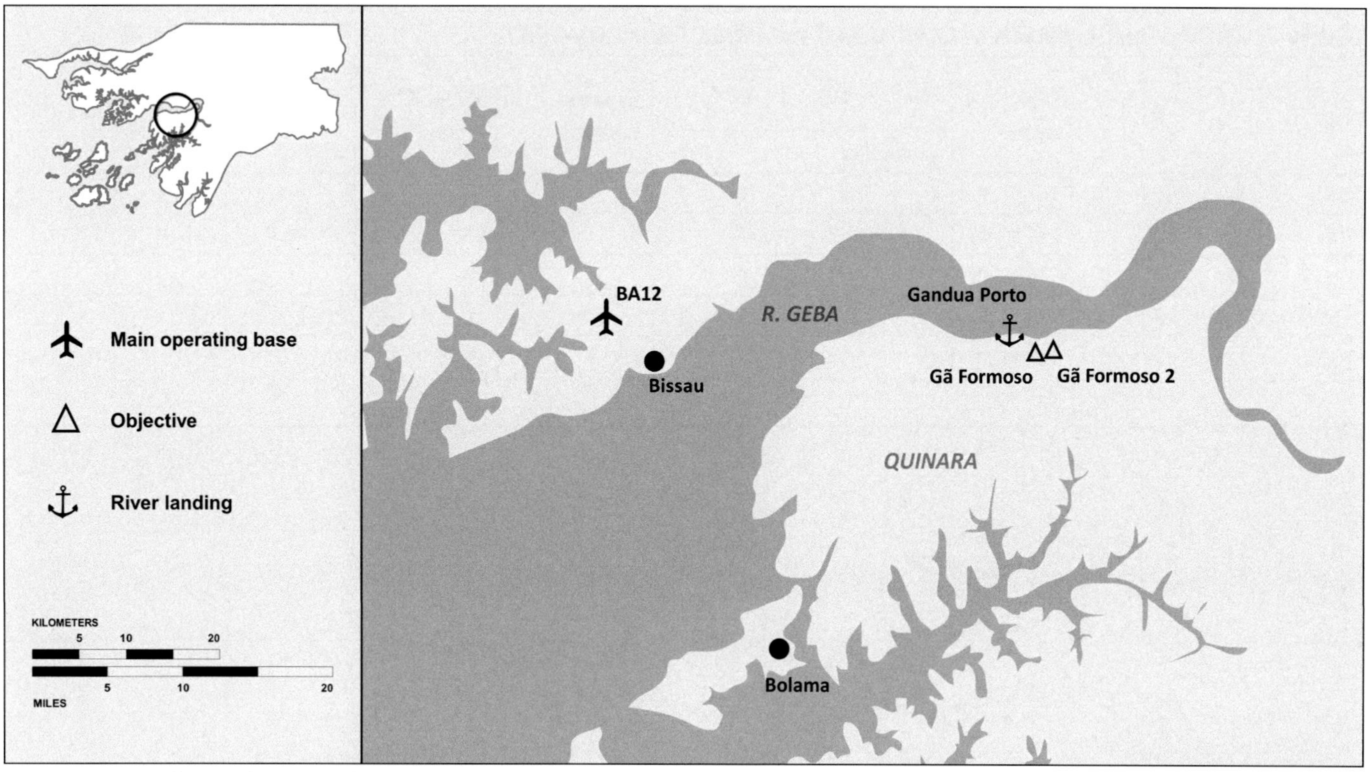

Operação Barracuda zona da acção, February 1967. (Matthew M. Hurley)

Geba River from Bissau – drew mounting scrutiny and concern from Bissalanca. In one instance a pair of G.91s, flown by *Tenente Coronel* Damásio and *Tenente* Egídio Lopes, were surprised by anti-aircraft fire from the Geba's southern bank while crossing the river at 2,000 feet on initial approach to BA12.[24] To eliminate the threat to aircraft flying near their main base or crossing the Geba (which bisected Western Guinea), the ZACVG conceived *Operação Barracuda*, a one-day air and paratrooper offensive in February 1967.[25] The mission order directed G.O. 1201 to:

DShK 12.7mm AAMG positions near a small village, targeted during *Operação Barracuda*. (National Defence Archive)

1. Neutralise the anti-aircraft threat in the Quinara region;
2. Prepare the *zona de acção* for a ground assault into the Gã Formoso forest;
3. Transport paratroopers by helicopter to the area of operations, in conjunction with near-simultaneous naval landings;
4. Interdict enemy movement in the *zona da acção*;
5. Provide logistics, command and control, and fire support as required.

A supplementary operations order directed the *páraquedistas*, upon landing, to clear and search their assigned objectives to further 'dismantle' insurgent infrastructure and organisation in the Gã Formoso area. Significantly, BCP 12 was also specifically tasked with finding and seizing at least one of the PAIGC's prized anti-aircraft weapons – an as yet unprecedented feat for Portuguese arms in Guinea.[26]

Operação Barracuda began at 0600 on 4 February. Twenty-five Portuguese aircraft (six G.91s, eleven T-6s, seven Alouette IIIs, and a PCV-configured Do-27) departed BA12 at minimum take off intervals, using both the runway and a new parallel taxiway to launch the fleet as quickly as possible and increase the likelihood of surprise. After the short flight across the Geba the G.91s unloaded their 50kg bombs on two anti-aircraft positions in and near Gã Formoso, silencing one of them, followed by T-6s which struck targets adjacent to the forest with 15kg and 50kg bombs, 37mm rockets, and 7.62mm machine gun fire. At 0620 the first platoon of paratroopers disembarked from six Alouette IIIs, accompanied by

Table 7: ZACVG Participation in *Operação Barracuda*, February 1967[32]											
Type	**No.**	**Flight hours**	**200**	**50**	**15**	**Napalm canisters**	**37mm rockets**	**20mm**	**.50in**	**7.62 mm**
			bombs (kg)					**rounds**		
G.91	6	7h 30	4	8		10			352	
T-6	13	39h 50		26	48		25			105
Do-27	2	12h 40					28			
Al-III	7	18h 15						855		
TOTAL	28	78h 15	4	34	48	10	53	855	352	105

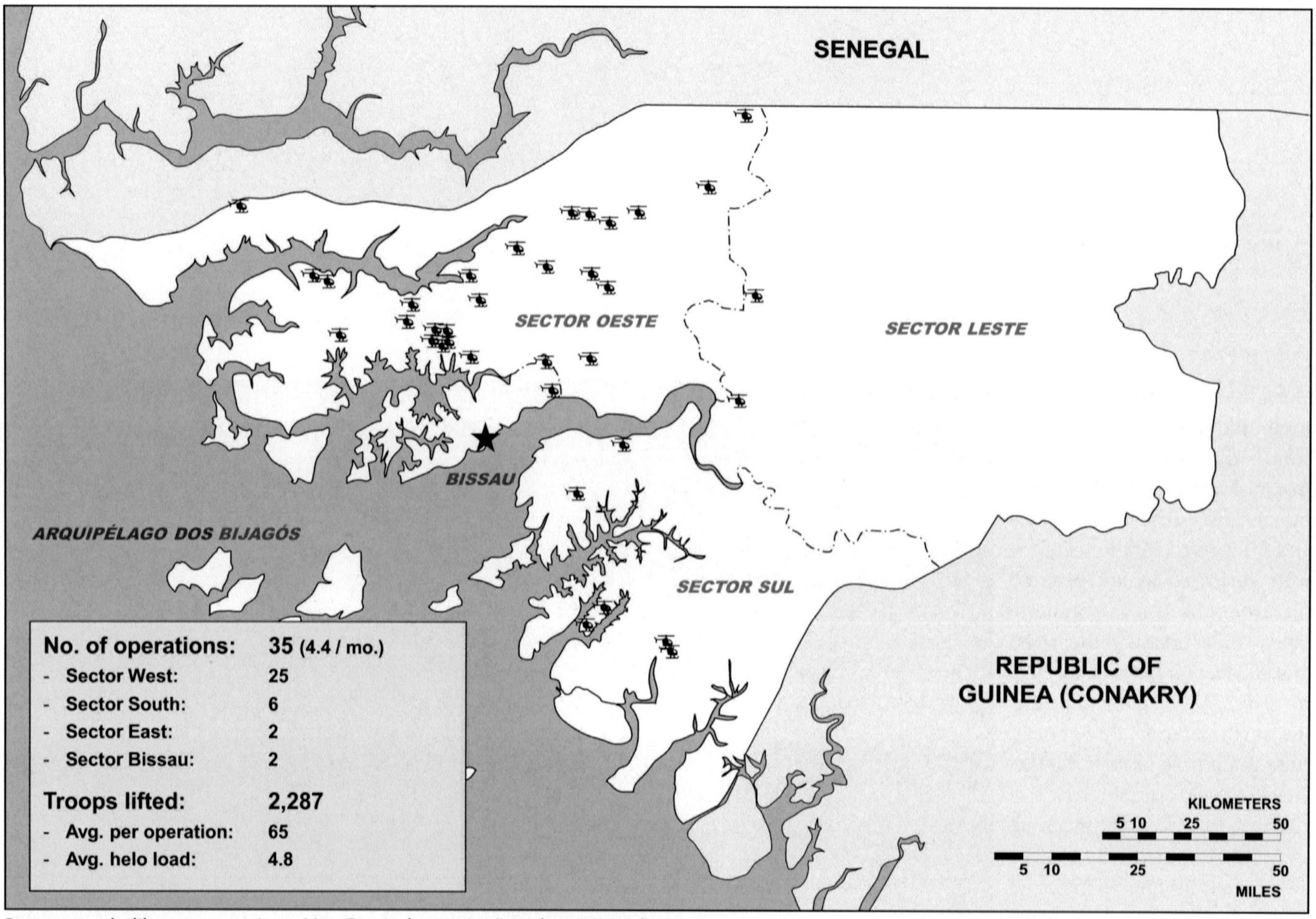

Portuguese heliborne operations, May-December 1967. (Matthew M. Hurley)

a *helicanhão*, with a second wave landing at 0630. The remaining paratroops arrived aboard naval launches at Ganduá Porto, on the Geba's southern bank, with two T-6s and a *helicanhão* supporting the landing. At 0900 the paratrooper groups joined together and began their sweep through the Gã Formoso forest, putting PAIGC militants there to rout. Having met their terrestrial goals while capturing a 12.7mm DShK AAMG, 'the fundamental objective of the operation', the paratroops withdrew to Ganduá Porto where they re-embarked at 1800 under the protection of two T-6s, a *helicanhão*, and a rocket-armed Do-27.[27]

Later analysis described *Operação Barracuda* as 'a perfectly executed operation, without any [Portuguese] casualties.'[28] Despite the air defence activity that had provoked the action, no aircraft were hit by defensive fire and Portuguese forces had, for the first time, seized a purpose-built anti-aircraft weapon from the PAIGC. Beyond these immediate effects, *Operação Barracuda* 'had as its main result the end of the enemy's prestige and arrogance in the area,' the after-action report proclaimed. While the losses inflicted on the insurgents were 'not spectacular', the purported psychological impact of the operation was rated 'highly rewarding'. Most importantly from the ZACVG's perspective, 'The capture of enemy anti-aircraft equipment, and the lowering of his morale and fighting strength, restored the Air Force's complete freedom of action in the Gã Formoso area.'[29]

In achieving those results, however transitory, the ZACVG and G.O. 1201 utilised virtually every aircraft at their disposal: a total of 28 G.91s, T-6s, Do-27s, and Alouette IIIs. During the one-day operation these aircraft expended 4,200kg of bombs, 53 37mm rockets, 855 20mm cannon shells, and over 500 rounds of .50in and 7.62mm machine gun rounds.[30] *Operação Barracuda* also demonstrated, once again, the value of low-altitude photographic reconnaissance missions carried out by the G.91s, which revealed detailed information regarding the location and layout of insurgent anti-aircraft positions.[31]

Operação Barracuda coincided with a renewed Portuguese push to reassert colonial control in the area north of the Geba River, part of a broader strategy implemented by *Brigadeiro* Schultz in December 1966.[33] Schultz's plan involved four complementary lines of action: securing the province's borders to prevent PAIGC reinforcement and supply; destroying insurgent forces within the territory; slowing the internal spread of subversion; and recovering the allegiance of prisoners, refugees, and populations formerly under rebel control.[34] Regionally, in the west (*Sector Oeste*) Schultz dispatched airmobile forces to interdict insurgent resupply in the coastal regions and force rebel forces into the Oio Forest, where they could be encircled and annihilated. This contrasted with the more positional 'aggressive defensive' posture Schultz ordered in the eastern half of the province (*Sector Leste*), but in the south (*Sector Sul*) he instructed his airmen to continue their vigorous reconnaissance and interdiction activities in preparation for continued air-ground operations.[35]

In accordance with Schultz's amended strategy and his November 1966 directive to 'increase heli-transported operations as much as possible,'[36] Bissalanca-based Alouette III helicopters and fixed-wing air support assets participated in at least 35 heliborne assault operations from May to December 1967, resulting in the destruction or abandonment of 10 insurgent bases and the reported deaths of nearly one hundred militants.[37] These operations soon revealed a general pattern, beginning with a preparatory phase. When practical, necessary preparations were accomplished at Bissalanca; for more distant objectives, the first phase of a heliborne assault involved the preparatory staging of airmobile forces, usually paratroopers or commandos, to forward bases. Transport helicopters and a Do-27 airborne command post (PCV) might also deploy forward, along with specialist personnel to facilitate air-ground coordination. At H-Hour, G.91s and/or T-6s would neutralise anti-aircraft resistance and strike enemy strongpoints; periodically, *helicanhões* or rocket-armed Do-27s participated in the opening attack, depending on aircraft availability and the anticipated threat. Transport helicopters would then be escorted to their landing zones by T-6s or *helicanhão*, with additional fire support and MEDEVAC assets standing by on airborne or ground alert. At the operation's conclusion, the airmobile forces re-embarked on Alouette IIIs or boarded surface transport for return to their staging areas or home garrisons.[38] Though this template betrayed the FAP's familiarity with and emulation of French *intervention héliportée* operations in Algeria, Portugal's helicopter assault tactics developed much further and closely presaged the 'Fireforce' model employed by Rhodesian forces against Zimbabwean nationalists in the 1970s.[39]

Portugal's helicopter offensive drew immediate attention and concern from the PAIGC leadership. In his memoirs, Luís Cabral (Amílcar's half-brother and PAIGC co-founder) acknowledged the initial shock of the heliborne attacks, which struck seemingly anywhere without warning, panicking local inhabitants and exerting 'a terrible impact' on PAIGC forces.[40] A party seminar in Conakry attributed at least part of this reaction to 'cultural traditions' and 'religious heritage', concluding that the technological novelty of helicopters aroused superstitions among some militants and cadres, provoking a sense of impotence.[41] The urgent need to confront this 'new desperate initiative of the *tugas*'[42] prompted Amílcar Cabral to issue a counter-helicopter 'manual' to his forces in June 1967. Acknowledging the damage already done by Portuguese helicopter raids and citing 'the heroic people of Vietnam' as both inspiration and exemplar, the document described Portuguese heli-assault tactics in some detail, including typical attack composition and timing, before turning to weaknesses and vulnerabilities that Cabral's militants could exploit. The manual also contained numerous detailed tactical recommendations, such as firing tables to determine effective ranges for various calibres of anti-aircraft weaponry.[43]

A FAP Alouette III and paratroopers on operations against the PAIGC. (Serrano Rosa Collection)

The document's central message, though, was one of encouragement; 'Helicopters can do nothing against a people united and determined to fight courageously for their freedom,' Cabral proclaimed hopefully in the first pages. 'Just as we have defeated the colonialist troops with their modern weapons and planes, so too will we defeat the helicopters they are now using.'[44] That promise proved empty, at least in the near term: despite over 70 helicopter assault operations from May 1967 through December 1968, and throughout a total of 3,500 helicopter sorties over Guinea during that same period, PAIGC anti-aircraft fire damaged only five Alouette IIIs while downing none.[45] 'We never got our men to face the helicopters, even after they had anti-aircraft weapons,' Luís Cabral later admitted.[46]

While Portugal's helicopter offensive gathered momentum, the ZACVG also maintained its counter-AD campaign in southern Guinea. By May 1967 it had identified the PAIGC's renewed anti-aircraft build-up in Cantanhez and Quitafine as 'the main threat to Portuguese aircraft,' necessitating a new round of defence suppression operations.[47] On 19 September FAP G.91s returned to Cantanhez for *Operação Tigre*, striking insurgent air defences that had re-emerged after *Operação Valquíria* (December 1966). A trio of G.91s delivered 200kg bombs and napalm against anti-aircraft weapons sites at Cacine and Darsalame, and post-damage assessment photos revealed direct napalm impacts against the first target. G.91s also strafed a second anti-aircraft gun emplacement at Cacine, silencing that position as well.[48] The regional threat remained, however, and at the end of the month Schultz directed the ZACVG to 'continue its independent actions to neutralise places where the enemy is strongest, with the priority on Quitafine and Cantanhez.'[49]

Quitafine accordingly received renewed ZACVG attention with a trio of air defence suppression operations in October and November 1967. The first and largest, *Operação Violeta*, was a five-day effort against PAIGC anti-aircraft emplacements threatening Portuguese aircraft over the Cassebeche area. From 6 to 10 October sixteen G.91 sorties pummelled their targets with 2.75in rockets, machine gun fire, 3,600kg of bombs, and six napalm weapons. At least two of the insurgent air defence sites received direct napalm hits, but heavy anti-aircraft machine gun fire persisted throughout the operation and one G.91 took significant damage from two 12.7mm rounds on the final day.[50] During the operation Portugal drew mild international ire for an errant raid that purportedly struck a village in the Republic of Guinea and killed 11 inhabitants – the

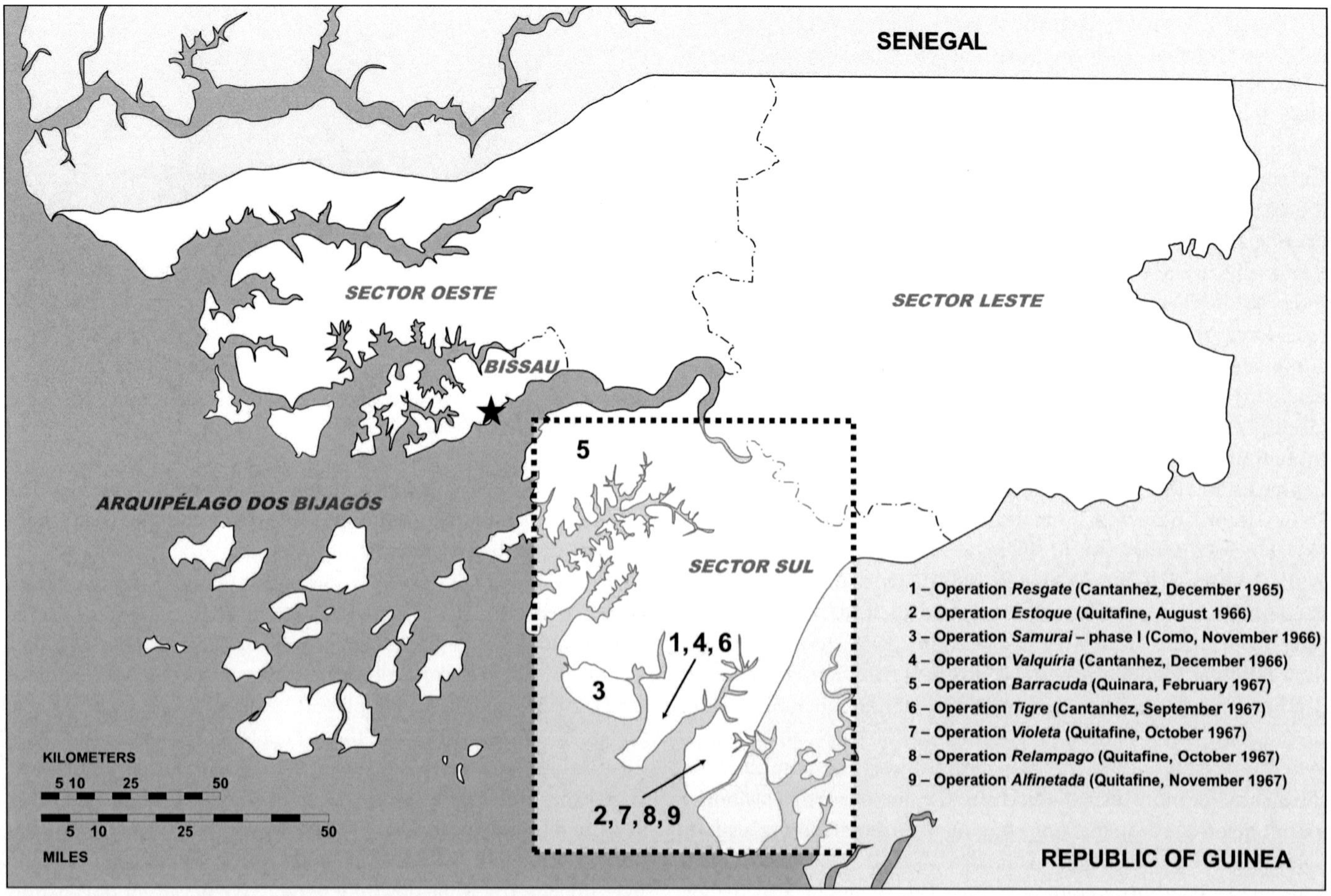

ZACVG counter-air defence operations, 1965–1967. (Matthew M. Hurley)

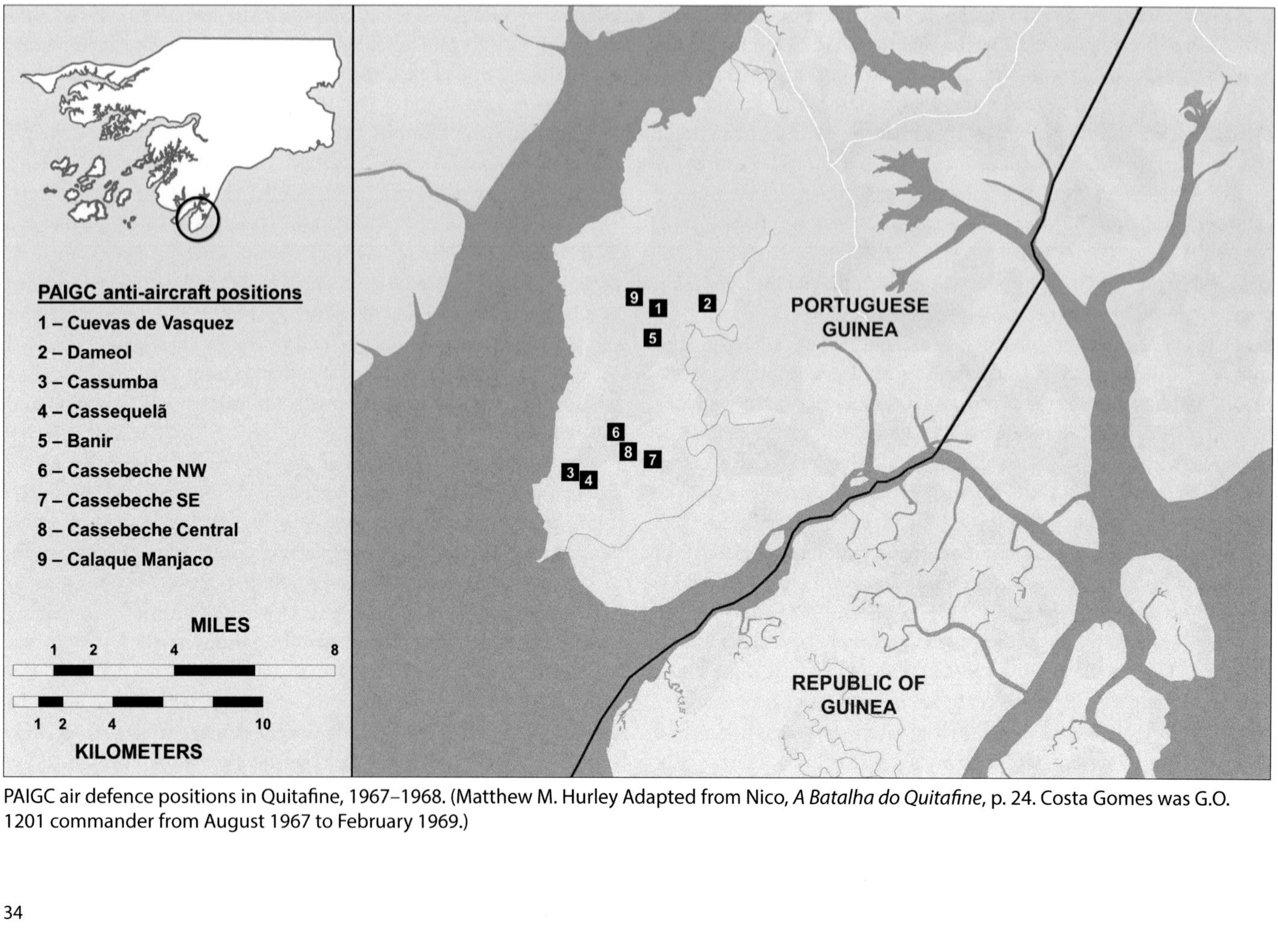

PAIGC air defence positions in Quitafine, 1967–1968. (Matthew M. Hurley Adapted from Nico, *A Batalha do Quitafine*, p. 24. Costa Gomes was G.O. 1201 commander from August 1967 to February 1969.)

AA positions in Banir targeted during *Operação Faísca*, January 1968. (José Nico Collection)

rated combat-ready throughout the first four months of 1968.[57]

Munitions availability and suitability also generated continuing concern. Ordnance shortages had previously compelled Portuguese G.91s to employ single-bomb attacks against anti-aircraft positions, a delivery profile that 'proved difficult and dangerous for the Fiat pilots.'[58] This issue was largely resolved when sufficient armament stocks began arriving in early 1968, after which FAP G.91s began carrying two each 50kg and 200kg bombs aboard each fighter, delivered in a single attack run. Depending on aircraft availability, up to four G.91s attacking in trail would hit a single target with a total of 16 bombs, and if necessary, the strike would be repeated until the objective was eliminated.[59]

However, the ordnance on hand was ill-suited to operations in Quitafine. 'We found, right at the start, that the bombs and fuses we used weren't very effective on that unstable ground,' *General* Nico recalled, since their explosive force was dissipated by the soft and sandy terrain. 'Even when the impacts took place relatively close to them, after the dust had settled and the earache had passed, the guerrillas continued to fire.'[60] Fortunately for the Portuguese airmen, the same soil characteristics that muted their weapons' effects also highlighted the air defence gun emplacements: their earthen revetments 'shone brightly under the intense Guinea sun and made target location far easier,' according to Nico.[61] Even so, as *Tenente Coronel* Costa Gomes countered, 'with the targets firing at us, the likelihood of placing a bomb in such a small circle was slim.'[62]

Despite these misgivings, the ZACVG responded to its charge with another series of counter-AD operations in southern Guinea during early 1968. Portuguese airmen ushered in the New Year with *Operação Faísca* (Operation Spark), a two-day attack on anti-aircraft positions identified in Dameol and Banir on the Quitafine Peninsula. From 1–2 January, G.91s delivered 5,400kg of bombs against the two sites during 19 attack sorties, destroying one 14.5mm ZPU in Banir and a 12.7mm DShK at Dameol. Returning Portuguese airmen reported the other sites 'possibly destroyed, having been completely abandoned by the enemy.'[63] During January 1968 G.91s also retaliated against anti-aircraft fire encountered by Portuguese aircraft supporting other operations, resulting in five reactive strikes across Quitafine and Cantanhez and the reported destruction of at least four more air defence weapons.[64]

These isolated successes failed to appreciably degrade the threat, however. Spirited anti-aircraft opposition in February prompted the ZACVG to mount another counter-AD campaign over Quitafine, a series of three operations optimistically christened *Operação Martelada* (Operation Hammering). The first round of *Operação Martelada* was launched in response to 'fierce' 12.7mm fire reported near the Quitafine locality of Calaque Manjaco on 8 February.

eighth alleged armed incursion by Portuguese forces since February 1965.[51] Regardless, follow-up raids against anti-aircraft sites in the Cassebeche vicinity took place during *Operação Relâmpago* (25–28 October) and *Operação Alfinetada* (24–26 November), the first of which reportedly killed five air defence gunners during a napalm attack.[52] Yet insurgent anti-aircraft sites continued to harass FAP aircraft over Guinea during the following months, stressing the severity of the continuing threat and presaging future Portuguese attempts to eradicate it.[53]

Between October 1967 and January 1968, G.91 reconnaissance missions identified five new or rebuilt anti-aircraft positions on Quitafine, the first a pair of 12.7mm DShK AAMG emplacements in the Cassumba and Cassequelã vicinities. Shortly thereafter, the PAIGC began work on two other sites designated Cassebeche and Cassebeche NW, while 'clustered' anti-aircraft positions appeared near Dameol and Banir, the latter apparently built to accommodate wheeled systems such as the 14.5mm ZPU-1 and ZPU-4. At the start of February, five new positions for 12.7mm AAMGs 'emerged overnight' in nearby Cuevas de Vasquez. Together, these deployments revealed the PAIGC's intention of 'creating and maintaining what we nowadays call a 'no-fly zone'' to discourage or deny FAP operations over Quitafine, according to *General* Nico.[54]

Portugal's Defence Minister informed *Brigadeiro* Schultz that he considered Quitafine 'an Air Force problem' and issued a 'definitive order' directing the ZACVG to neutralise the air defence threat on the peninsula. Corresponding instructions tasked G.O. 1201 with 'neutralising the AAA positions installed by the PAIGC at Quitafine.'[55] The order put G.O. 1201 commander *Tenente Coronel* Francisco Costa Gomes into a state of disbelief: 'Damn, for this job, the 'Air Force' is me plus the six Fiat pilots!' he fretted.[56] Only the G.91s were likely to survive the expected threat without suffering excessive damage, but too few were available to mount and sustain any concerted air offensive in the region: of the eight jets originally sent to Bissalanca, an average of just over half that number were

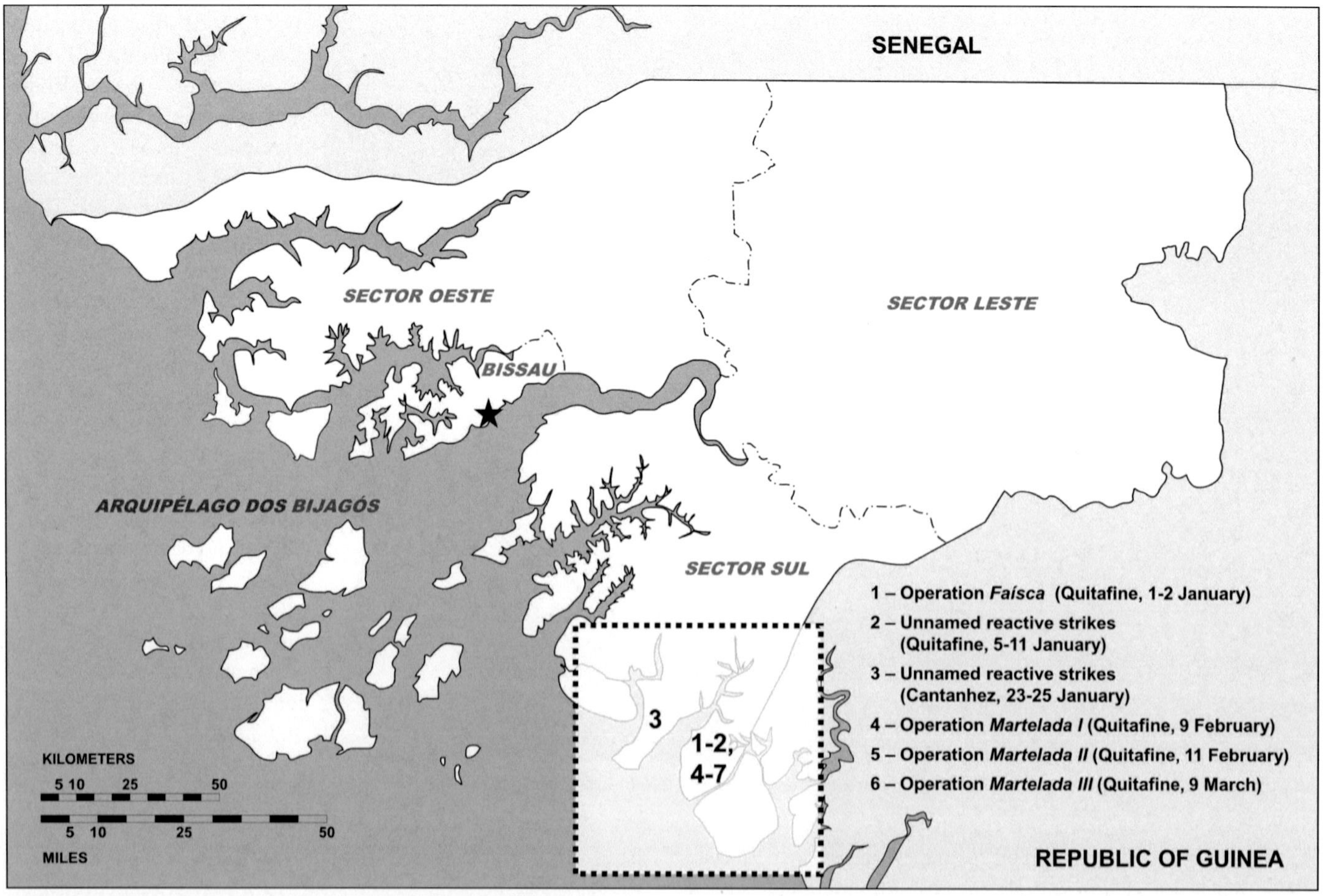

ZACVG counter-AD operations, January-May 1968. (Matthew M. Hurley)

Although G.91s struck two anti-aircraft positions immediately after the incident, the ZACVG commander's desire to respond more forcefully led to the initiation of *Operação Martelada I* on 9 February.[65] At 1255 four G.91s departed BA12, each carrying four 50kg and two 200kg bombs, to strike PAIGC AAMG positions in Cassebeche as well as Calaque Manjaco. Meeting only sporadic and ineffectual resistance, they blasted the sites with 24 bombs in less than 30 seconds, and a second wave at 1600 found the gun emplacements abandoned.[66] Bissalanca-based G.91s flew a total of 10 sorties for *Martelada I*, delivering 4,800kgs of bombs and destroying two of the air defence positions jeopardising operations over the Quitafine Peninsula.[67]

Just two days later, on 11 February, the ZACVG launched *Operação Martelada II* in response to renewed heavy machine gun fire directed against G.91s flying over Cassebeche. Nine Fiat sorties struck PAIGC 12.7mm DShK sites in the area with eight 50kg bombs, six 200kg bombs, and eight napalm canisters, reportedly destroying one gun emplacement and forcing the evacuation of two others. Follow-on reconnaissance later in the day encountered no opposition.[68] The satisfactory results of *Operaçãoes Martelada I* and *Martelada II*, coinciding with improved munitions availability, induced the ZACVG and G.O. 1201 to plan future G.91 strikes in waves of four to five aircraft delivering maximum bomb loads in quick succession. The concentrated violence of these attacks often compelled insurgent anti-aircraft gunners to abandon their positions or relocate; assuming that they and their weapons survived the initial assault.[69]

The mounting peril arising from BA12-Bissalanca made the air base a tempting target for the PAIGC, leading to an unprecedented insurgent attack against the installation. During a six-minute raid commencing at 2330 on 18 February 1968, 10 mortar rounds and rocket-propelled grenades fired from outside the security perimeter impacted within BA12. The hit-and-run attack left two dead and 12 wounded among a group of militia camped on the base, but failed to impact on any aircraft and caused only 'negligible' material damage; in fact, the following morning BA12 launched more than 30 sorties in support of ongoing operations, including a company-sized air assault in west-central Guinea.[70] Nonetheless, the PAIGC farcically declared the attack a 'great success' and claimed the destruction of two aircraft, three hangars, and the control tower, later awarding the 'Black Star of the Party' to each of the 13 participating militants.[71] Obvious propaganda aside, the attack underscored the PAIGC's ability to infiltrate heavily armed militants into Bissau and its environs, conduct an attack, and withdraw without being intercepted.[72] The raid was also a blunt reminder of the PAIGC's mandate to 'shell airfields, carry out ambushes there, and attack aircraft as they take off,' in accordance with a 1965 party directive.[73] Indeed, the PAIGC had unrealistically claimed over 20 earlier attacks against outlying Portuguese airstrips; in one case allegedly rendering the airfield at Cufar 'unusable to aviation' with mortar fire.[74]

Attacks against its airfields, whether actual or fictitious, did not disrupt the ZACVG's counter-AD campaign in Quitafine, and G.O. 1201's Fiats returned to the Cassebeche area for *Operação Martelada III* on 7 March 1968. A four-plane wave of G.91s delivered twelve 50kg bombs, six 200kg bombs, and two napalm canisters against a ZPU-4 quad-mounted 14.5mm anti-aircraft gun, destroying it. The Fiats then strafed four nearby DShK 12.7mm AAMG positions, prompting the gunners to relocate to more secure sites.[75] Follow-on strikes later that day and the next encountered neither opposition nor viable targets, and photo reconnaissance subsequently confirmed the 'brutal annihilation of the complex' which 'broke the enemy's ability to react,' according to *General* Nico.[76]

Detail of a A ZPU-4 position in Cassebeche, targeted during *Operação Martelada* III. (José Nico Collection)

The same anti-aircraft position following an attack by Portuguese G.91s. (National Defence Archive)

Operação Martelada III would be the ZACVG's last pre-planned counter-AD operation for 10 months, although sporadic reaction strikes against PAIGC anti-aircraft fire continued. The ZACVG's counter-air defence activity thus far had apparently succeeded: reported incidents of opposing anti-aircraft fire declined from 110 in 1966 to 29 in 1968, with the steepest drop recorded in the Southern sector incorporating Como, Cantanhez, and Quitafine.[77] A meeting of Schultz's commanders in April 1968 approvingly noted a 'significant decrease' in hostile fire directed against Portuguese aircraft, one of several developments suggesting 'an imbalance to the opponent.'[78] Better still for the pilots of G.O. 1201, not a single Portuguese plane had been brought down by hostile fire for all of 1965, 1966, 1967, and the first half of 1968.[79]

The ZACVG did suffer accidental losses during those years, however (see Appendix III). On 21 July 1966, a ZACVG Do-27 (FAP 3485) on a routine training flight and mail run strayed into Senegalese airspace and crashed offshore. The pilots, *Ensigns* José de Sousa and Manuel Lima Leite, were rescued by a German vessel and briefly detained in Dakar before being returned to Bissau on 4 August.[80] Early the following year, on 22 February, *Esquadra 121* suffered its first operational G.91 loss. The squadron commander, *Major* Armando dos Santos Moreira, was dive bombing a suspected anti-aircraft position near Gã Pedro in the Quinara region when his aircraft (FAP 5407) was damaged by shrapnel from his own 200kg fragmentation bomb, possibly due to a premature detonation. With his wingman *Tenente* Egídio Lopes escorting him, Moreira attempted to nurse his plane back to Bissalanca, but severe elevator and rudder damage forced him to eject from an altitude of 2,000 feet while on long final approach. *Major* Moreira was recovered and evacuated to metropolitan Portugal for convalescence, but his

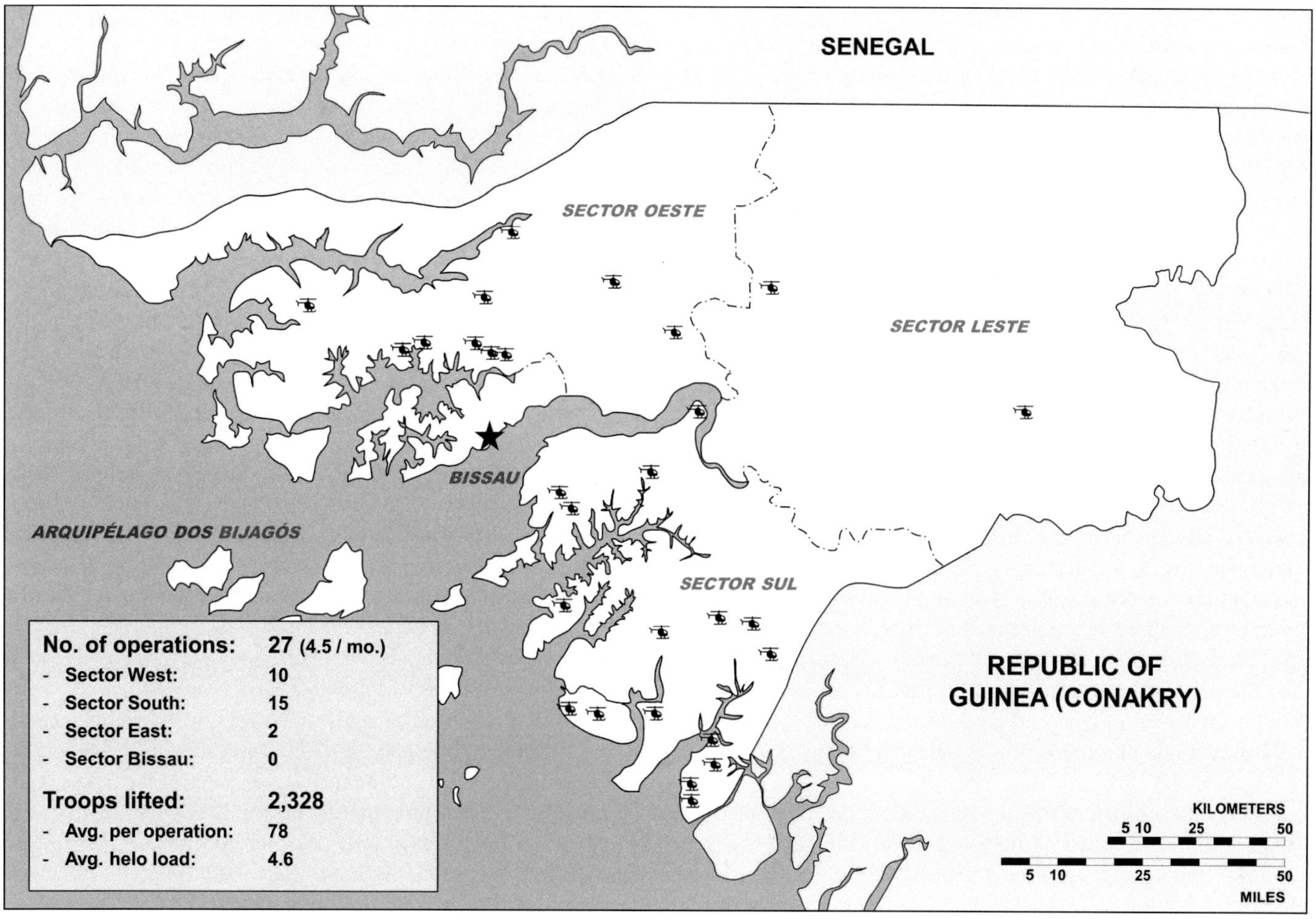

Portuguese heliborne operations, January–June 1968. (Matthew M. Hurley)

FAP Alouette IIIs were very active during the first half of 1968, especially in assault transport operations. (Helder Ferreira Collection)

Table 8: ZACVG Attack and Fire Support Sorties, 1965–1967

	1965	1966	1967
ATIP, Pre-planned Independent Attack	113	596	1,328
ATIR, Armed Reconnaissance	53	295	138
ATID, Directed Independent Attack			78
ATAP, Close Support Attack	52	666	650
ATAC, Accompanying Attack		131	357
AESC, Escort Attack		269	564
TOTAL	218	1,957	3,115

aircraft was a total loss.[81] Finally, on 15 June 1968 a T-6/Harvard IIB (FAP 1791) suffered engine failure and crashed between Chéché and Madina do Boé, in southeast Guinea. The following day heli-transported Portuguese paratroops executed *Operação Recolha* (Operation Recovery) to retrieve the damaged aircraft, which was later scrapped.[82]

As *Esquadra 121*'s G.91s occupied themselves with the counter-AD campaign, the Alouette IIIs of *Esquadra 122* carried the intensifying air assault offensive. ZACVG records reveal an additional 27 heliborne assault operations from January to June 1968, with a greater proportion occurring in the restive south.[83] Two of them, *Operação Ciclone I* (Quitafine, 10 January) and *Operação Tufão* (central Como, 20 March), were the largest heliborne assault operations in Guinea to date, each involving the movement of 200 paratroops in eight waves of five Alouette IIIs with the usual G.91/T-6, *helicanhão*, and Do-27 PCV support. Do-27s took damage from anti-aircraft fire during both operations, as did a cannon-armed Alouette III supporting *Operação Tufão*, underscoring the persistent air defence threat over southern Guinea.[84] Schultz and his air force commanders appeared more than willing to face those risks, committing more aircraft and personnel to these operations than the previous norm. In fact, compared to those of 1967, the average helicopter assault conducted during the first half of 1968 was a third larger in terms of sorties flown and troops transported (see Appendix IV).[85]

In January 1968 the ZACVG also launched a series of pre-planned strikes against suspected insurgent infrastructure and support networks throughout Guinea. *Operação Fogachol* (Operation Wildfire) struck the village of Quitafine on 8 January, while *Fogacho II* hit the Tafor-Canefaque area the following day. During each attack, seven G.91s deployed two 350 litre napalm canisters apiece, and the structures targeted in both operations were 'practically destroyed.'[86] In central Guinea, Portuguese T-6s carried out *Operação Dá-lhe Agora*, a three-day series of raids against suspected insurgent centres located in Dambol, Banir, and Cauali. From 21 to 23 January the T-6s flew 12 missions, closely coordinated with G.91 activity occurring elsewhere in the Oio and Bafatá regions.[87] The ZACVG returned to Como on 4 February 1968 for *Operação Crepúsculo*, a strike against three PAIGC encampments in the Caiar area. Four G.91s and three T-6s delivered 2,970kgs of bombs on their targets, resulting in 'great explosions… producing rolls of black smoke and intense fire about the trees.' The extent of observed secondary detonations led to speculation the attack had successfully destroyed an insurgent ammunition storage depot.[88]

Operação Crepúsculo would be G.O. 1201's last independent pre-planned strike operation until November 1968, punctuating a period of intense ZACVG activity during a dynamic and uncertain phase in the war. The addition of the G.91 and *helicanhão*, along with a near doubling of T-6 flight hours, spurred explosive growth in the number of aerial attacks: fire support, strike, armed overwatch, and armed reconnaissance missions flown from BA12-Bissalanca increased ninefold from 1965 to 1966, and grew by an additional 60 percent the following year.[89] According to PAIGC sources, the Quitafine Peninsula alone suffered some 2,000 air attacks during 1967, an aerial onslaught that 'nearly paralysed' the PAIGC. Foreign press reported the reinvigorated air offensive drove many local inhabitants from insurgent dominated villages, with thousands fleeing to neighbouring Senegal or the Republic of Guinea. Those villagers abandoned their crops in the process, forcing some remaining militants to hunt game and forage for edible plants rather than face starvation. Even more worrisome, some within the PAIGC began to openly question the party's strategy and the wisdom of fighting on, while more committed cadres faced the grim prospect of trying to persuade terrified villagers to remain in their 'liberated' enclaves despite the risk of continued aerial bombardment.[90]

Portugal's multi-pronged aerial offensive spurred major changes in the insurgents' organisation and operations.[91] Their semi-permanent base areas, encampments, and support facilities within Guinea had featured prominently on the ZACVG's targeting list since the war's beginning, so in 1967–68 Amílcar Cabral and his commanders began to dismantle them. 'We reduced the bases, dividing them into twos and threes, and finally we ordered [their] elimination,' Cabral later recalled.[92] The PAIGC leader

Table 9: PAIGC *Bi-grupo* Organisation and Armament, 1967–1968[96]

	Bi-grupo (normal)	*Bi-grupo* especial (reinforced)
Combatentes (Personnel)	44	54
Pistola (Pistols)	4	12
Espingarda (Rifles)	14	6
Pistola-metralhadora (Sub Machine Guns)	22	24
Metralhadora ligeira – (Light Machine Guns)	2	6
Metralhadora pesada (Heavy machine guns)	1	2
Lança-granada foguete ('LGr Fog' – Rocket Launchers RPG-2/7) or *Canhão sem recuo* ('Can S/R' – Recoilless Rifle, 82mm)	2	6
Morteiro, 60/82/120mm ('Mort' – Mortars)	1	2
When required, *bi-grupos* could be augmented by dedicated PAIGC artillery or anti-aircraft teams.		

President Américo Thomaz's visit to Guinea in 1968. (Virgílio Teixeira Collection)

also felt that sedentary camp life bred complacency and 'reduced the offensive capacity of the combatants,' and so directed a more nomadic disposition. From an offensive perspective, this itinerant arrangement also facilitated the rapid concentration of dispersed insurgent forces for larger operations – an ability that 'guaranteed the enemy near impunity,' according to the Portuguese command.[93]

At the same time, the PAIGC's unit articulation was further refined and its armament improved. Their standard manoeuvre formations, *bi-grupos*, were complemented by 'special' or reinforced *bi-grupos* serving under each of the PAIGC's Front or Inter-Region commands. The heavier *bi-grupos* operated as 'intervention forces' for larger operations and offensives that, the insurgents hoped, would 'be decisive in the current phase of the fight' given the new weapons available from the Communist Bloc.[94] These included the RPG-7 rocket-propelled-grenade launcher, initially observed in November 1967; the T-21 'Tarasnice' 82mm recoilless rifle, first reported in June 1968; and 120mm mortars, which debuted two months later.[95] The PAIGC assigned many of its new acquisitions to special artillery and anti-aircraft teams, which could be employed on independent missions or in support of larger operations involving multiple units.

With these improvements the PAIGC's full-time military wing, the EP, operated as a 'highly flexible semi-mobile army' within Portuguese Guinea after 1967, supported by nearly 30 base camps located not within the territory, but in neighbouring Senegal and the Republic of Guinea.[97] Those secure sanctuaries and the EP's 'permanent mobility'[98] enabled nearly 120 armed attacks throughout Guinea during the first five months of 1968, including a succession of noteworthy assaults during which insurgent units again demonstrated improved initiative, firepower, and tactics. One PAIGC attack – a raid against Bissássema de Cima, just 20km from Bissau – involved some 200 militants armed with mortars, rocket-propelled grenades, and recoilless cannons, rivalling the scale and intensity of the largest Portuguese helicopter assault operations during the same period.[99]

The escalation of insurgent violence did not prevent the President of Portugal, Américo Thomaz, from spending six days in Guinea during February 1968. The Portuguese head of state's visit proceeded without incident, and he received an outwardly enthusiastic welcome at each carefully selected stop, earning Lisbon a qualified propaganda success. The PAIGC, however, dismissed the event as 'one of the greatest failures ever recorded in Portuguese colonial history,' noting that Thomaz and his sizeable security entourage only 'visited some places in the small part of our national territory still provisionally occupied by colonialist troops.'[100] The nationalist party's dismissal of the Presidential visit reflected wider perceptions that, by the time Schultz relinquished command on 20 May 1968, his forces 'had lost the capacity to intervene, and, above all, lost the initiative.'[101]

In reality, the war for Guinea had settled into a strategic stalemate.[102] Unable to uproot the PAIGC from its strongholds, Schultz's forces increasingly turned to fortifying and reinforcing their own enclaves, from which they struck the insurgent enemy predominantly from (or through) the air.[103] Portuguese units were increasingly confined to their bases or immediate environs due to incessant ambushes and mine laying, while demonstrable improvements to insurgent tactics and firepower degraded their morale.[104] Only airpower in its myriad roles had prevented the situation from deteriorating further, and in

1968 the meagre complement of aircraft serving in the province was universally regarded as 'the decisive military factor' in the war.[105] The ZACVG's efforts had prevented the insurgents from consolidating their territorial gains, and according to one American assessment, so long as the Portuguese maintained 'absolute mastery of the air' the PAIGC would be unable to expel Lisbon's troops from their bases or the major towns. Until they could, any discussion of independence for Portuguese Guinea would remain a theoretical exercise.[106]

Brigadeiro Schultz had played his 'air power card' to great effect,[107] but not decisive effectiveness, and while prolonged warfare may have suited the insurgents it became a serious drain on Portuguese resources.[108] 'We have followed a strategy designed to harass the Portuguese and drain their economy,' PAIGC official Gil Fernandes later summarised, 'To combine effective military pressure in the colony and economic pressure in metropolitan Portugal has been our formula for victory.'[109] From a fiscal perspective, the strategy appeared to be working: by 1968 direct costs associated with the war in Guinea approximated $350,000 US a day, or more than one billion annually in 2023 US dollars.[110] That figure represented 44 percent of Portugal's defence expenditures for 1968 – and the defence budget accounted for more than a third of all state spending that year.[111] All told, Portuguese defence outlays tripled between 1959 and 1968 to support a military establishment that had more than doubled in size during that same period, from 79,000 to 182,500 uniformed personnel.[112]

Filling the expanding ranks proved a growing challenge, however. In 1961, the incidence of draft evasion in Portugal was 12 percent; in 1967 it surpassed 19 percent, with over 16,000 registrants failing to report for conscription.[113] Opposition to serving in the three African wars, combined with stagnant social and economic conditions at home, also prompted a wave of emigration from Portugal, depleting the relevant demographic still further. Simultaneously, desertion among those already in uniform rose to 1,402 in 1967, with nearly as many again absconding the following year.[114] As for the officer ranks, applications and accessions to the *Academia Militar* also plummeted as the wars dragged on. In 1968 just 149 applicants 'competed' to fill 430 openings, and only 58 were ultimately admitted to the full course, an abysmal 13 percent of requirements. In comparison, nearly 90 percent of academy vacancies from 1960 to 1963 had been filled by qualified candidates.[115]

Despite these constraints, Schultz managed an impressive build-up of Portuguese forces in Guinea. The number of troops assigned to the province increased by 50 percent during his tenure, from 15,000 to more than 22,000, while the ZACVG's aircraft inventory grew by more than a third.[116] However, those reinforcements underscored the ultimate defect in Schultz's strategy: his reliance on a military solution to the problem of Portuguese Guinea.[117] The outgoing commander found himself 'a classic Clausewitzian general [caught] in the web of counter-subversion,' and as Schultz himself later confessed, he fell into the equally classic trap of trying to defeat an insurgency through force alone.[118] While he understood many of the military aspects of COIN, including the advantages of a robust aviation enterprise, he preferred firepower to persuasion much like his American contemporary in Vietnam, General William Westmoreland.[119] As a result, 'Shultz committed great stupidities,' PAIGC field commander Manuel 'Manecas' dos Santos later stated. 'He did not conduct a modern guerrilla war, did not conduct work with the population. On the contrary, the work he undertook was repression, and here repression increased resistance and became, almost objectively, our ally.'[120]

Frustrated in his initial goals, Schultz fell back on a predominantly static defensive strategy punctuated by brief offensives conducted chiefly through the aerial domain. His strategy grew increasingly dependent on the air forces available to him as the war progressed, and by mid-1968 aircraft and heliborne units made up the majority of Portugal's offensive capability in Guinea. Yet it was not enough: despite the rising number of missions flown, bombs dropped, and targets destroyed, PAIGC influence continued to spread throughout his tenure while Portuguese authority receded.[121] 'In this way our actions did not fit what was intended,' the outgoing governor-commander later conceded.[122] The situation called for a commander who could regain the initiative and find a satisfactory way out of the Guinea 'quagmire.'[123] In his search for that outcome, Schultz's replacement, António de Spínola, would fundamentally alter not only the course of the war, but also the political destiny of the Portuguese state and the fate of its empire.

4
The 'Cornerstone'

> The Air Force, due to its high fire potential and potential for rapid reaction, is effectively the 'cornerstone' of operational activity in the Guinea Theatre of Operations. (*Brigadeiro* António de Spínola, Portuguese Guinea governor/commander, 10 December 1968)[1]

Brigadeiro António Sebastião Ribeiro de Spínola assumed the functions of provincial Governor and *Comando-Chefe das Forças Armadas da Guiné* (CCFAG – Commander-in-Chief of the Armed Forces of Guinea) on 20 May 1968, bringing with him a reputation for dynamism, imagination, and resolve. The new commander cut a flamboyant figure with a 'swashbuckling manner,' sporting his trademark monocle and riding crop on frequent (and often unannounced) visits throughout Guinea, sometimes within the PAIGC's purported *zonas libertadas*.[2] He disdained personal comforts, even foregoing air conditioning despite Guinea's oppressive heat; one foreign journalist described walking into his office from the climate-controlled anteroom 'like entering a tepid oven.'[3] Famously volatile and caustic towards his staff, Spínola was equally unflinching when confronting his own superiors, and on the battlefield he purposely projected an aura of fearlessness, often 'plunging forth unarmed at the head of the troops' to the delight of frontline soldiers.[4]

Spínola already had four decades of military experience as a cavalryman when he arrived in Bissau. In the late 1930s then *Tenente*, Spínola received his first exposure to combat while organising aid to Francoist forces during the Spanish Civil War. During the Second World War he also participated in a Portuguese Army 'study and observation mission' to Nazi Germany, which included visits to officer combat training schools and frontline positions outside besieged Leningrad.[5] From 1961 to 1964 Spínola commanded a

General Spínola, a veteran of Portuguese COIN operations in Angola, was chosen by Salazar to reinvigorate Portugal's campaign for Guinea and reverse its losses there. (United Press Europix)

cavalry battalion in Angola, where he was praised for his bravery and effectiveness in the field, earning him national admiration and the attention of Portuguese Prime Minister, António de Oliveira Salazar.[6] Spínola had been a proponent and practitioner of conventional warfare throughout his career, but as the official now responsible for restoring Portugal's deteriorating prospects in Guinea, the new provincial governor and commander championed an entirely new strategy better suited to the politico-military dilemmas confronting him there. As Spínola explained to Salazar before accepting the post, the only way to prevent Portugal's expulsion from Guinea was through a campaign of economic development, political reform, and 'social revolution' benefitting its inhabitants. Only in this manner could Lisbon rekindle or reinforce their allegiance, while preparing them 'to assume their responsibilities in local administration on an equal footing with the metropolitan Portuguese.'[7]

First, however, he would have to confront the immediate challenge awaiting him there. Three months after his arrival, Spínola acknowledged that the military situation in Guinea revealed 'a sad reality.'[8] The enemy's forces had seized the military initiative, he reported in October 1968, being more motivated, increasingly better armed, and better adapted to local conditions and terrain. As a result, the insurgents controlled or actively contested three-fifths of the province, threatening Portuguese forces with an imminent 'military collapse'. Were that to occur, the new CCFAG warned, 'an unstoppable wave of support for the liberation movements' would deprive Lisbon of not only Guinea, but the more lucrative colonies of Angola and Mozambique as well, thereby threatening the future of the Portuguese state itself.[9]

In formulating his strategy to forestall Lisbon's imperial collapse, Spínola explicitly acknowledged something his predecessors in Guinea had not: that 'Revolutionary war, the kind we are facing in Guinea, is primarily psychological and is characterised by the conquest of people.'[10] The problem of insurgency eluded a purely military solution, he recognised, instead calling for 'a genuine, clear, and decisive social revolution' in conjunction with 'programmes which substantiate the just aspirations of the people.'[11] Those programmes, ultimately intended to demonstrate the advantages of remaining under Portuguese rule, were collectively labelled *Por uma Guiné Melhor* (For a Better Guinea).[12]

The centrepiece of Spínola's 'Better Guinea' initiative was civic action, specifically immediate measures intended to satisfy 'the people's most urgent desires.'[13] The new governor directed the construction or renovation of schools, medical posts, roads, and interior ports to facilitate trade, with the ultimate aim of securing 'a better future' in which Portugal's local subjects could 'fully realise [their] legitimate desire for progress.'[14] Within three years primary school enrolment jumped to around 120,000 students, compared to mere hundreds a decade earlier; an 'extensive network of hospitals, maternity clinics and first aid posts' was established throughout Portuguese controlled territory; government subsidised agricultural cooperatives initiated willing Guineans into the cash economy; and Portuguese-sponsored *Congressos do Povo* (People's Congresses) gave the populace at least a semblance of political representation while demonstrating Spínola's 'commitment to non-violent evolutionary change under the Portuguese flag.'[15] Through these and similar civic programmes, Spínola hoped to deprive the enemy of 'the force of their reason and, with this, the people – which is the end goal of the counter-subversion plan.'[16]

When Spínola arrived in Guinea in 1968, the military initiative had swung to the increasingly better-trained and better-equipped insurgents. (Reg Lancaster/Express Hulton Archive/Getty Images)

To secure and support the 'Better Guinea' campaign Spínola directed the establishment of defended villages in Portuguese controlled territory, known locally as *aldeamentos,* or less frequently *reordenamentos.* Reminiscent of the 'strategic hamlet' initiative in Vietnam and similar COIN initiatives,[17] the CCFAG intended the *aldeamentos* to physically separate the populace from the PAIGC, thereby depriving the insurgents of their main source of information, food, and local sanctuary. The Portuguese also launched a renewed psychological campaign intended to induce the inhabitants of Guinea, 'clearly and simply for their primitive

Spínola launched an economic and social reform programme in Guinea (the 'Better Guinea' initiative) in an attempt to regain the allegiance of disaffected inhabitants. (António de Spínola Collection)

A primary school in Guinea. Education was one of the areas that received Spínola's attention as part of his 'Better Guinea' programme. (National Defence Archive)

minds', to accept resettlement and participate in government sponsored reforms.[18] The central message of that campaign, according to the governing CCFAG directive, was a simple one: 'With us Heaven, with the enemy Hell.'[19]

As Spínola repeatedly asserted, however, the importance of civic reform 'does not diminish the keenness of the military problem, since we cannot ignore the fact that although these kinds of wars are not won on the battlefield, they can certainly be lost there.'[20] As a result the new CCFAG ordered a series of fundamental changes to Portuguese military organisation, deployment, and operations in Guinea. Most dramatically, military realities compelled Spínola to consolidate Portuguese forces further into fortified encampments and adjoining *aldeamentos*. The CCFAG directed this realignment to ensure 'strict economy of resources' given the improbability of additional reinforcements, while 'respecting the principle of concentration' in areas likely to yield positive results.[21] However, retrenchment necessarily ceded even more territory to nominal insurgent control, especially in the south and east, delighting the PAIGC and its sympathisers. Party chief Amílcar Cabral touted the Portuguese withdrawals as 'decisive victories' for the PAIGC's militants,[22] for example, while insurgent field commander João Bernardo 'Nino' Viera later boasted 'We can advance for many kilometres without catching sight of the enemy.'[23]

Overseas Minister Silva Cunha's much-publicised visit to Guinea, March 1970. Silva Cunha (centre) is accompanied by Spínola. (António de Spínola Collection)

To counter those claims, Portugal continued its own attempts to visibly demonstrate territorial dominance. In yet another loudly publicised VIP visit, Overseas Minister Joaquim da Silva Cunha visited Guinea for nine days in March 1970. During his tour Silva Cunha accompanied Spínola to a succession of carefully planned stops, viewing the progress of the latter's *Guiné Melhor* programme and hoping to demonstrate Portuguese authority and freedom of movement throughout the province. 'He paid detailed visits to all parts of the territory, was enthusiastically greeted everywhere, [and] gave the lie to the tales of 'occupation', 'advances' and 'control' that the enemy had put about,' an Overseas Ministry account asserted.[24] Some senior Portuguese officers took issue with the official narrative,

During his tenure in Guinea Spínola restructured the organisation, disposition, and employment of Portuguese forces there. He often accompanied troops during operations. (Alvaro B. Geraldo Collection)

however, including *Coronel* Abecasis, who noted that Silva Cunha's visit 'meant nothing more than political prose.' One of the Minister's stops was Madina do Boé, a garrison the PAIGC claimed to have 'liberated' the previous year, but which had in fact been deliberately evacuated as part of Spínola's retrenchment scheme.[25] That particular stopover highlighted the fluid and ephemeral nature of territorial control in the conflict: 'It was true, [Silva Cunha] went to Madina do Boé,' Abecasis observed, for '*helicanhão* overflights temporarily chased away the true [insurgent] occupants of the barracks.' Once the Overseas Minister and his entourage departed, however, PAIGC forces returned 'promptly.'[26]

Yet Portugal's withdrawal from outlying garrisons such as Madina do Boé created new opportunities for the ZACVG, since consolidation on the ground simplified operations in the air by more cleanly delineating secured areas from contested or insurgent dominated territory. When the redeployment of surface forces resumed in late 1968, Spínola simultaneously directed the FAP to 'compensate the most vulnerable sectors of our disposition with timely fire support.'[27] He also ordered the expansion of areas reserved for 'intervention' by mobile artillery, river units, and most especially air and airmobile forces. The previous CCFAG had established *zona de livre intervenção da Força Aérea* (ZLIFAs, Air Force free intervention zones) for similar purposes, and Spínola quickly implemented new procedures governing them to ensure 'air activity should be more responsive to the commander-in-chief's orders.'[28] In March 1969, however, Spínola introduced a new arrangement, the *Zona de Intervenção do Comando-Chefe* (ZICC, Commander-in-Chief Intervention Zone). Seven ZICCs were established at that time, largely corresponding to the PAIGC's 'liberated' regions or terrain recently vacated by Portuguese ground forces, and now designated as 'areas where the Air Force could act by direct order of the commander in Bissau, without lengthy coordination with local commanders.' In this manner, ZICC procedures permitted the ZACVG to act swiftly when emerging intelligence or tactical conditions dictated a rapid response.[29]

To manage assigned air assets more efficiently, Spínola also conceptually split ZACVG assets between those dedicated to 'direct unit support' – logistics, liaison, reconnaissance, and fire support– and the aerial component of the CCFAG's 'manoeuvre' or 'intervention' force, capable of independent attack and airmobile operations. He emphasised the latter, given the 'precariousness of

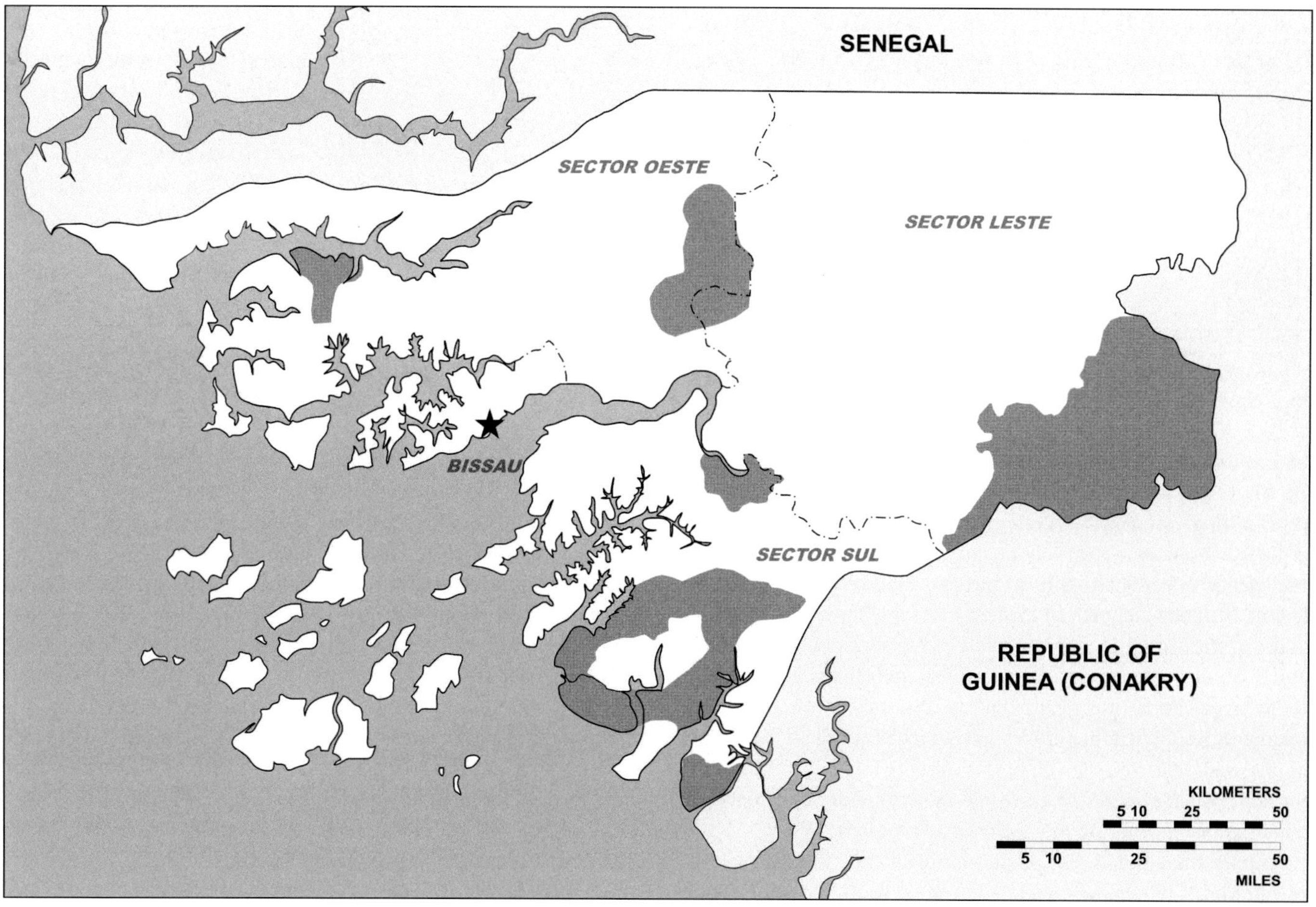

Commander-in-Chief Intervention Zones, August 1970. (Matthew M. Hurley based on CTIG/2REP, 'SUPINTREP 14,' SGDN/2REP/088/0363/010, ADN.)

A propaganda poster celebrating Silva Cunha's visit to Guinea and proclaiming Portugal's continued rule over the entire province. (José Matos Collection)

land resources and their limited ability to react in good time.' Thus, the Air Force, Spínola acknowledged, comprised the 'cornerstone' of his military strategy,[30] a strategy resting on the twin imperatives of interdiction and 'intervention' to capitalise on time-sensitive intelligence or tactical opportunities. Specific tasks reliant on air activity included stepped-up logistical and intelligence support, air attack or air assault in the most vulnerable sectors (especially the PAIGC's *zonas libertadas*), and, somewhat ambiguously, 'retaliation in the areas bordering neighbouring countries, from which the insurgents resupplied their forces and launched attacks.'[31] As Spínola emphasised, however, the aim of this strategy was not annihilation, but rather 'to guarantee the space and time necessary to achieve the primary objectives of the socio-economic programme.'[32]

Despite his emphasis on civic improvements and reforms on the ground, Spínola was soon confronted with the resumption of the war for aerial supremacy. On 28 September 1968, a pair of G.91s used rockets to silence unspecified 'heavy weapons' that had fired on them during an armed reconnaissance mission near Guileje, adjacent to a key insurgent infiltration corridor from the Republic of Guinea.[33] Three months later, on 6 January 1969, four G.91s struck a 14.5mm ZPU-4 covering a PAIGC attack against the nearby barracks of Gadamael, at the northern edge of the Quitafine Peninsula.[34] Results of the latter attack were confirmed by Portuguese forces inspecting the area three days later, who reported 'the air force acted precisely and destroyed the anti-airgun' while damaging other heavy weapons used in the preceding barracks attack. Portuguese forces also found 'heads, legs, arms, and camouflage pieces all over the area,' concluding that 'next to the anti-air position, all personnel operating the gun would have died.'[35] As further proof of success, the Gadamael garrison presented G.O. 1201 commander *Tenente Coronel* Costa Gomes with the destroyed ZPU-4's optical sight, recovered by Portuguese troops during their inspection.[36]

Although sporadic incidents occurred elsewhere in the province, the most intense anti-aircraft environment remained southern Portuguese Guinea, particularly the Quitafine Peninsula abutting the border with the Republic of Guinea. At the end of 1968 a pair of G.91s patrolling the area reported sighting a ZPU-4 in the abandoned village of Cassebeche, surrounded by five to six 12.7mm AAMG emplacements. Given the difficulties to date in destroying anti-aircraft weapons via air attack alone, *Brigadeiro* Spínola ordered a paratroop assault to ensure the threat's elimination following an initial round of air strikes. However, the CCFAG further directed the operation be delayed in hopes the PAIGC would concentrate additional air defence assets in the area. The first part of Spínola's plan to 'let them grow and pull them out by hand' indeed came to pass, as insurgent forces continued to strengthen their air defences around Cassebeche over the next two months.[37] Pulling them out would prove more difficult, however, as 'the element of surprise was traded for a long lead time and an obvious and oversized operation against an alerted and well-prepared enemy.'[38]

As with earlier operations involving paratroops, the plan to sweep PAIGC air defences from the Cassebeche area involved a

Aerial view of Gadamael, on the Quitafine Peninsula. The village was near the site of a G.91 strike against a PAIGC ZPU-4 anti-aircraft system in January 1969. (National Defence Archive)

preparatory air bombardment followed by a helicopter assault. The opening strike committed G.91s to suppress known or suspected anti-aircraft positions, a key enabler for the subsequent ground operation. Then ZACVG chief and BA12 commander *Coronel* Manuel Diogo Neto recalled 'It was the opinion of some more experienced pilots that if it were possible to destroy the ZPU right away the [PAIGC] defence would collapse, facilitating the action of the paratroops.'[39] The draft plan called for two paratroop companies to be heli-transported to landing zones north and south of the target area. These paratroops were to advance on and destroy the PAIGC emplacements, supported by a Do-27 command post, a pair of *helicanhões*, four T-6s, and the refuelled and re-armed G.91s. Forward assets, including the T-6s and PCV, would be temporarily based at Catió, 45km from the zone of action.[40] All ZACVG assigned G.91s, 10 of 11 Alouette IIIs, and most fixed-wing transports were committed to the operation, as were 34 of the 35 pilots assigned and present at BA12; only one aviator failed to participate, due to illness.[41] With over 25 aircraft and 240 paratroops taking part, the operation – named *Operação Vulcano* in anticipation of 'the festival of fire in which we would participate and attend',[42] was set to be the ZACVG's largest combined strike and air assault effort to date.[43]

The objectives set for *Operação Vulcano* went beyond air defence suppression. The operations order directed FAP forces (including the paratroops) to eliminate the entire PAIGC organisation in or around Cassebeche, neutralising any enemy personnel who resisted; capture or destroy PAIGC weapons and materiel; and gather intelligence.[44] However, planning for *Operação Vulcano* was hindered by several issues that would come to complicate its execution and ultimate outcome. One of the most fundamental challenges was CCFAG's lack of intelligence on the strength and disposition of PAIGC militants in Quitafine, an area Portuguese surface forces had generally avoided during the previous year. The available information proved distressingly vague and sporadic, only alluding to the presence of multiple 'heavily armed' insurgent groups on the peninsula. Even so, Spínola inexplicably halved the number of paratroops assigned to the mission, considering a single company sufficient, and 'nothing convinced him of the need to employ the two available,' Diogo Neto recalled.[45] Worse for the FAP, enemy anti-aircraft guns in the area had multiplied 'like mushrooms' in the weeks since the first were identified, threatening the success of the initial strikes and subsequent aerial support activities.[46] *Operação Vulcano* was nonetheless scheduled for 7 March 1969, despite the heavy opposition Portuguese forces expected to encounter.

The day prior, 6 March, 60 paratroopers flew by C-47 from BA12-Bissalanca to the forward airfield in Catió, where four T-6s also stood by to support the next day's operation. Early on 7 March, a series of staging flights on four Do-27s delivered 40 paratroops – earmarked as the second helicopter assault wave – to their forward

During *Operação Vulcano* (March 1969), all ZACVG assigned G.91s were employed against enemy AA positions in southern Guinea. (José Nico Collection)

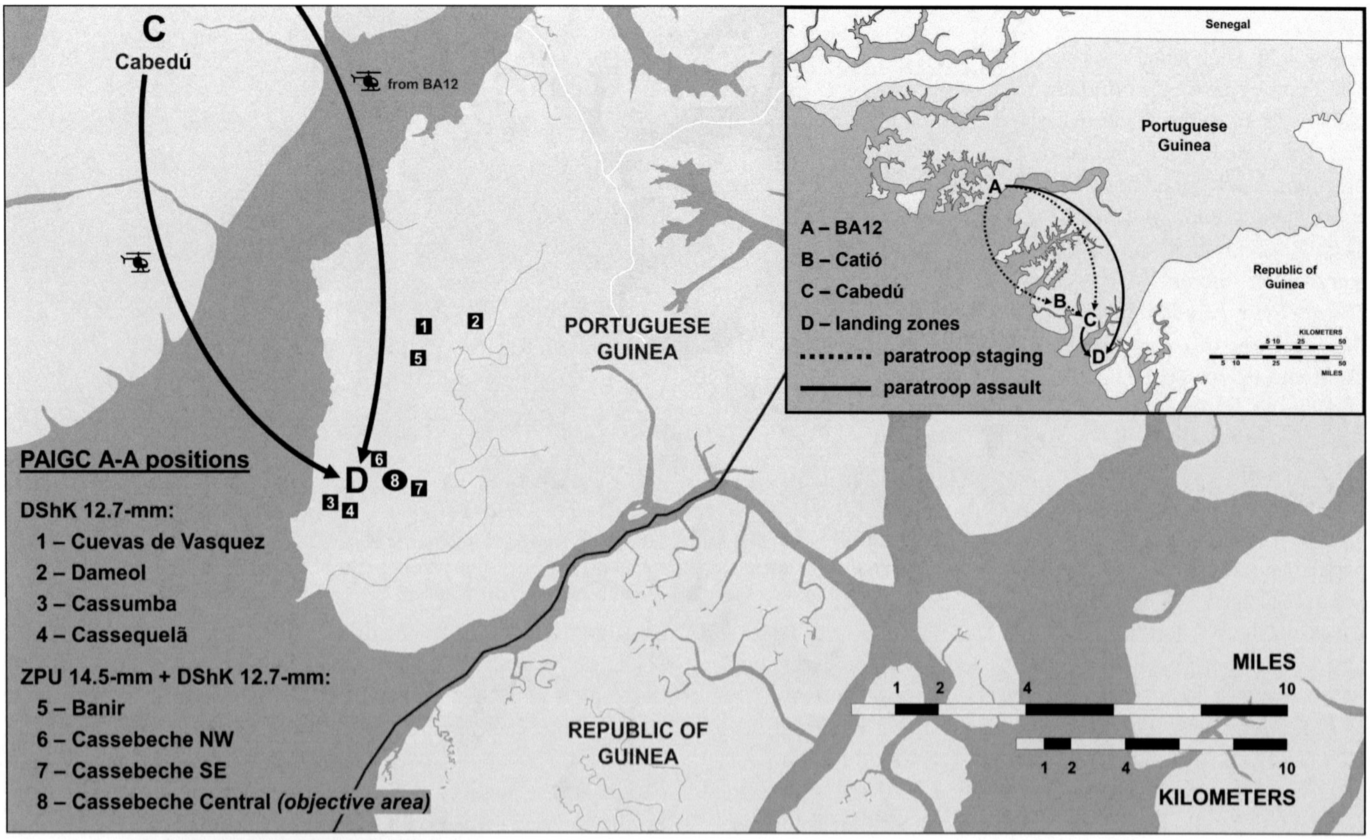

Operação Vulcano, March 1969. (Matthew M. Hurley)

Coronel Diogo Neto, ZACVG commander during Operation *Vulcano*. (National Defence Archive)

jumping-off point at Cabedú. This second wave included 20 newly arrived paratroops from BA12, leaving 40 from the previous day's movement as a ready reserve force at Catió. The first wave of the heli-assault, also comprising 40 paratroops, was to proceed directly from BA12 to the objective area on eight Alouette IIIs upon completion of the initial air bombardment. After delivering the first wave, the same eight helicopters were to fly to Cabedú and return to the zone of action carrying the second wave of 40 paratroops. The mission of both paratroop formations was to advance on Cassebeche, complete the destruction of PAIGC anti-aircraft assets located there, and eliminate any other insurgent positions, concentrations, or heavy weapons in the vicinity.[47]

Operação Vulcano proper began at 0700 on 7 March with the departure of a Do-27 tasked to conduct visual reconnaissance of the target area. Upon the pilot's report of optimal weather conditions, 10 Alouette IIIs, including two *helicanhão* gunships, took off from BA12 with the initial wave of 40 paratroopers.[48] Their success hinged on the ZACVG's ability to first suppress the air defence threat, lest the PAIGC's anti-aircraft guns savage the slow-moving helicopters and supporting piston-engined aircraft. That task fell to the seven available G.91s, the first three of which lifted off from BA12 at 0848 armed with general purpose bombs and their .50in machine guns. The trio climbed to 8,000 feet for the 11-minute flight to Cassebeche, 120km away. Skirting the border with the Republic of Guinea to attack from the sun, the G.91s immediately encountered defensive fire from at least seven active AA positions, housing six 12.7mm DShK AAMGs and one quad-barrelled 14.5mm ZPU-4. Concentrating on the ZPU, the G.91s delivered twelve 50kg and six 200kg bombs against the position, with G.O. 1201 commander *Capitão* Fernando de Jesus Vasquez reporting a direct hit. One of the DShK emplacements was also destroyed, and with the qualified success of the first strikes ZACVG commander Diogo Neto, flying FAP 5408 for this mission, optimistically concluded 'the hardest part was done.' As no further anti-aircraft activity was detected immediately following the initial strikes, the ZACVG commander mistakenly concluded all air defence activity had been suppressed, and he transmitted that assessment to the circling PCV.[49]

Two minutes after the G.91s completed their attack, the vanguard assault landed under the protection of a rocket-armed Do-27 and two *helicanhões*. The first paratroops disembarked at 0901 and began their march towards the PAIGC positions just over a kilometre away. At 0916 the second-strike mission – a pair of G.91s carrying the same ordnance as the first trio – began attacking the air defence 'cluster' at Cassebeche, in the process identifying a seventh AAMG position. Four minutes later the second wave of paratroops landed and started out towards the objective area, immediately encountering small arms fire from the now alerted PAIGC militants. At 0927 a third G.91 formation, again a pair, struck the air defence sites around Cassebeche, silencing a second DShK. By this time, however, the paratroops began taking RPG and machine gun fire, and the Do-27 PCV reported three active anti-aircraft emplacements, one of which struck that aircraft in the wing.[50]

The mounting air and ground resistance indicated the PAIGC had quickly recovered from the shock of the opening attacks, a realisation that made Diogo Neto 'apprehensive'. Failure to eliminate the PAIGC's anti-aircraft capability precluded the use of T-6s and *helicanhões*to support the paratroops, for fear that 'due to their low speed, they would be uselessly massacred.'[51] Even the G.91s remained at risk, a point emphasised when their fourth mission of the morning encountered renewed 12.7mm fire, severely damaging one aircraft. 'Under these conditions, it was no longer possible to achieve the objectives set, as they all presupposed an advance without significant resistance,' *General* Nico later recalled, reflecting a growing worry that Portuguese forces had 'trapped ourselves' in a rapidly deteriorating tactical position.[52]

Twenty-five of the paratroop reserve were committed to the stalled ground operation while three G.91s returned for a fifth raid against the stubborn AA positions, this time with rockets and machine gun fire, but at least two of the sites remained active.[53] The reinforced paratroops resumed a cautious advance but were halted again by intense enemy fire when they were within 500 metres of their objective.[54] A further pair of G.91s was summoned to suppress PAIGC defences and quell the lingering anti-aircraft threat, but a second jet was hit and damaged by 12.7mm fire, losing engine power and returning to BA12 for an emergency landing. Following that development 'we were down to five Fiats,' Diogo Neto recalled, and 'we had to consider the possibility of breakdowns, losses from AA fire, and accidents.' He also fully realised, however, that 'without air support, the recovery of ground forces would be seriously compromised.'[55]

The three Portuguese paratroop columns had linked up by 1330, following a seventh G.91 attack against the persistent AA guns which were also being used against the paratroops in a surface fire role.[56] Shortly afterwards another trio of G.91s appeared overhead,

Capitão Alberto Cruz, one of the G.91 pilots who participated in *Operação Vulcano*. Cruz flew two strike missions during this major operation in southern Guinea. (Alberto Cruz Collection)

Table 10: *Operação Vulcano* – G.91 Attack Missions[66]

Wave	G.91 aircraft	Take off	Time over Target	Ordnance (each aircraft)
1	5408 (Neto) 5405 (Cruz) 5412 (Vasquez)	0848	0915	2 x 200kg GP bombs 4 x 50kg GP bombs 4 x .50in machine guns
2	5247 (Amaral) 5410 (Nico)	0902	0915	2 x 200kg GP bombs 4 x 50kg GP bombs 4 x .50in machine guns
3	5416 (Barbosa) 5414 (Balacó)	0915	0928	2 x 200kg GP bombs 4 x 50kg GP bombs 4 x .50in machine guns
4	5414 (Amaral) 5410 (Nico)*	1000	1013	8 x 2.75in FFAR 4 x .50in machine guns
5	5414 (Neto) 5412 (Cruz) 5405 (Vasquez)*	1042	1055	8 x 2.75in FFAR 4 x .50in machine guns
6	5416 (Barbosa) 5427 (Balacó)	1137	1150	8 x 2.75in FFAR 4 x .50in machine guns
7	5416 (Amaral)	1300	1315	2 x 200kg GP bombs 4 x 50kg GP bombs 4 x .50in machine guns
8a	5416 (Barbosa) 5408 (Balacó)	1350	1405	2 x 200kg GP bombs 4 x 50kg GP bombs 4 x .50in machine guns
8b	5427 (Nico)	1405	1420	2 x 300kg napalm
9	5412 (Neto) 5414 (Vasquez)	1450	1505	2 x 200kg GP bombs 4 x 50kg GP bombs 4 x .50in machine guns

* aircraft damaged by PAIGC AA fire

two of them delivering napalm against an especially troublesome DShK position. The attack failed, however, leaving at least three AA machine gun sites now manned and active, while the paratroops continued to receive heavy fire from multiple directions.[57] With the air defence threat unsuppressed, the ground element immobilised, and two of the precious G.91s out of the fight, Diogo Neto prudently ordered the withdrawal of all ZACVG elements, including the paratroops, effectively aborting the operation.[58] Portuguese forces vacated the peninsula by 1521, and by 1830 all personnel and aircraft had returned to Bissalanca, once again ceding Quitafine to the insurgents.[59] The tension at BA12 that night was 'knife-edged,' Diogo Neto later recalled. 'What could have been a big 'roar' had failed for lack of means to carry out the final assault,' alluding to *Brigadeiro* Spínola's earlier decision to employ only one paratroop company.[60]

Operação Vulcano involved 20 G.91 sorties in nine attacks, and of the seven participating pilots all but one flew three strike missions during the six-hour operation (*Capitão* Alberto Cruz flew only two). In total, the Fiats delivered 7,200kg of bombs, 1,400 litres of napalm, 56 2.75in rockets, and several thousand .50in machine gun rounds, representing 'a remarkable effort at the level of our meagre arsenal,' Diogo Neto reflected.[61] For that effort the ZACVG claimed four 12.7mm DShK sites neutralised and, more importantly, the destruction of the 14.5mm ZPU.[62] Intercepted communications listed insurgent casualties at 19 dead and 32 wounded, leading Amílcar Cabral to label the engagement 'the Cassebeche disaster.'[63]

In exchange, two of the ZACVG's seven G.91s were hit by anti-aircraft fire: FAP 5410 suffered nose and wing damage leading to the loss of hydraulic controls, while FAP 5405 took tail damage causing partial engine failure. A Do-27 performing airborne command post duties was also hit in the wing by 12.7mm fire. All three aircraft successfully returned to BA12, but the available G.91 fleet was reduced to five during a critical juncture.[64] *General* Nico later wrote 'From then on, at certain times the continued presence of the G.91 in the Action Zone could only be ensured with isolated aircraft.'[65]

If the PAIGC considered the event a 'disaster,' the result 'did not leave anyone satisfied' on the Portuguese side, either.[67] Follow-on analysis and enemy activity indicated at least two AA weapons remained operational in the Cassebeche vicinity, with several other air defence 'clusters' located elsewhere on the Quitafine Peninsula.[68] In fact, on 9 March 1969 – just two days after *Operação Vulcano* – four enemy AA positions near Cassebeche fired on Portuguese aircraft flying a nighttime mission, with a similar incident occurring the following week.[69] *General* Nico later concluded 'We had all the conditions to destroy the anti-aircraft system and inflict a heavy blow on the PAIGC, but the result, although positive, fell far short of our expectations.'[70] Factors leading to that unsatisfactory outcome included, among others, the months long delay following initial target identification; coordination and synchronisation snags; the decision to employ a single paratroop company for the ground assault; and an underestimation of PAIGC capabilities in the objective area.[71] As then *Coronel* Diogo Neto observed, 'In the future we had to be more careful; we couldn't get caught between a sword and the wall, without a way out.'[72]

For their part, the insurgents limped away from Cassebeche with a harsh reminder that 'aviation remained the only means by which [the Portuguese] could cause us problems,' according to Luís Cabral.[73] Ironically, Portuguese authorities in Guinea also worried about the threat of enemy bombing. One of Spínola's most immediate challenges upon arrival involved Portuguese Guinea's vulnerability to aerial infiltration and, potentially, air attack from hostile neighbouring states. The threat was almost as old as the war itself, as FAP airmen logged their first sighting of an unidentified jet in territorial airspace on 23 July 1963.[74] Portuguese ground forces, meanwhile, 'frequently' reported mysterious aircraft near their bases and encampments, especially at night. Anti-aircraft tactical control radars provided tentative corroboration to some reports,[75] but most derived exclusively from the visual observations of ground forces, and Portuguese troops were known to be susceptible to 'Enemy Helicopter Fever.' Nevertheless, a renewed spate of sightings, beginning in 1966, led CCFAG to order *Operação Ver Para Crer* (Operation Seeing is Believing) on 25 May 1967.[76]

During *Operação Ver Para Crer* Alouette IIIs lifted a platoon of paratroops into the Pache area of Western Guinea, where they investigated reports of unidentified nighttime helicopter activity presumably conducted by, or on behalf of, the PAIGC. On-the-spot assessments and analysis of evidence collected at the site led the ZACVG commander to conclude 'a small enemy helicopter had possibly landed at Pache a few times,' but attributed most sightings to 'confusion with our planes flying at night, or with planets that change their brightness due to the passage of clouds.'[77] At that time Portuguese authorities did not believe the PAIGC possessed aircraft of its own, instead 'very rarely' using a pair of helicopters owned and operated by wealthy civilian sympathisers.[78] In fact, Amílcar Cabral himself had in 1964 concluded aircraft of any sort were beyond the party's resources and capabilities.[79] Portuguese military authorities expected that to change, however, given a spate of reports through 1969 alleging pilot training for PAIGC militants in the USSR and purported plans to provide them with 'MiG aircraft' based in the Republic of Guinea.[80]

The risk of aerial intervention also grew with the air forces of neighbouring states increasingly hostile to Portugal's imperial

A Soviet MiG–17. The Soviet Union supplied 10 of these fighter-bombers to the Republic of Guinea in the early 1960s. (Alexey Tolmachev Collection)

A Republic of Guinea Antonov-14 that mistakenly landed at Aldeia Formosa (Quebo), Portuguese Guinea, in March 1968. The plane was then flown to BA12-Bissalanca, where it was impounded and ended up abandoned on the apron. (Virgílio Teixeira Collection)

One of the AAA platoon's quadruple 12.7mm guns defending BA12-Bissalanca. (Historical Archive of Air Force)

persistence. The Republic of Guinea received 10 MiG-17F (NATO 'FRESCO C') fighter-bombers from the Soviet Union in the early 1960s, and they formed the offensive core of Conakry's *Force Aérienne de Guineé* (FAG or air arm) until the mid-1980s.[81] Although Senegal maintained only a small inventory of helicopters, transports, and light aircraft throughout the 1960s, these assets could be used to shuttle arms and personnel for the insurgents.[82] As the governments of both nations steadily increased their moral and material support for the PAIGC throughout the latter half of the decade, the Portuguese increasingly worried that 'the Enemy can be reinforced with air resources from other countries, intervening openly in the current conflict.'[83]

Several incidents predating Spínola's arrival aggravated those concerns. On 24 April 1968 a pair of Portuguese T-6s were 'bounced' by unidentified aircraft over the Guileje corridor, just a few kilometres from the border with the Republic of Guinea. One of the pilots, *Tenente* Oliveira Couto, recalled being surprised by two swept-wing jets that manoeuvred aggressively against the T-6s, one passing close enough to induce wake turbulence. Bissalanca's G.91s had been idle that day, however, leading to speculation they had encountered MiG fighters from the Republic of Guinea, which had probably crossed the densely-forested border inadvertently.[84] Just a month earlier, on 26 March 1968, a Soviet-built Antonov-14 *Pchelka* light transport (NATO An-14 'CLOD') in FAG markings landed in error at Aldeia Formosa, a forward airfield near the border, presumably due to an instrument malfunction. Portuguese authorities flew the aircraft to BA12 and released the six Malian passengers immediately, but the two FAG crewmen were detained as leverage to secure a prisoner swap for five Portuguese servicemen held by Conakry.[85] The pilot and mechanic were eventually repatriated some three years later, after Portugal had secured the release of its own prisoners through more direct means, but the aircraft 'ended up rotting' on the apron at BA12.[86] There it joined a Westland Wessex, marked as the property of Bristow Helicopters, a British concern with extensive operations in Nigeria. On 10 September 1967 this particular helicopter was spotted in flight over northern Guinea by a FAP C-47 crew, leading to its interception by G.91s and a forced landing at Bula. After a few hours there, the Wessex flew under *helicanhão* escort to Bissalanca.[87] The incident led to renewed speculation alleging PAIGC helicopter operations, especially since Bristow had in 1966 sold two of the aircraft to Ghana, a major PAIGC benefactor.[88]

Regardless of the intent behind these incidents, they reinforced the incoming CCFAG's perception that a 'surprise attack, or even a simple low-level flyby over our troops' could cause 'sudden demoralisation and consequent entry into panic.'[89] Spínola feared that 'such a raid, whether flown by insurgent pilots or foreign aircrews, would result in 'truly catastrophic consequences.'[90] Correspondingly, upon his arrival the new CCFAG renewed long-standing demands for improved defence against air attack. Perhaps the most obvious solution was the improvement of anti-aircraft artillery coverage over Bissau, BA12, and other critical Portuguese installations, especially in light of the trouble AAA had given FAP

The *Oficinas Gerais de Material Aeronáutico* (OGMA, Aeronautical Material General Workshops) tested methods of firing AIM-9B Sidewinder missiles from FAP G.91s, but the combination proved ineffective against targets at low and medium altitudes and was never adopted. (OGMA)

A U.S. Army soldier aims an FIM-43C 'Redeye' anti-aircraft infrared-guided missile launcher during a training exercise in 1973. Lisbon repeatedly tried to obtain this system, despite the American embargo on arms deliveries to Portugal. (U.S. National Archives)

airmen. As early as January 1962 – a full year before the war's formal onset – the first Portuguese AAA platoon (*Pelotão AAA* 43) was installed at Bissalanca, equipped with a mix of 12.7mm machine guns and Bofors L/60 40mm guns.[91] This meagre force represented Portugal's entire air defence commitment to Guinea for the rest of the decade following the withdrawal of FAP F-86 Sabres in 1964.[92] However, the AAA platoon struggled to overcome 'a huge shortage of personnel' and obsolete weaponry unsuited to meeting any credible air threat.[93]

Spínola called for a dramatic increase in available AAA, and by 1970 his requirements had grown to a total of six platoons to be deployed throughout the province.[94] No reinforcements would be forthcoming until at least 1971, however, leaving a frustrated CCFAG with just one poorly-equipped and under-manned platoon at his disposal.[95] To boost Guinea's air defence array, the FAP operations directorate recommended acquiring man-portable, infrared-guided FIM-43 'Redeye' surface-to-air missiles (SAMs) from the United States.[96] The 'Redeye', in service with American forces since 1967, had been designed to protect frontline troops from low-flying tactical aircraft, although it was only marginally effective against fast jets.[97] Spínola's forces, however, were unlikely to receive the system so long as U.S. arms restrictions against Portugal remained in effect.[98]

In 1964 the American embargo had forced the withdrawal of Portugal's F-86F Sabre contingent from Guinea, leaving the ZACVG without an air-to-air fighter to defend against aerial attack. Its G.91 fleet – the only jet aircraft available in 1968 – was 'not designed for that mission, but only for tactical support,' Portugal's aviation minister recognised.[99] To redress the gap, the FAP considered arming the ground attack jets with AIM-9B 'Sidewinder' infrared-guided air-to-air missiles. Portugal had received 440 of the weapons from the United States in the early 1960s, specifically to equip the FAP's F-86F Sabres,[100] and in May 1969 Spínola concurred in the 'necessity to augment the Fiat G.91's armament with Sidewinders, with the intent of increasing its aerial combat potential.'[101] Tests to that effect, however, revealed the G.91 to be 'at a clear disadvantage compared to the performance of likely enemies,' notably the MiG-17, with or without missiles.[102] During those same tests, the AIM-9B proved ineffective against targets at low and medium altitudes, reaffirming the American experience in air-to-air combat over Vietnam. Consequently, in April 1970 the head of the FAP's operations directorate, *Coronel* António da Silva Cardoso, recommended against further attempts to arm the G.91 with missiles or employ it as an air combat fighter.[103] Although the notion generated additional discussion within the FAP and Defence Ministry, the proposal never produced operationally viable results.[104]

By January 1970, the solution to the ZACVG's air combat deficiencies seemed to lay in the acquisition of a new fighter aircraft. In his annual situation estimate for that year, Spínola requested a minimum of 16 French Dassault Mirage V interceptors.[105] This, however, represented a long-term project requiring years of international negotiations, type training, and infrastructure improvements (see Chapter 5).

Even an advanced fighter like the Mirage, however, would be worthless as an interceptor without adequate warning of an inbound attack. Although two AN/TPS-1D air surveillance radars had been providing limited coverage for Bissalanca since 1964, they operated under a number of crippling limitations. Already obsolete, the radars were plagued by poor power availability and maintenance problems, exacerbated by difficulties in obtaining spare parts. As a result one of the pair was soon cannibalised to keep the other in operation.[106] Two additional AN/TPS-1D sets were later sent to Guinea, but both soon ended up inoperative and/or cannibalised themselves.[107] Even in working order, the AN/TPS-1D gave only 4 to 7 minutes' warning of an intruder flying at 3,000 feet and 450 knots, leaving inadequate time to initiate an intercept.[108] Nothing better was available in 1970, however, so the ZACVG requested four additional sets of the same type to be deployed throughout the province.[109]

Absent adequate warning or viable defensive options, the best the ZACVG could do in the near term was improve physical protection at its own facilities. The threat of air attack against Bissalanca in particular, reinforced by the PAIGC's 18 February 1968 guerrilla raid against the base, led the FAP *Chefe do Estado-Maior da Força Aérea* (CEMFA, Chief of Staff) *to direct that BA12 undertake* 'an urgent study of measures to protect aircraft against possible attacks from outside.' Effective dispersal was virtually impossible due to the number of aircraft assigned and available parking surfaces,[110] so base officials recommended building a limited number of aircraft shelters and hardened dispersal pads at Bissalanca to compliment the requested surveillance radars, fighter aircraft, and AAA units.[111] In April 1970 a joint Army and Air Force study mission reiterated those requirements, and also proposed the creation of an Air Warning Centre and Anti-Air Operations Centre at BA12. Unfortunately, the recommended improvements entailed expenses well beyond the FAP's budget.[112] As a result, and despite repeated appeals from all affected commands, few of the theatre's air defence needs were ever fulfilled.

In the meantime, Spínola's own war against PAIGC air defences continued. In September 1969 aerial reconnaissance revealed a new ZPU-4 position in Cassebeche, indicating insurgent efforts to reconstitute their depleted air defences on the Quitafine Peninsula. Three aircraft formations of G.91s visited that locality on three consecutive days from 24–26 September, resulting in the destruction of the quad-barrelled anti-aircraft system.[113] Undeterred, the PAIGC

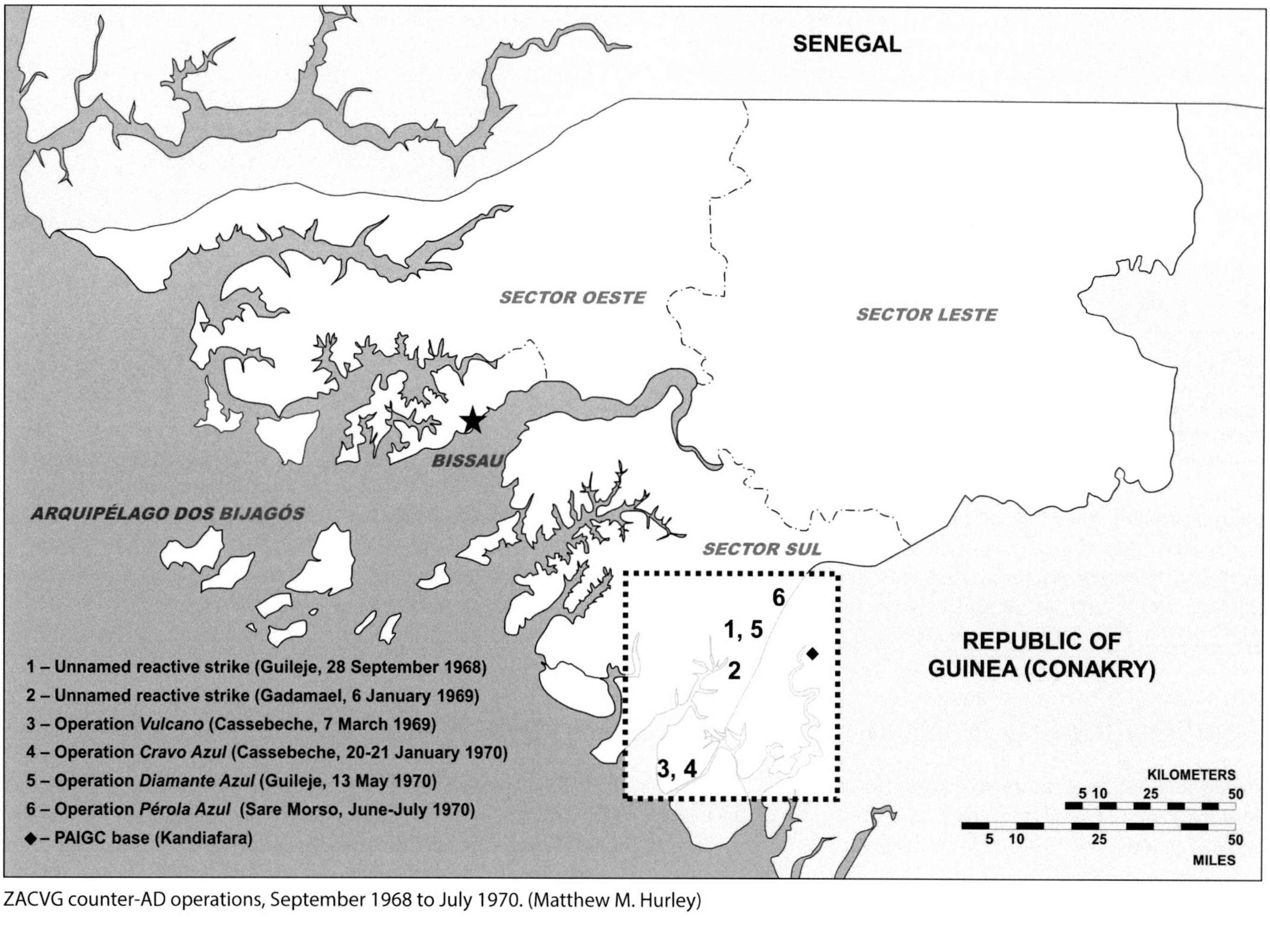

ZACVG counter-AD operations, September 1968 to July 1970. (Matthew M. Hurley)

A Soviet-made M1939 37mm anti-aircraft gun used by the PAIGC in southern Guinea. (Casa Comum/Mário Soares Foundation)

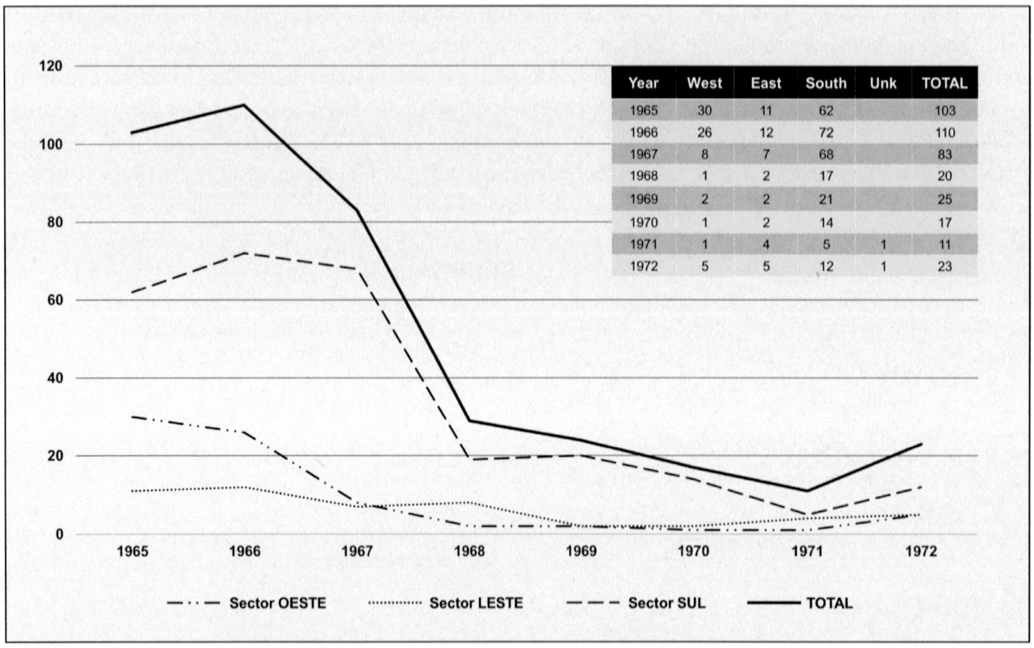

Year	West	East	South	Unk	TOTAL
1965	30	11	62		103
1966	26	12	72		110
1967	8	7	68		83
1968	1	2	17		20
1969	2	2	21		25
1970	1	2	14		17
1971	1	4	5	1	11
1972	5	5	12	1	23

Reported air defence activity, 1965–1972. (Matthew M. Hurley based on COMCHEFE Guiné, 'SUPINTREP no. 35,' Anexo H, 20 April 1971, SGDN/2REP/088/0364/024, ADN; COMZAVERDEGUINÉ, SITREP circunstanciados nos. 01/69 through 53/72, 08 January 1969 – 31 December 1972, SGDN/2REP/096, ADN.)

continued to commit its air defence assets to Cassebeche, and on 20 January 1970 a G.91 formation reported ineffective ZPU-4 and DShK fire originating from the site.[114] That incident triggered *Operação Cravo Azul*, an immediate response launched that same afternoon. At 1500 four G.91s departed BA12 at 'maximum load' and struck the site, reporting the destruction of a ZPU-4 and a pair of DShK AAMGs. To ensure definitive success, ZACVG commander *Coronel* Diogo Neto ordered a follow-on attack at 1005 the following day – again with four G.91s. Post-strike reconnaissance revealed no further indications of insurgent activity in Cassebeche, and some Portuguese aircrew heralded *Cravo Azul* as the successful conclusion of the 27 months long 'Battle of Quitafine.'[115]

Despite that initial optimism, G.91 pilots reported nine subsequent AAMG firing incidents throughout the remainder of 1970, including seven over Quitafine or along the nearby border with the Republic of Guinea. Additionally, small arms fire was directed against light aircraft and helicopters on at least four occasions.[116] Worse yet for Portuguese airmen, that year the PAIGC began using Soviet-made M1939 37mm anti-aircraft guns, more than doubling the reach of insurgent air defences.[117] Their presence was first revealed on 12 May by G.91 pilots patrolling the south-eastern border, who observed flak detonations above them while flying at a supposedly 'safe' altitude. A subsequent C-47 reconnaissance sortie confirmed the presence of four 37mm AA guns, two ZPU-4s, and four DShK AAMGs in the Guileje vicinity, having presumably originated from the PAIGC's cross-border base in Kandiafara, Republic of Guinea.[118]

A planning session that evening resulted in *Operação Diamante Azul* the next day. On 13 May two waves of four G.91s each struck the assembled weapons; the first carrying 600kg of general purpose bombs per aircraft, and the second armed with 750lb depth charges converted into demolition bombs. Post-strike reconnaissance revealed the PAIGC weapons, or what remained of them, had been returned to Kandiafara.[119] At the end of June 1970 a G.91 identified additional 37mm AA cannons at Sare Morso, on the border with the Republic of Guinea 10km northeast of Guileje, prompting *Operação Pérola Azul*. Twenty-four G.91 sorties struck the site in the first week of July, with apparent success, as no further 37mm AAA sightings or activity were reported in Guinea until May 1972.[120]

The FAP's years long counter-AD campaign, consisting of no fewer than 17 named operations and multiple reactive strikes since December 1965, had achieved several notable successes. Immediate effects included the neutralisation of air defence weapons and their operators, and in the course of these missions the ZACVG claimed more than 50 anti-aircraft guns destroyed or damaged. This attrition was reflected in the reduced amount of anti-aircraft fire threatening ZACVG operations: the frequency of aerial opposition fell from 110 incidents reported in 1966 to just nine in 1971. Although the number rebounded to 23 in 1972, two-thirds of all reported episodes

The Berliet Tramagal was one of the most important vehicles used by the Portuguese forces in Africa during the 1960s and 1970s. The French-designed truck was produced under licence in Portugal from 1964 until 1974, first in a 4x4 version and then in a larger 6x6 version. In Guinea, as in Portugal's other overseas possessions, the Tramagal were used extensively for cargo and troop transport. Given the PAIGC's increasing use of road mines, sandbags were strategically placed to cushion the effects of an explosion and prevent serious injury to the occupants. Versatile, reliable, and powerful, the Berliet was employed extensively during the war for Guinea, where it reputedly saved many lives. "Everyone wanted to ride it," veterans of the ground war there recalled. (Artwork by Paulo Alegria)

Thirty-eight General Motors Fox armoured cars, produced in Canada during the Second World War, were supplied to Portugal in 1957. Their Browning 7.62mm coaxial machine guns were replaced by 7.92mm calibre weapons, and at the end of 1959 the first reconnaissance squadron of eight Fox vehicles was activated for service in Guinea. Despite its relative obsolescence the Fox proved reliable and robust, qualities much appreciated by Portuguese Army personnel. The Fox reconnaissance squadron assigned to Guinea was installed at Bafatá, and these vehicles were used to great tactical effect in notable actions throughout the territory. (Artwork by Paulo Alegria)

The Unimog 400/411 series was a family of all-terrain vehicles produced by Daimler and marketed by Mercedes-Benz, and the Unimog 411.115 was a customized version produced specifically for Portugal. The 411 became an all-purpose workhorse for Portuguese ground troops in Africa, capable of carrying up to 10 armed soldiers. Its elevated cabin and bed allowed occupants to better detect nearby movement or potential threats, although this advantage was negated in the heavy rainforests of Guinea and northern Angola. The vehicles were poorly protected against mines or ambush, but their general sturdiness and offroad versatility ensured extensive use in Africa. (Artwork by Paulo Alegria)

Beginning in 1963 the PAIGC employed Soviet-made Goryunov SG-43 7.62mm medium machine guns against both ground and air targets. First deployed during the Second World War, the simple and reliable SG-43 has since been adopted by over three dozen armies worldwide and has been produced under license in China, Poland, Czechoslovakia, and Egypt. With an effective anti-aircraft range of 800 metres, this weapon especially threatened slow, low-flying Portuguese aircraft and helicopters. Despite its long career during the war for Guinea, its use was suspected as the cause for only one aircraft loss – a T-6 shot down in January 1964, during Operation *Tridente*. (Artwork by David Bocquelet)

By mid-1964 the PAIGC began using the Soviet-designed 12.7mm DShK (*Degtyaryova-Shpagina Krupnokaliberny* or "Degtyaryova-Shpagina large-calibre") anti-aircraft machinegun. First fielded by the USSR in 1938, the DShK has since gone on to serve in the armed forces of over 100 nations and insurgent groups. With an effective anti-air range of 1,000 metres, the DShK proved a deadly threat during the 1954 siege of Dien Bien Phu and against American aircraft overflying the Ho Chi Minh Trail traversing Laos, Cambodia, and South Vietnam. In Guinea, PAIGC DShK fire brought down a FAP G.91 in July 1968 and damaged several other aircraft throughout the war. (Artwork by David Bocquelet)

With an effective anti-aircraft range of three kilometres, the M1939 37mm automatic anti-aircraft gun could fire armour-piercing and fragmentation shells at a sustained rate of 80 rounds per minute, or twice that for burst firing. The USSR first deployed the M1939 just prior to the Second World War, and it has since seen service with over 60 nations' armed forces. Its use was first reported in Guinea during 1970, but the M1939's weight (over one metric tonne) and size (5.5 metres total length) limited its deployment there to prepared anti-aircraft positions. (Artwork by David Bocquelet)

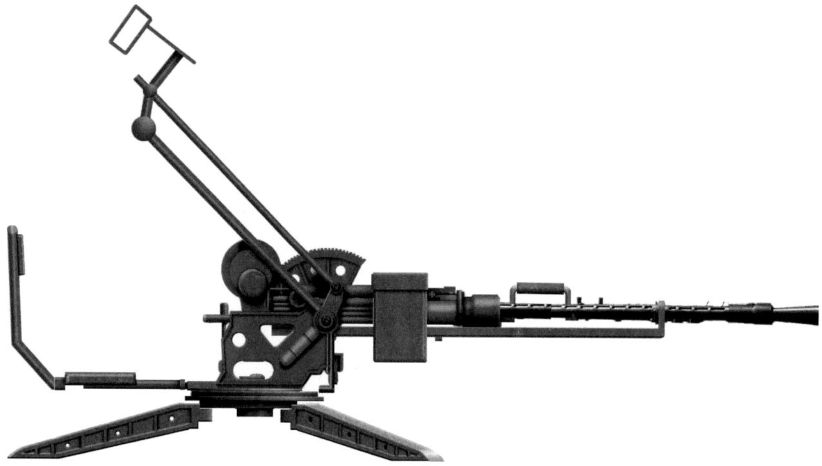

The Soviet-designed ZPU series of anti-aircraft machineguns (*zenitnaya pulemotnaya ustanovka*, or "anti-aircraft machinegun mount") first entered service immediately following the Second World War. All ZPU variants used the 14.5mm KPV heavy machinegun (*krupnokaliberniy pulemyot Vladimirova*, or "Vladimir's large-calibre machinegun"), which could engage aerial targets out to an effective range of 1,400 metres. The ZPU-1 mounted a single KPV capable of firing 600 rounds per minute. (Artwork by David Bocquelet)

The ZPU-2 was the twin-barrel variant of the Soviet *zenitnaya pulemotnaya ustanovka* series of anti-aircraft machinegun mounts. Used extensively by communist forces during the Korean War, the ZPU-2 could fire 14.5mm high explosive/incendiary-tracer (HEI-T) or armour-piercing incendiary (API) rounds at a rate of 1,200 rounds per minute. Its 1,400 metres effective anti-aircraft range was more than doubled by its 3,000 metres reach against ground targets. (Artwork by David Bocquelet)

Mounting four 14.5mm heavy machineguns, the ZPU-4 was the deadliest member of the ZPU family, capable of firing 2,400 HEI-T or API rounds per minute. The ZPU-1, -2, and -4 have been used by more than 70 nations and non-state militant groups, and they have seen service in every major conflict from Korea to the war in Ukraine. (Artwork by David Bocquelet)

In 1967 Portuguese authorities first received intelligence regarding the delivery of Soviet Projekt-183 patrol boats to the PAIGC (better known as 'P-6'). These craft were based in the port of Conakry and were similar to those used by the Republic of Guinea Navy. Armed with twin 25mm 2M3 autocannons installed in turrets mounted fore and aft, PAIGC P-6s were crewed by militants trained in the Soviet Union. Capable of speeds exceeding 40 knots, the P-6 could rapidly attack lightly defended craft, but the PAIGC's boats generally sat docked in Conakry and never ventured into Portuguese Guinea waters. In November 1970 these boats, along with all Republic of Guinea naval vessels, were destroyed by Portuguese forces participating in Operation *Mar Verde*. (Artwork by David Bocquelet)

In 1971 the Portuguese corvette *Jacinto Cândido* (F476), carrying two 40mm anti-aircraft guns and an MLA-1B air surveillance radar, arrived at Bissau to defend the city and its vital port facilities from air attack. This *João Coutinho*-class corvette had just entered service with the Portuguese Navy (1970) when Spínola requested the vessel's deployment, although its meagre anti-air capability offered little defence against the expected threat. Following the *Ultramar* wars this corvette enjoyed a long career in the Portuguese Navy, serving until 2018. (Artwork by David Bocquelet)

Aerospatiale SE.316B Alouette IIIs of the FAP were used in Guinea for a wide variety of missions, including armed reconnaissance and force escort missions, for which some were fitted with a 20mm cannon. In a troop transport role, each Alouette III typically carried five soldiers and their individual equipment (four in the rear seat and one facing backwards from the front to the pilot's left). Alternatively, the French-built helicopter could lift two stretcher patients and two medical attendants during MEDEVAC missions. This Alouette III, FAP 9338, suffered a serious accident in Guinea in July 1970: it crashed in bad weather, killing its crew and occupants, which included four members of Portugal's parliament. (Artwork by Paulo Alegria)

In Guinea the T-6/Harvard/SNJ series of armed trainers was routinely used for interdiction, fire support, naval and ground escort, airborne command and control, and armed reconnaissance. By the mid-1960s, however, they had already proven vulnerable to even light surface fire. Consequently, when the first Fiat G.91s arrived in mid-1966, the FAP's T-6s were relegated to missions deemed less threatening. This T-6, FAP 1975, carries a Browning 7.7mm machine gun and a 50-litre napalm canister under each wing. (Artwork by Paulo Alegria)

Seven Douglas B-26 Invader medium bombers were illegally sold to Portugal in 1965, before U.S. authorities discovered the scheme and arrested the pilot responsible for the transfers. Two of the covertly acquired aircraft saw service in Guinea beginning in March 1971, when aircraft 7104 and 7106 deployed to Bissalanca for an operational evaluation. During three months of combat appraisal the B-26s logged approximately 200 hours over Guinea, providing valuable experience for subsequent operations in Angola, where the aircraft were ultimately based. FAP Invaders received an aluminium paint scheme with white upper surfaces and a dark blue separation fillet along the fuselage. The section of nose fairing facing the cockpit was painted anti-reflective black. (Artwork by Paulo Alegria)

All Fiat G.91s in Guinea were assigned to *Esquadra* 121, which was responsible for attack, fire support, and airborne command and control. Alongside the G.91 "Tigres" flight, the squadron also flew T-6s ("Roncos") and Do-27s ("Cafeteiras"). The G.91s fulfilled critical attack and reconnaissance roles, and with external fuel tanks they could quickly reach nearly any point in the Portuguese colony. This G.91 carries two 350-litre napalm tanks, one under each wing. (Artwork by Paulo Alegria)

The Fiat G.91-R4 debuted in Guinea in mid-1966, dramatically improving the ZACVG's offensive potential. The R4 variant was initially delivered to the West German Luftwaffe after Greece and Turkey reneged on their purchase agreements, and later offered to Portugal on favourable terms. The G.91's flight characteristics and aerodynamic stability made it an excellent gun platform, and it carried three Vinten F.95-MK3 70mm cameras in the nose to collect detailed imagery. This G.91 was one of the first to arrive in Guinea and retained the Luftwaffe colour scheme of dark grey-green on the upper surfaces, and bluish-grey below. This aircraft, FAP 5407, was damaged by shrapnel from its own 200kg fragmentation bomb during a February 1967 mission; the pilot, *Major* Santos Moreira, was compelled to eject while attempting to return to BA12-Bissalanca. (Artwork by Paulo Alegria)

From 1968 FAP G.91s received a new paint scheme in overall light blue-grey, although insignia and serial number placement remained unchanged. On 28 July 1968, G.O. 1201 commander Lieutenant Colonel Francisco da Costa Gomes flew one of two freshly repainted jets on a photoreconnaissance mission in southern Guinea. While attempting to locate reported anti-aircraft positions along the international border, Costa Gomes' aircraft (serial 5411) was hit by 12.7mm fire allegedly originating from Republic of Guinea territory. The impacting rounds ruptured the fuel line, igniting the engine and tail section and forcing Costa Gomes to eject. (Artwork by Paulo Alegria)

Between 1965 and 1970 the FAP received fourteen Nord N.2501D Noratlas from the Luftwaffe to augment its fleet of N.2502A/B/F aircraft purchased from France and Israel. Two of these ex-German Noratlas (6423 and 6424) were assigned to *Esquadra* 123 in Guinea, performing airlift, liaison, and assault transport duties. Portuguese N-2501D models retained their German camouflage in two shades of green and grey, and for *Ultramar* service these aircraft also sported dayglo colours on the nose, wingtips, engine cowlings, and rudder. The Noratlas of *Esquadras* 92 (Luanda) and 123 (Bissalanca) also featured squadron insignia beneath the cockpit window, as seen here. (Artwork by Paulo Alegria)

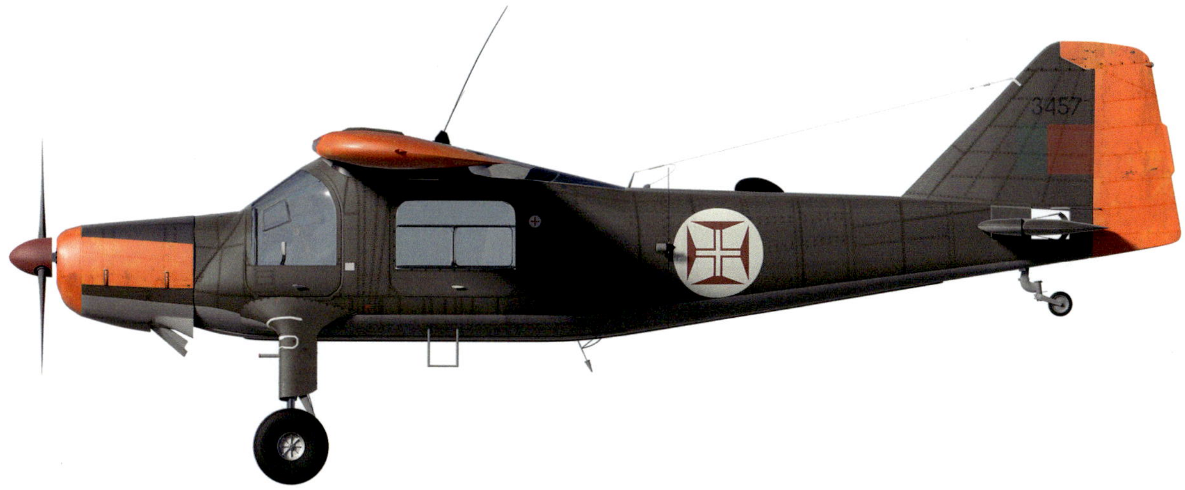

Portugal acquired 152 Dornier Do-27 light utility aircraft (149 for the FAP and three for Guinea's civil aviation service, the TAGP) between 1961 and 1979. During the war a dozen of these rugged, versatile craft were typically present in Guinea, where they performed light transport, visual reconnaissance, liaison, command and control, MEDEVAC, and light attack/escort duties. Six Do-27s were lost to operational accidents or hostile fire during approximately 30,000 sorties flown throughout the conflict. (Artwork by Paulo Alegria)

The Republic of Guinea received 10 MiG-17F (NATO "FRESCO C") fighter-bombers from the Soviet Union in the early 1960s, and for more than two decades they formed the offensive core of the *Force Aérienne de Guineé*. Initially based in Conakry, the FAG's MiG-17 fleet suffered from low operability rates despite pilot and technician training in the Soviet Union. Portuguese forces attempted to destroy these fighters at Conakry airport during November 1970's Operation *Mar Verde* but, unknown to the Portuguese, the MiGs had been moved to a different airfield prior to the raid. (Artwork by Paulo Alegria)

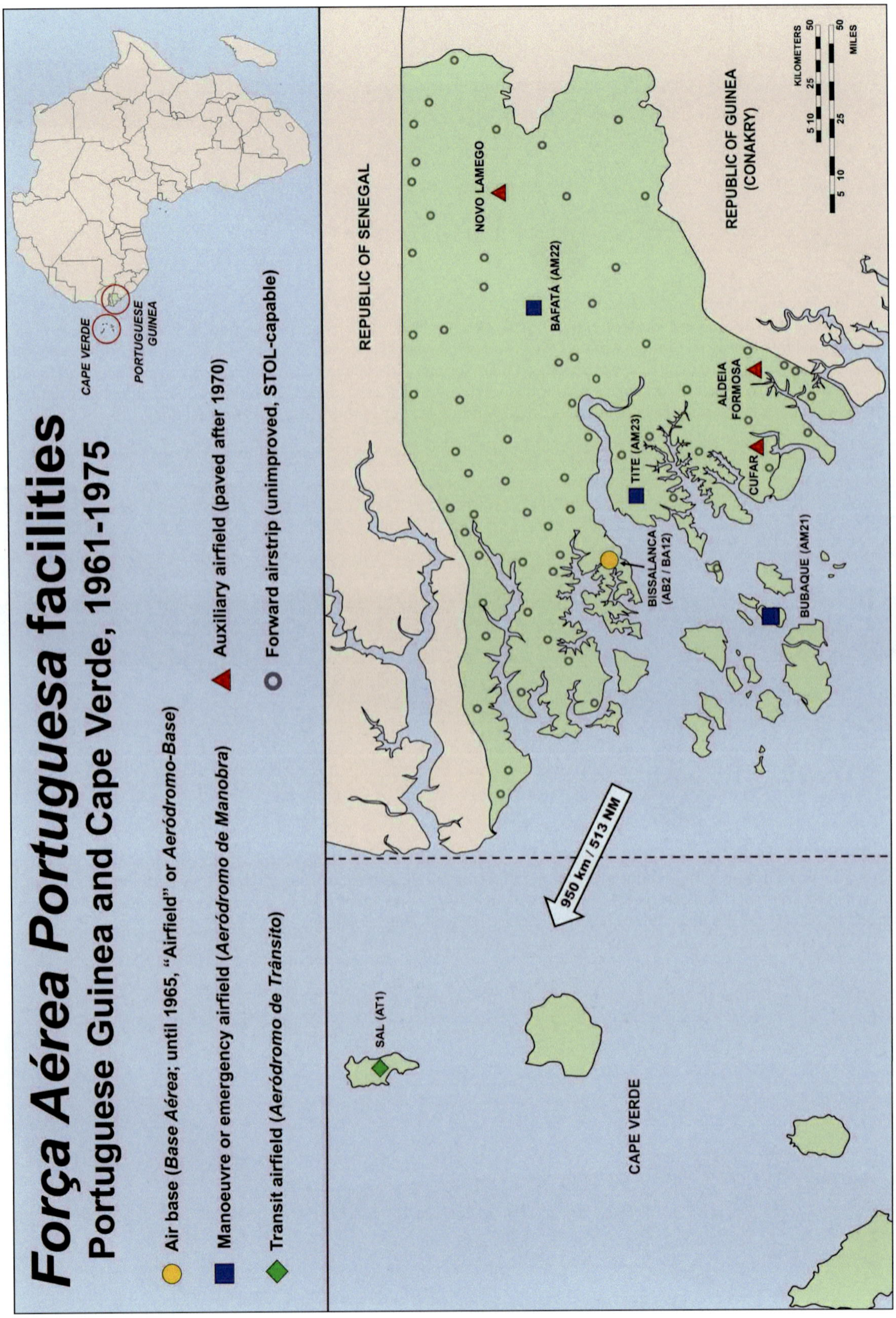

FAP installations, Guinea-Cape Verde theatre 1961–1975. (Matthew M. Hurley)

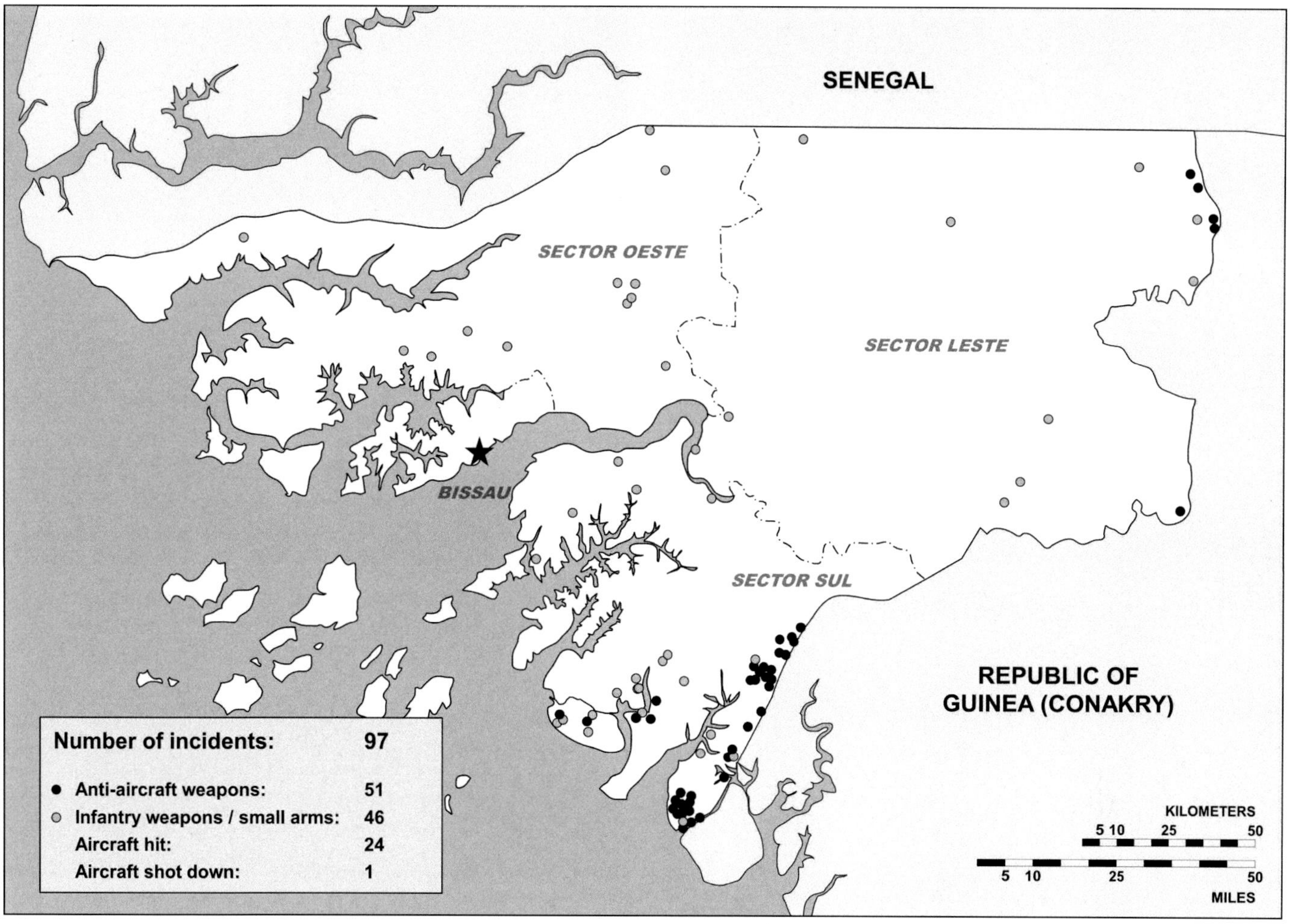

PAIGC air defence activity, 1968–1972. (Matthew M. Hurley based on COMZAVERDEGUINÉ, SITREP circunstanciados nos. 01/69 through 53/72, 08 January 1969 – 31 December 1972, ADN/SGDN/2REP/096.)

G.91 no.5411, a few days before it was shot down near the border with the Republic of Guinea. (José Nico Collection)

following *Operação Pérola Azul* (July 1970) through to the end of 1972 involved small arms fire or other infantry weapons rather than dedicated anti-aircraft weaponry, and most of the latter originated from sites across the frontier with the Republic of Guinea.[121] In fact, virtually all of the PAIGC's true 'anti-aircraft' fire – from purpose-built DShK, ZPU, or 37mm AA guns – targeted aircraft over the border zones of southern and eastern Guinea.

For the insurgents, the air defence battle revealed systemic shortcomings in their ability to neutralise the FAP, despite the influx of effective weaponry and foreign expertise. The failure of his anti-aircraft strategy to 1971 prompted Amílcar Cabral to chastise his forces for their 'lack at courage to shoot at planes, despite knowing that the more shots are fired against the planes, the more fearful the aviators are.'[122] Also telling, and most significantly for Portuguese airmen, throughout the years 1965 to 1972 the FAP lost only one aircraft to hostile fire over Guinea. On 28 July 1968, G.O. 1201 commander *Tenente Coronel* Francisco da Costa Gomes was flying one of two G.91s conducting photoreconnaissance north of Guileje. While attempting to locate and photograph reported anti-aircraft positions along the international border, Costa Gomes' aircraft (Fiat 5411) was hit by 12.7mm fire allegedly originating from Republic of Guinea territory. The impacting rounds hit the fuel line, igniting the engine and tail section, forcing the G.O. 1201 commander to eject. His aircraft then crashed four kilometres from the border, near the Portuguese barracks at Gandembel.[123] After evading enemy patrols and navigating a minefield, Costa Gomes managed to reach the barracks where a soldier challenged the

The detached tail section of G.91 no.5411, shot down by the PAIGC on 28 July 1968. (Casa Comum/Mário Soares Foundation)

Position of no.5411's crash site within Portuguese Guinea territory, 4km from the Republic of Guinea border. (National Defence Archive)

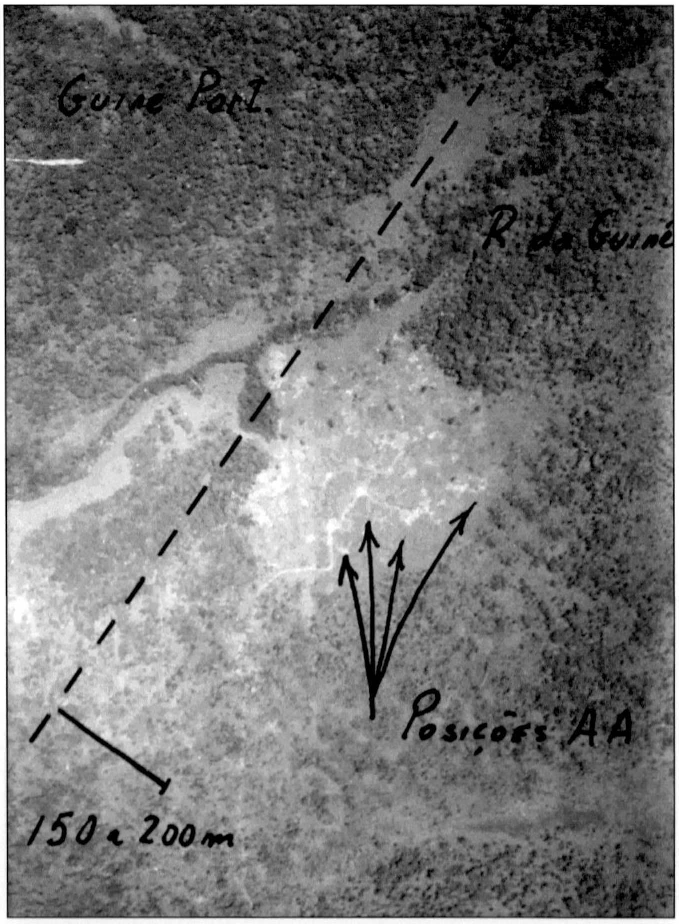

PAIGC anti-aircraft gun positions about 200 metres from the border with Portuguese Guinea. G.91 no.5411 was presumably hit by 12.7mm fire from one of these positions. (National Defence Archive)

haggard, unknown figure in a dirty flight suit who looked 'too old to be a pilot.' Once his identity and status were verified, the G.O. 1201 commander was returned to Bissalanca without further incident.[124]

In raw numerical terms, the counter-AD effort represented only a small part of the FAP's overall activity in Guinea. From Spínola's assumption of command on 20 May 1968 through to the end of 1972, Portuguese airmen flew nearly 12,408 attack, fire support, and armed reconnaissance sorties over Guinea, of which just 67 – about one-half of one percent – were specifically allocated to pre-planned air defence suppression operations.[125] Sortie counts alone, however, belie the significance of the air defence struggle to both sides of the conflict. The PAIGC had staked much of its political credibility on the ability to win and hold 'liberated' areas, but the validity of its claims diminished with every FAP aircraft that flew unmolested above them. For their part the Portuguese increasingly relied on air power to project force – and by extension, political authority – throughout the territory; failure to do so risked its continued viability as an imperial power. In this round the Portuguese had won a qualified victory, having by mid–1970 re-established air supremacy, albeit temporarily. This ultimately compelled the PAIGC to look elsewhere for an answer to the bane of Portuguese airpower, but in the meantime the FAP was free to commit additional aviation resources to other endeavours.

5

'Everything was hanging on them, one way or the other'

> We had, on the one hand, 40,000 ground troops, who endured the hardships they had to endure: remoteness, discomfort, in short, the constant danger... On the other hand, 50 or 60 pilots, 70 at most. Everything was hanging on them, one way or the other. (General José Lemos Ferreira, BA12 commander, 1971–74)[1]

While the battle for air supremacy raged, the ground war expanded in scope and intensity. By 1968 the PAIGC claimed control of two-thirds of Guinea's territory, citing as evidence Spínola's consolidation of forces and consequent abandonment of some isolated garrisons.[2] Their operations had also become more lethal: although the total number of attacks against Portuguese forces decreased by almost a third from 1969–1970, they caused nearly 45 percent more casualties.[3] According to the *Chefe do Estado-Maior-General das Forças Armadas* (CEMGFA, Chief of the General Staff of the Armed Forces), General Venâncio Deslandes, the PAIGC's greater combat effectiveness reflected four complementary developments:

1. materiel reinforcement, both qualitative and quantitative;
2. manpower reinforcement, including the use of foreign specialists;
3. military reorganisation, which improved tactical control and flexibility;
4. advances in intelligence, planning, and tactical leadership.[4]

These improvements reflected the PAIGC's continued effort to transform its armed wing into 'a conventional military structure'.[5] Driven by the need to counter Spínola's military and socio-political initiatives as well as the influx of heavy weapons, the PAIGC 'completely remodelled its structure' during 1970–71.[6] The new arrangement eliminated the 'guerrilla' designation, replacing those units with *Forças Armadas Locais* (FAL, Local Armed Forces). Its 'regular' force, the *Exército Popular* was further divided into regionally assigned 'corps' composed of two or more *bi-grupos*, with specialised sections attached as required. 'It is a set of forces which involves the cooperative employment of several units,' a CCFAG analysis summarised, 'having infantry, artillery and rockets, allowing distribution of massed manpower to conduct the war effort where the Party intends.'[7] An intelligence estimate from the same period assessed the EP's overall strength at some 6,000 personnel (4,800 within Guinea and 1,200 in neighbouring states) divided into 73 *bi-grupos*, 30 artillery groups, and two commando groups.[8]

To counter the PAIGC's growing potency Spínola, like his predecessors, turned increasingly to his aviation arm. Although the ZACVG mounted only one pre-planned attack operation (ATIP – see Appendix VI) in 1969,[9] that number grew to 22 the following year, followed by 45 in 1971.[10] Those operations involved nearly 3,000 strike sorties, the vast majority carried out by G.91s or T-6s, accounting for a third of all attack and air support missions logged from 1969 to 1971. Unsurprisingly, pre-planned airstrikes focused on areas of increased PAIGC activity in the southern and western sectors, where the insurgent party and its militants were most active.[11]

Many of the remaining attack and fire support sorties were flown in support of the continuing 'helicopter war' in Guinea. From August 1968 to the end of 1971 the ZACVG oversaw nearly 160 heliborne operations, again concentrated in the west and south, lifting nearly 15,000 troops in over 3,000 'hops'. Virtually all were supported by fixed-wing and rotary-wing aircraft performing reconnaissance, preparatory bombardment, fire support, command and control, and MEDEVAC. Over time, every type in the ZACVG inventory played an active role in Portugal's helicopter campaign, even a pair of B-26s briefly assigned to BA12 for combat evaluation.[12] By 1971 the combined air-ground assaults had assumed a 'vital role' in Spínola's strategy, according to a visiting journalist, who observed that 'the Alouettes are rarely idle. Barely a day goes by without all the operational craft being sent out at one time or another.'[13]

Together, ZACVG operations of all types accounted for over 40,000 sorties during the first three and a half years of Spínola's

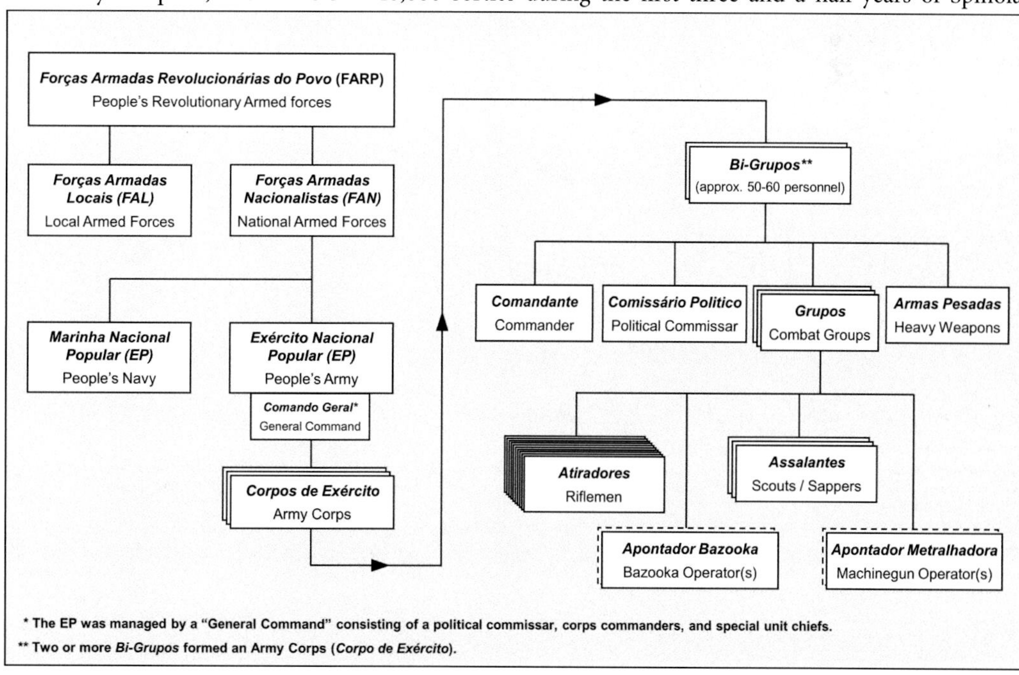

PAIGC military structure, 1971. (Matthew M. Hurley based on CCFAG, 'Estudo da situação operacional e logística do TO da Guiné e evolução prevista para 1970–1971,' January 1970, CEMGFA/017/0036/028, AND; Amílcar Cabral, 'Para a reorganização dos ExércitosNacionais Populares,' 1970, Pasta 04602.052, FMS, www.casacomum.org/cc/visualizador?; Amílcar Cabral, 'Forças Armadas Revolucionárias do Povo – Bases e componentes,' 19 September 1970, Pasta 04343.002.007, FMS; Aniceto Afonso and Carlos de Matos Gomes, *Guerra Colonial* (Lisbon: Editorial Notícias, 2000), 160.)

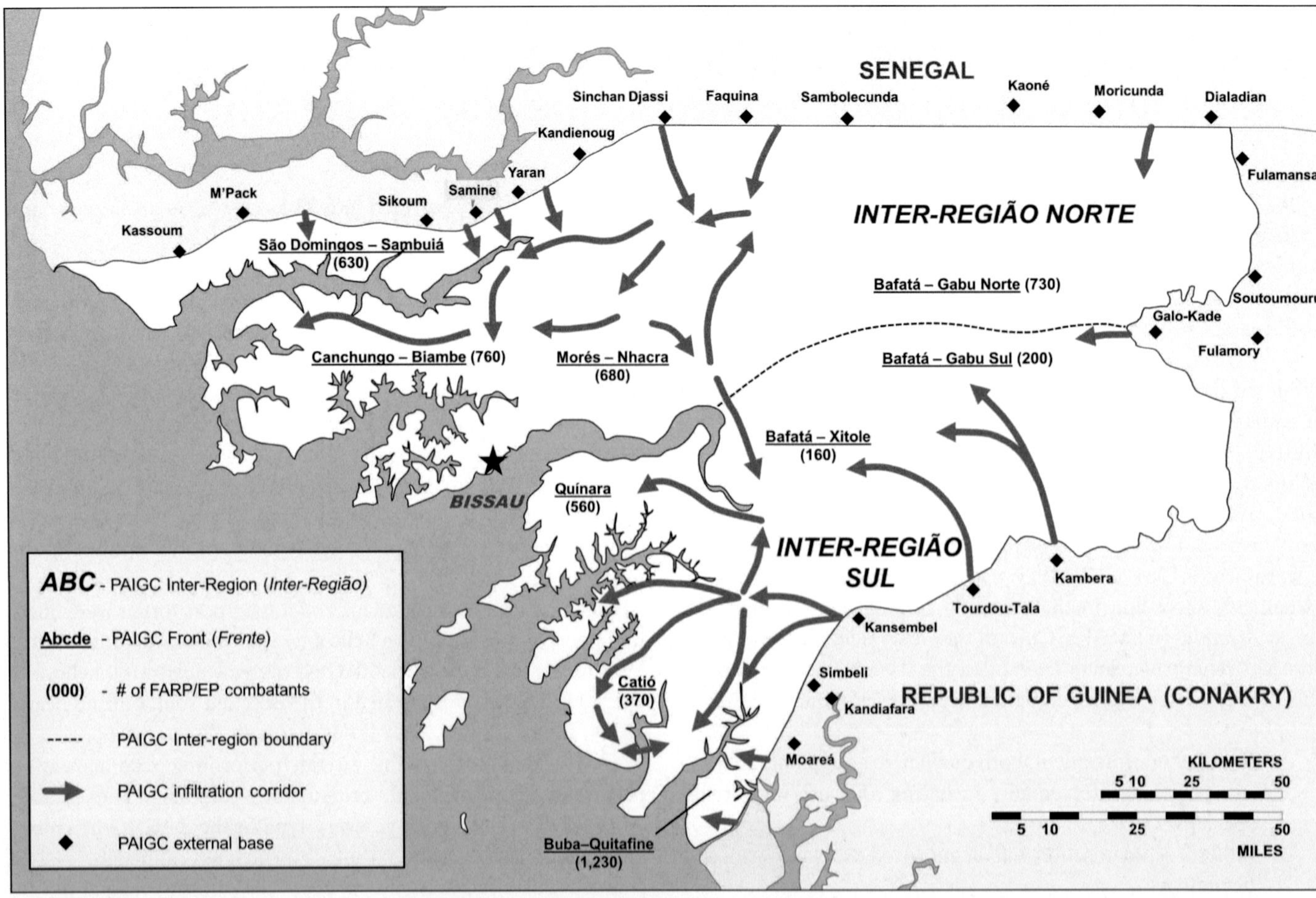

'Regular' FARP/EP deployments, 1970 (not counting local militia). (Matthew M. Hurley based on CCFAG, 'Estudo da situação operacional e logística do T.O. da Guiné e evolução prevista para 1970–1971,' January 1970, CEMGFA/017/0036/028, ADN; CCFAG, 'SUPINTREP no. 35, Aditamento no. 1 (evolução da actividade e da situação do IN no TO referente a 1970),' 20 April 1971, SGDN/2REP/088/0364/024; CCFAG, 'SUPINTREP 32: Ordem de batalha do PAIGC – Instrução, táctica e logística,' June 1971, SGDN/2REP/088/0364/023, ADN; CECA, *Resenha Histórico-Militar das Campanhas de África*, 6-II-II, p. 399.)

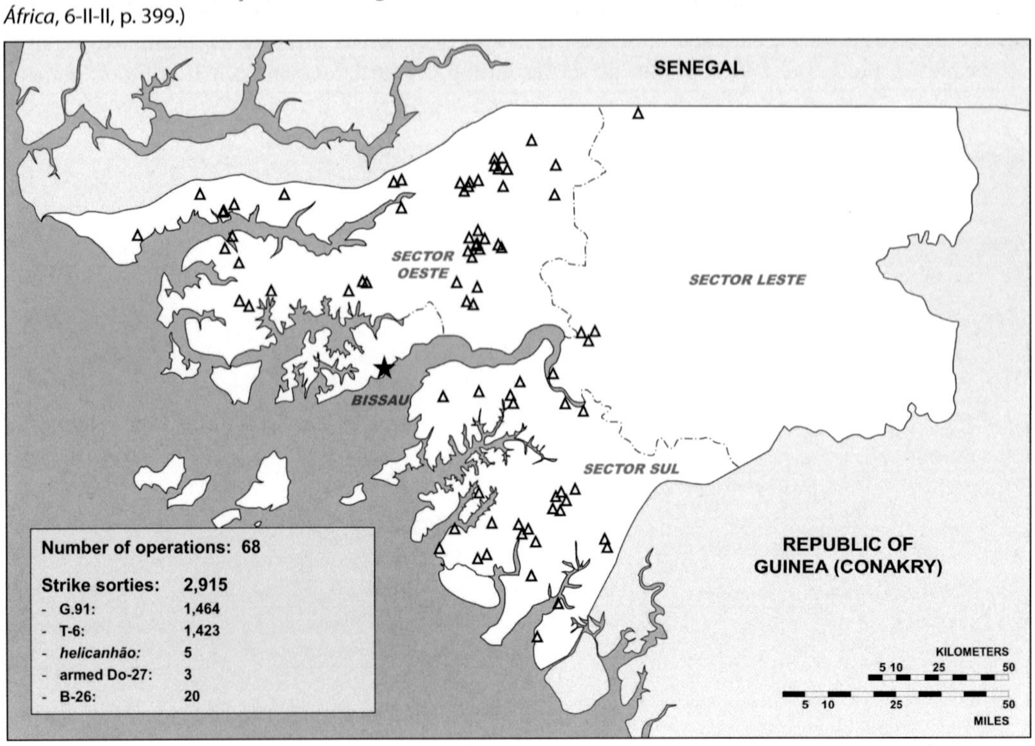

Independent ZACVG strike operations, 1969–1971. (Matthew M. Hurley based on COMZAVERDEGUINÉ, SITREPs circunstanciados nos.19/69 through 01/72, 12 May 1969 to 2 January 1972, ADN/SGDN/2REP/096.)

command (July 1968 to December 1971 – see Appendix II), reaching a peak annual total of 11,320 during 1971. The most heavily tasked aircraft in BA12's inventory during this period were the Do-27 (14,047 sorties) and the Alouette III (12,185), indicative of their utility across multiple mission sets and the centrality of aerial logistics to both Portugal's war effort and its civil support programmes. In terms of mission type, the three transportation categories – assault, general, and MEDEVAC – flew more than half of the total, accounting for 22,899 of the 40,639 sorties reported in daily ZACVG situation reports from 1968 to 1971. This was an impressive tally for a force struggling to maintain a fleet of around 40 operational aircraft, although several new arrivals at BA12 helped to relieve the demands placed on individual planes and those who serviced them.[14]

Spínola had petitioned for more aircraft since October 1968, when he submitted a request for an additional eight G.91s, four T-6s, and six Do-27s, along with two types new to the province: six Sud Aviation SA330 'Puma' helicopters and three (later four)

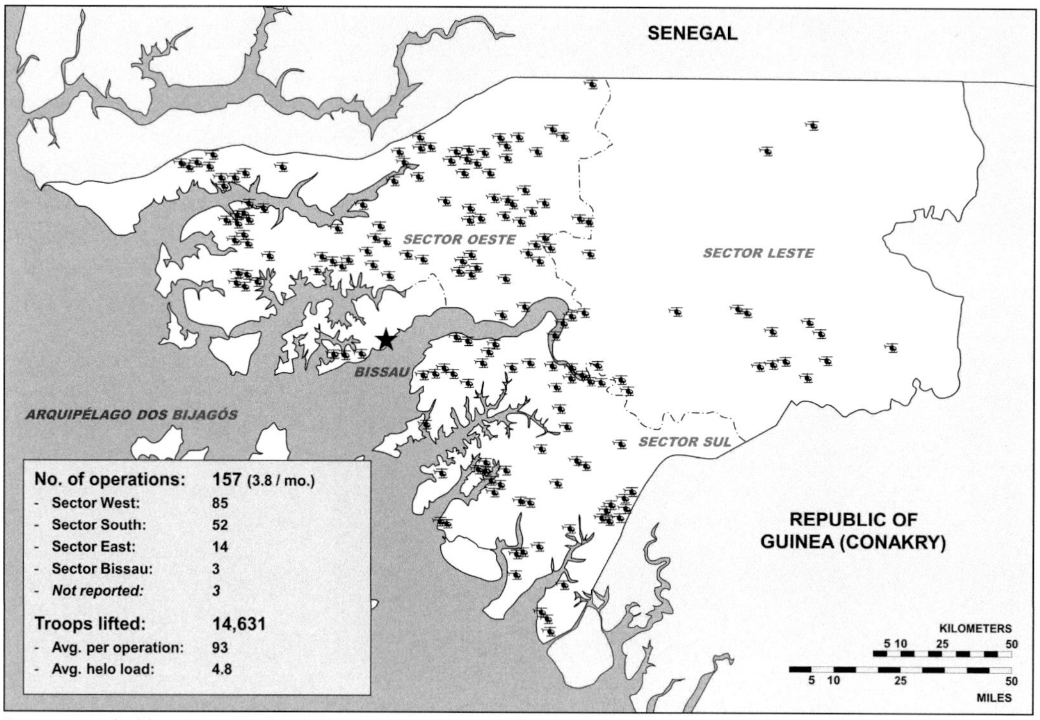

Portuguese heliborne operations, August 1968 – December 1971. (Matthew M. Hurley based on COMZAVERDEGUINÉ, SITREPs circunstanciados nos. 19/69 through 01/72, 12 May 1969 to 2 January 1972, ADN/SGDN/2REP/096.)

From August 1968 to the end of 1971 the ZACVG conducted nearly 160 heliborne operations. (Helder Ferreira Collection)

Nord Aviation 'Noratlas' transports.[15] Spínola put particular emphasis on the additional helicopters to permit 'timely and beneficial exploitation of information regarding the encampment or deployment of armed enemy groups,' and called for a fleet that would ensure the operational availability of 12 Alouette IIIs or their equivalent on demand.[16] Most of his requests were fulfilled by the end of 1970, with the exception of the helicopters, of which he received six new Alouette IIIs in lieu of the larger Pumas; and the G.91s, of which four were provided instead of the eight requested.[17] These reinforcements increased the number of G.91s at BA12 to ten, and raised the Alouette III inventory to 14.[18]

Introduction of the Noratlas[19] provided an immediate and noteworthy boost to the ZACVG's airlift capacity. The French-built transport was 'very stable, robust, and therefore well behaved in turbulence as befits Africa,' according to onetime *1ª Região Aérea* commander *General* Rui Tavares Monteiro.[20] The type had been designed for austere environments, with landing gear intended for rough field operations and easy cargo handling through the rear-opening clamshell doors. It could also carry over twice the cargo, or 50 percent more troops, than the C-47s already serving in Guinea, and its theatre debut freed the venerable Dakotas for additional night bombing and photoreconnaissance missions.[21] The FAP had been forced to 'scrounge' its Noratlas fleet from varied sources during the 1960s, ultimately acquiring six N-2502A versions from the civil airline *Union Aéromaritime du Transport* (UAT), six N-2502F models from the Israeli *Kheil HaAvir*, three N-2502Bs from *Air Algérie*, and 13 military variants (N-2501D) from retiring *Luftwaffe* stocks. Although the military 2501 version could operate from shorter runways, the FAP elected to use the turbojet-augmented 2502 civil variant in Africa given its greater cargo and passenger capacity. Three of these were sent to BA12, where they flew their first missions at the end of January 1971.[22]

Attack operations were temporarily augmented by an operational evaluation of B-26 Invader medium bombers, which Portugal clandestinely acquired in 1965, circumventing U.S. arms restrictions.[24] Two of these aircraft deployed to BA12 from March to June 1971, where they conducted 55 bombing, overwatch, reconnaissance, and instrumentation support sorties, including participation in at least nine ZACVG strike operations.[25] Additionally, beginning in February 1970 the P2V-5 Neptune made its return to the Guinea-Cape Verde theatre when one of the maritime patrol bombers was detached to AT1, the FAP's air transit base on Sal Island, Cape Verde.[26] The most significant improvement to the air force's capabilities, however, resulted from the purchase of two Boeing 707-3F5C jetliners for transoceanic airlift. Until 1971 the FAP had relied on its ageing fleet of Douglas DC-6 piston-engined transports, which proved distressingly prone to engine failure and other maintenance issues, but U.S. and UK arms embargoes against Portugal limited replacement options.[27] In August 1970, however, U.S. President Richard Nixon relaxed restrictions governing the sale of 'non-lethal dual-use items which are preponderantly employed for civilian use' to Portugal.[28] This led to a convoluted arrangement

Do-27s were the most heavily-utilised aircraft in BA12's inventory from 1966 to 1973. The versatile light utility craft were tasked for a wide variety of roles including general transport, airborne C2, MEDEVAC, and even fire support. (Virgílio Teixeira Collection)

Table 11: Status of ZACVG Requests (as of May 1971)

Request	Date presented	Resolution
8 x Fiat G.91	October 1968	Four provided in 1970
4 x T-6	October 1968	Fulfilled, May 1969
3 x Noratlas	October 1968	Fulfilled, end of 1970
6 x SA-330	October 1968	Six Al-III provided *c.*March 1969 instead
6 x Do-27	May 1969	Fulfilled, June 1969
1 x Para company	May 1969	Established in June 1970

Table 12: ZACVG Theatre Transport Capacity, 1971[23]

	Do-27*	Alouette III**	C-47	Noratlas 2502
Equipped troops	4	5	20	30
Passengers	5	6	25	45
Maximum cargo	350kg	300–500kg	1,900kg	4,500kg
Stretchers	2 (+1 seated)	2	12 to 15	30

* When armed, transport capability was limited to 150kg or two passengers.
** On most missions, no passengers were carried on armed Alouette IIIs.

A *Luftwaffe* Noratlas (N-2501D). Portugal bought 13 examples of this model from West Germany. (José Matos Collection)

that permitted FAP acquisition and use of the Boeing jets, and the first 707 arrived in Portugal on 16 October 1971, with a second following on 14 January 1972.[29] The 707's introduction immediately improved Lisbon's ability to reinforce its overseas outposts, including Guinea. 'One of the two aircraft was always on a mission,' historian John Cann related, 'and the reliability and flexibility of the plane made a dramatic difference in the logistic picture.'[30]

Despite the new acquisitions, most of the ZACVG's aircraft were 'unsuited to the missions assigned,' according to a 1971 CEMFGA assessment. These included the antiquated T-6s, which were neither designed nor intended for prolonged combat service, and the Do-27s, whose carrying capacity could satisfy only half of the theatre ground commander's requirements.[31] Both types were also considered excessively vulnerable and difficult to maintain. In April 1971 the *Comissão Técnica da Força Aérea* (Air Force Technical Commission) initiated a study of replacement options, ultimately recommending a single airframe to replace both aircraft: the Reims FTB-337G 'Milirôle', a licence-built French derivative of the Cessna O-2A 'Skymaster' then in USAF service for observation and forward air control (FAC).

The Milirôle's cargo capacity and passenger accommodation were comparable to the Do-27, and its STOL capabilities were only slightly inferior to the versatile German design. However, the Milirôle exceeded both the T-6 and Do-27 in range, ceiling, and endurance, making it a more attractive surveillance and command post platform. For light attack duties the Milirôle could carry 7.62-mm mini-guns, small bombs, or rocket pods from four underwing mounts, and its utilisation cost per hour

A P2V-5 Neptune deployed to AT1 on Sal Island, Cape Verde. (Touricas Collection)

One of the two Boeing 707-3F5C jetliners used by the FAP for transoceanic airlift. (Austin J. Brown Collection)

The Reims FTB-337G 'Milirôle'. Portugal secured a deal to purchase this aircraft from France in 1974, but by the time the first were delivered the FAP had ceased combat operations in Africa. (Robert Ver Collection)

was less than half that of the Do-27 or T-6. In 1972 the FAP identified a requirement for 114 aircraft, including 24 to replace the 11 Do-27s and seven T-6s then assigned to BA12-Bissalanca. While discussions with France successfully yielded a procurement deal, however, none of the new aircraft were delivered to Portugal until after the war for Guinea had ended.[32]

Despite recent reinforcements the ZACVG still needed additional helicopters as well, and in December 1970 *Ministro da Defesa Nacional* Sá Viana Rebelo reported an operational requirement for 36 Alouette IIIs in Guinea, more than double the number then assigned.[33] The prospects of achieving that objective dimmed, however, following a spectacular act of sabotage in metropolitan Portugal on 8 March 1971. Early that morning members of the communist *Acção Revolucionária Armada* (ARA), the armed wing of the Portuguese Communist Party, infiltrated the FAP base at BA3-Tancos, 100km northeast of Lisbon. The four saboteurs, one of them a FAP conscript assigned to the base, detonated 20 explosive devices inside the only maintenance hangar then in use, the other being under renovation.[34] Fourteen of the 28 aircraft packed inside were destroyed outright or damaged beyond repair, including one new Puma helicopter and four Alouette IIIs. Another 10 Alouettes were damaged, while five fixed-wing light aircraft were destroyed and three damaged.[35] The loss directly affected Spínola's reinforcement scheme and was later characterised as 'the biggest single catastrophe of the ten-year military struggle' by a senior Portuguese intelligence officer.[36]

The Tancos raid generated a flurry of unwanted press attention on Lisbon's African wars, compounding the negative publicity received over other aspects of its *Ultramar* campaigns. Perhaps the most acrimonious public debate concerned Portugal's continued military attacks against ostensibly neutral African states. During the Guinea conflict, these were prompted by the surge in weapons and materiel provided to the PAIGC from its foreign sponsors through Senegal and the Republic of Guinea, and the insurgents' growing use of base areas in those countries.[37] Marine *Comandante* Alpoim Galvão groused, 'We were always chasing the enemy, but since the borders in Guinea were not closed, it was like emptying a bathtub without turning off the tap.'[38] Frustrated by the PAIGC's unchallenged use of foreign sanctuaries, in December 1968 Spínola directed his forces to 'develop retaliatory actions (artillery fire and special operations) on the border areas of neighbouring countries.'[39] Although *Ministro da Defesa Nacional* Sá Viana Rebelo ordered Spínola to respect international frontiers and 'defeat the enemy within our borders,'[40] the war occasionally spilled over into Senegal and the Republic of Guinea, often involving ZACVG aircraft. Former FAP *Chefe do Estado-Maior* (1977–84) *General* José Lemos Ferreira later recalled. 'There was never authorisation for this, either direct or indirect. There were actions, but not sanctioned by higher authority... The same thing happened in Mozambique in Angola.'[41]

One attack into Senegalese territory resulted in the brief involvement of French airpower indirectly supporting Portugal's foes. On 25 November and 7–8 December 1969 Portuguese forces allegedly shelled a PAIGC depot at Samine, Senegal, killing six civilians and wounding nine.[42] To deter continued cross-border barrages President Leopold Senghor ordered reinforcements to Senegal's southern frontier, invoking defence agreements with France to secure the use of six Dakar-based *Armée de l'Air* Noratlas transports and their crews. On 12 December these French aircraft ferried 1,200 Senegalese troops to Ziguinchor airfield, 13km from the border with Portuguese Guinea.[43] This show-of-force (and a U.N. Security Council Resolution condemning Lisbon's actions[44]) failed to deter future Portuguese incursions, however, and from January to July 1970 Senegal complained of an additional 16 commando raids and artillery barrages, as well as eight airspace violations by FAP aircraft.[45] Ultimately, Amílcar Cabral conceded that these activities 'did have an effect on Senegal's attitude. Senghor closed the PAIGC hospitals in Senegal, blocked the passage of arms and reinforcements, and even subjected medicines and food for the PAIGC to strict controls.'[46]

The Republic of Guinea likewise protested Portugal's 'premeditated aggression,' accusing Lisbon's forces of five artillery barrages and three air strikes against its territory during 1969,[47] but the most dramatic and contentious Portuguese attack by far took place late the following year. In a bold attempt to decapitate the PAIGC leadership and foment a coup in the Republic of Guinea, Portuguese forces staged an amphibious invasion of Conakry on 22 November 1970. The 'clandestine'[48] operation, named *Mar Verde* (Green Sea), was conceived and led by Portuguese Marine *Comandante* Alpoim Calvão. He proposed a nighttime landing of marines, African commandos led by Portuguese officers, and members of the dissident group *Front de Libération Nationale de Guinée* (FLNG) in the port of Conakry. Once ashore, the assault force was to assassinate Republic of Guinea President Sékou Touré, initiating an FLNG-led coup; destroy PAIGC facilities located in Conakry, including its headquarters; arrest PAIGC leader Amílcar Cabral; rescue Portuguese prisoners-of-war being held at *La Montaigne* prison; and, in order to ensure a safe withdrawal, destroy the MiG-17 fighters of the *Force Aérienne de Guinea* and potentially hostile watercraft. Due primarily to poor intelligence and lack of indigenous support, however, the only objective met was the successful recovery of all 26 Portuguese prisoners.[49]

ZACVG participation in the operation itself was minimal, although in the days prior G.91s flew photoreconnaissance

Portuguese prisoners in a Conakry prison controlled by the PAIGC; in November 1970 they were liberated as part of *Operação Mar Verde*. (National Defence Archive)

Portuguese assault and support craft off Conakry during *Operação Mar Verde*. (Luis Costa Correia Collection)

missions against 19 PAIGC bases within the Republic of Guinea, in preparation for air strikes to take place after Touré's overthrow.[50] Since that never occurred, FAP activity during the operation was limited to a single P2V-5 Neptune flying from Cape Verde, which patrolled for enemy vessels while Portuguese forces sailed to and from Conakry.[51] Nonetheless, *Mar Verde* had an enduring impact on FAP operations in Guinea. The most immediate effect was the morale boost generated by the repatriation of the sole Portuguese aviator in captivity, *Furriel* António Lobato. The T-6 pilot had been taken by the PAIGC on 22 May 1963 following a midair collision and crash, spending the next seven and a half years in Guinean prisons. As the longest held of the 26 Portuguese POWs kept in Conakry, and the only pilot among them, Lobato's liberation raised the spirits of FAP personnel even though the circumstances of his release remained an official secret.[52]

The operation failed to neutralise the MiG threat, however. Just two days prior to *Operação Mar Verde*, the Republic of Guinea's MiG-17F fighters and MiG-15UTI fighter-trainers had relocated to Labé, 150km from Conakry, for reasons that are unclear.[53] Realising that 'one of the factors for success, air dominance, was severely compromised,' Calvão aborted the operation and ordered his assault teams to regroup at the port for the return voyage to their staging base on Soga Island.[54] Republic of Guinea officials did attempt to sortie aircraft against the invaders, but it was not until 0900, nearly seven hours after the initial landing, that a single MiG-17 appeared over the port of Conakry. In a stunning display of operational incompetence, its pilot misidentified and inadvertently strafed the Cuban freighter *Conrado Benitez* instead of the six withdrawing Portuguese vessels.[55] At 0930 the fighter overflew the flotilla at high altitude but took no action to halt or disable it. All Portuguese

Nigerian dictator Major General Yakubu Gowon promised military aid to Conakry after the Portuguese invasion. (Keystone Press Agency)

craft returned safely to Soga, the assault force having suffered only minimal casualties throughout the operation.[56]

Despite this poor showing, the survival of the MiG fleet concerned Spínola. On 26 January 1971 the general[57] informed *Ministro da Defesa Nacional* Sá Viano Rebelo that he feared aerial retaliation against Portuguese installations in Guinea, and not necessarily from Conakry's fighters alone. Despite Lisbon's public insistence the fighting had been a purely internal matter between rival factions, Touré immediately appealed to all friendly capitals to dispatch military forces, especially combat aircraft, to help repel 'a new series of enemy incursions.'[58] In response, Spínola warned, Nigeria had reportedly placed its fighters and bombers at Touré's disposal, and he also received word that the chief of Algeria's air force travelled to Conakry, suggesting that nation's willingness to intervene as well. Unspecified military assistance from Libya, Egypt, and the United Arab Republic was also said to be en route.[59]

It was the prospect of Nigerian involvement that concerned Spínola the most. Nigerian dictator Major General Yakubu Gowon, expressing 'deepest shock and indignation at the invasion of Guinea by foreign forces,' promised 'any assistance that [Touré] may ask for, military or otherwise.' It was a credible threat: Gowon commanded a battle-tested army perhaps 200,000 strong, by far the largest standing force in sub-Saharan Africa. But Portugal had alienated and angered the Lagos regime by providing significant military support to the losing Biafran side during Nigeria's recently concluded civil war (6 July 1967 – 15 January 1970).[60] Hoping to secure the friendship of at least one friendly post-colonial African state and eager to weaken the staunchly anti-colonialist Nigerian regime, Lisbon had willingly provided vital logistical support, military expertise, and even combat aircraft to the secessionist Biafrans.[61]

Those aircraft included four T-6Gs purchased from French scrap yards and restored to flying condition in Portugal. Lisbon's inability to secure overflight authorisation from most African countries required those aircraft to be dismantled and shipped by sea to Bissau, where they were reassembled and flown to rebel-held airfields by Portuguese pilots[62] (one of them, Gil Pinto de Sousa, was captured by Nigerian forces on 2 November 1969 and held until September 1974).[63] Bissalanca also facilitated the transfer of Gloster 'Meteor' jet fighters and combat-capable Fouga 'Magister' jet trainers to Biafra, leading to one Meteor abandoned at the base and the destruction there of a transport carrying Magister components, apparently due to sabotage by a crew member.[64] Additionally, Lisbon established an air logistics hub on the Portuguese-held island of São Tomé, through which arms, ammunition, mercenaries, and relief supplies were delivered to Biafra. Without these, the rebellion 'would have collapsed long before it did,' earning Lisbon the enduring ire of Nigeria's rulers.[65] *Mar Verde* presented them with an opportunity for retribution, with the added political cover of a U.N. Security Council Resolution calling for support to Conakry.[66]

A Gloster 'Meteor' jet fighter, intended for service in the Biafra's insurgent air force but abandoned in Bissalanca while en route. (José Nico Collection)

Table 13: FAP Fighter Requirements vs Existing Types, 1971

	1971 requirement[82]	G.91[83]	F-86F[84]
Max airspeed	Mach 2 at 40,000 ft (1,150kts/2,130kph)	Mach .87 at 5,000 ft (565kts/1,045 kph)	Mach 1.04 at 35,000ft (600kts/1,110 kph)
Time to climb to 40,000ft/12,000m	5 minutes	7 minutes (to 25,000ft)	9 minutes
Combat radius	300NM/555km	150NM/280km	250NM/460km
Armament load	3,000kg/6,600lb	680kg/1,500lb	905kg/2,000lb
Air-air missiles	Y	N	Y*
Air-ground missiles	Y	N	N
GP bombs	Y	Y	Y
Air-ground rockets	Y	Y	Y
Cannon	Y	N	N
Machine guns	N	Y	Y

*Portugal began arming its F-86F fleet with Sidewinder missiles in 1962, but none of them were ever sent to, or used in, its African territories.[85]

The expected intervention prompted Spínola to petition Lisbon for 'immediate reinforcement with bombing planes capable of night flight' to deter or avenge any attack against Portuguese interests in Guinea. Spínola specifically asked for aircraft with sufficient range to reach the Republic of Guinea's main airfields at Conakry, Labé, and Faranah from the FAP transit base on Sal.[67] Faranah was a target of particular interest: in late February 1971, three months after *Mar Verde*, Portuguese authorities received word of runway construction there to accommodate Ilyushin Il-28 jet bombers, three of which were operated by Nigeria.[68] From Faranah, the Soviet-built Il-28 (NATO 'Beagle') could easily carry a bomb load of 3,000kg to strike any target in Portuguese Guinea.[69] Reports of their impending deployment there ultimately proved unfounded, but Portuguese authorities received a jarring reminder of the air threat just two weeks earlier. On 13 February 1971, two fighter-type aircraft identified as MiG-17s originating from Republic of Guinea airspace crossed the border to overfly Bissau and its environs 'in a provocative way,' presumably on a photoreconnaissance mission against BA12 and the Port of Pidjiguiti.[70] Conakry denied all responsibility,[71] and various theories about the planes' and pilots' nationality circulated among the armed forces. The MiGs were variously thought to belong to the Republic of Guinea or Nigeria and piloted by personnel from those nations, Algeria, or Tunisia.[72] Spínola even concluded that the demanding mission profile could only have been executed by 'highly specialised pilots, who, of course, must be Russian.'[73]

Confusion over the planes' origin, ambiguity regarding their mission, and uncertainty over whether the flight had even occurred revealed crippling deficiencies in Portugal's ability to monitor and control the airspace over Guinea. 'The complete lack of detection radars denies us any chance of reacting, even if we had suitable planes or anti-aircraft equipment,' Spínola protested to his Defence Minister while repeating earlier calls for reinforcement.[74] At his urging the corvette *Jacinto Cândido* was assigned to defend the port and city of Bissau with its two 40mm anti-aircraft guns, two 76mm dual-purpose guns, and MLA-1B air surveillance radar.[75] This was only a stopgap measure, however, and the scant air defences at Portugal's disposal left Guinea 'at the mercy of enemy air attack,' the CCFAG complained.[76] At the time Portugal had only one anti-aircraft battery in Guinea, with its 1940s-era radar, 40mm cannon, and 12.7mm machine guns covering BA12. Three additional batteries arrived between late February and July 1971, covering Bissau with 9.4cm AAA and three critical outposts (Nova Lamego, Aldeia Formosa and Nhacra) with lighter 40mm and 12.7mm guns.[77] They were hamstrung by the limitations of their obsolescent Mark VI air search radars, however, whose restricted range and poor serviceability made it 'difficult to act in a timely manner,' according to one battery commander. 'It was, indeed, a most deficient system.'[78]

To provide a more robust air defence, Portuguese authorities in Bissau and Lisbon renewed their efforts to procure and field a suitable air superiority fighter. According to a 1971 ZACVG

France's Mirage 5 fighter was the preferred option for future FAP operations in Africa. (Dassault)

assessment the G.91 'does not possess the necessary attributes for this mission,'[79] but the FAP's sole air defence fighter – the F-86F – could only be deployed in open defiance of American restrictions. Therefore, *Secretário de Estado da Aeronáutica*[80] José Pereira do Nascimento proposed the purchase of 30 new aircraft – 27 new fighters plus three two-seat operational trainers. He specified a rapid climb rate, Mach 2 speed at altitude, and air-to-air missile armament to satisfy the air defence interceptor role, while projected ground attack requirements included a 3,000kg combat load and 300NM combat radius with five minutes' time in the target area.[81]

Of the suitable Western types then in production, all American and British designs[86] were immediately discounted due to continuing arms restrictions, as was Sweden's J35 'Draken,' given Stockholm's sympathetic policies towards the PAIGC.[87] This left France's stable of Dassault 'Mirage' fighters – the delta-winged Mirage III and Mirage 5, and the swept-wing Mirage F1. Since the F1 was not yet in production and was likely too expensive, Pereira do Nascimento proposed the combat-proven Mirage III or its simplified Mirage 5 derivative as 'the aircraft whose characteristics are closest to the proposed specifications.'[88] French officials stonewalled the request, however, concerned over the geopolitical repercussions of supplying Portugal with frontline combat aircraft that would certainly be used in Africa. Paris was particularly unwilling to strain relations with Senegal, which hosted a permanent French garrison and airbase. By May 1972 Portugal and France had made no progress towards a Mirage deal, and the issue lay dormant for nearly a year. Despite renewed Portuguese overtures in 1973 and 1974, however, the Mirage family of fighters never saw service with the FAP.[89]

Portugal's inability to defend Guinea from aerial attack remained a source of anxiety for the rest of the war, reflecting the general state of Lisbon's military position there. 'This picture of manifest setbacks is deteriorating at a worrying pace,' Spínola warned in June 1971,[90] and the chief of the Portuguese armed forces, *General* Venâncio Deslandes, drew a similar conclusion during a visit to the province later that month. He too acknowledged the worsening military climate, noting that Portuguese forces 'are not sufficient to guarantee the permanence of the successes obtained' and admitting that their PAIGC opponents 'may try to impose a solution by force, creating unfavourable situations that are difficult or impossible to reverse.'[91] Spínola, however, had never based his strategy solely on military outcomes. He continued to insist that 'The expression 'military victory' is meaningless in this type of conflict,' as he told the Superior National Defence Council in May 1971. 'The problem can only be resolved in the political field, and I want to believe that such a solution is still viable.'[92] This included opening a dialogue with Portugal's opponents, an effort he felt necessary to avoid 'a prolonged and pointless agony.'[93]

Spínola had already attempted local negotiations with PAIGC elements in the 'Manjaco ground' of Western Guinea. At the beginning of 1970 he initiated contacts with party leaders in the region to negotiate their surrender and the integration of local PAIGC forces into Portuguese units.[94] The CCFAG was by all accounts genuinely enthusiastic about this *Chão Manjaco* initiative, and Overseas Minister Silva Cunha described him as 'euphoric with the results he was expecting.'[95] The venture ended in tragedy, however, when three Portuguese Army *majors* and their interpreters were brutally murdered by PAIGC elements during a peace foray on 20 April 1970.[96] 'It was a hard blow that we suffered,' Spínola informed *Ministro da Defesa Nacional* Sá Viana Rebelo the following day, 'as they were a team of exceptional valour and determination.'[97]

By that time planning for *Mar Verde* was already underway, offering Spínola another opportunity to radically reshape the war after the apparent collapse of his peace initiative.[98] The raid's international repercussions and escalating warfare within Guinea precluded any real movement towards a negotiated settlement until 1972, when diplomatic efforts vis-à-vis Senegal resumed. These led to a meeting at Cap Skirring between Spínola and Senegalese President Senghor on 18 May, during which the two discussed a ceasefire and 10-year transitional period to prepare for Guinean independence.[99] With the 'massacre of the majors' still on their minds, Portuguese forces prepared a substantial operation to protect their commander during the Conference. Unknown to President Senghor, a flight of G.91s sat alert at BA12, ready to bomb 'the entire area' at the first sign of any threat to the CCFAG. Meanwhile, 10 Alouette III helicopters and two Noratlas transports stood by to lift 130 Portuguese paratroops to Cap Skirring, where they would 'collect the bodies,' including Spínola's if necessary. The meeting ended without incident, however, as did a follow-up encounter several days later.[100]

Encouraged, Spínola travelled to Lisbon at the end of the month to brief Portuguese Prime Minister Marcelo Caetano on his diplomatic progress. He did so with high hopes: Caetano was thought to be less rigid and dogmatic on colonial matters than his predecessor, long-time Portuguese strongman António de Oliveira Salazar, who had suffered a debilitating stroke in August 1968.[101] By 1972, however, Caetano's imperial outlook had apparently hardened. During a 28 May audience he forbade further diplomatic efforts to resolve the conflict in Guinea, telling a dumbstruck Spínola 'For the overall defence of the overseas territories it is preferable to leave Guinea through a military defeat with honour than through an agreement with terrorists that would justify other negotiations [in other territories].' If Portuguese forces were militarily defeated after fighting to their full potential, the Prime Minister reasoned, 'such a defeat leaves us with the legal and political possibilities intact to continue to defend the rest of the overseas territories.'[102] Realising

In 1972, Spínola sought a political solution to the Guinea problem through the mediation of Senegal's President Senghor, but Lisbon rejected the peace initiative. (Revista do Povo Collection)

Portuguese Prime Minister Marcelo Caetano rejected any negotiated solution in Guinea, fearing it would set an irreversible precedent for the rest of Portugal's colonial empire. (Overseas Historical Archive)

this policy meant sacrificing his troops' lives and the army's prestige, Spínola glumly concluded that Caetano had squandered Lisbon's 'last opportunity to resolve the problem of Guinea with honour and dignity.'[103]

His subordinate commanders had more immediate worries, noting with concern the increase in PAIGC military capabilities and the introduction of new enemy weapons. According to Portuguese assessments, in 1972 these included additional 37mm anti-aircraft cannon, BM-21 122mm multiple rocket launchers, BTR-40 armoured personnel carriers, and even PT-76 light tanks.[104] Additionally, the insurgents had begun conducting more ambitious operations with larger formations, corresponding to their long-established intention to initiate a conventional war of manoeuvre.[105] The obvious implication, G.O. 1201 (and later ZACVG) commander *Coronel* José Lemos Ferreira concluded, was that the PAIGC now believed an outright military victory was within its reach, but 'What they needed was something that would nullify the Air Force.'[106]

To this end insurgent air defences briefly reappeared within Guinea's borders during 1972. In May, for example, 37mm anti-aircraft guns opened fire against a pair of G.91s patrolling the southeast frontier and the Quitafine *zonas libertadas*.[107] Those fighters escaped unharmed, but eight other Portuguese aircraft were damaged by insurgent action during the year. In February and August, unspecified anti-aircraft fire presumably originating from the Republic of Guinea struck a total of three G.91s patrolling the northeast frontier, resulting in slight damage.[108] Two Do-27s were hit by small arms fire in the interior during March, as was a T-6 the month before, while three Alouette IIIs took damage from mortar, RPG, and automatic weapons fire in November-December. The ZACVG reported a total of 23 'actions against aircraft' throughout 1972, but only two resulted in serious material damage or injury to Portuguese personnel. Significantly, those incidents involved infantry weapons and mortars rather than purpose-built anti-aircraft systems.[109]

For their part, PAIGC propagandists claimed 10 fixed-wing planes and eight helicopters destroyed by insurgent action from 1969 through to 1972, including six aircraft allegedly destroyed during raids against forward airstrips (see Appendix III).[110] The documentary record and lack of evidence offered by insurgent sources, however, reveal the ZACVG had not lost a single aircraft to enemy action since *Tenente Coronel* Costa Gomes' G.91 was shot down in 1968. It continued to lose aircraft in accidents, however, and from 1969 to 1972 two each T-6s, Do-27s, and Alouette IIIs crashed in Guinea, resulting in 14 fatalities (including the six pilots) and the total loss of all aircraft involved.[111] These mishaps raised the number of FAP planes and helicopters lost in Guinea since 1962 to 23, although three at most were destroyed by hostile fire (see Appendix III).[112]

Despite their own propaganda, the PAIGC acknowledged the 'absence of an effective anti-aircraft defence.'[113] Consequently, the insurgent leadership actively sought out more effective air defence weapons from its sponsors in the Communist Bloc and Amílcar Cabral travelled to the Soviet Union in July 1972 for that very reason.[114] His efforts would ultimately be rewarded, but in the interim the ZACVG was able to prosecute its air war against the PAIGC without serious impediment. During 1972 FAP aircraft flew a total of 10,643 sorties over Guinea in all mission areas – a six percent reduction from the previous year, but still the second highest annual total of the war to date.[115] Attack and fire support sorties numbered 3,029 during 1972 (all but two flown by ZACVG G.91 and T-6s) – 15 percent fewer than 1971, but a greater effort compared to 1969 or 1970.

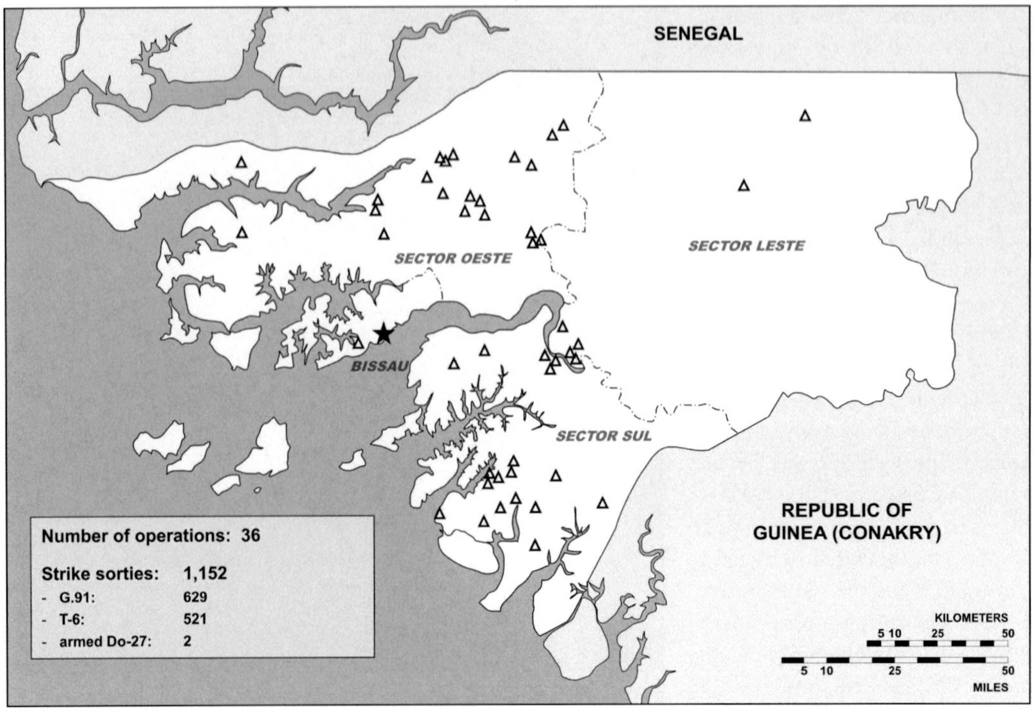

Independent ZACVG strike operations, 1972. (Matthew M. Hurley based on COMZAVERDEGUINÉ SITREP Circunstanciados Nos.01/72 through 01/72, 2 January 1972 to 31 December 1972, ADN/SGDN/2REP/096.)

Finally, ZACVG Alouette IIIs airlifted over 6,000 troops during 75 heliborne operations in 1972, compared to 58 analogous missions in 1971 and 41 in 1970.[116]

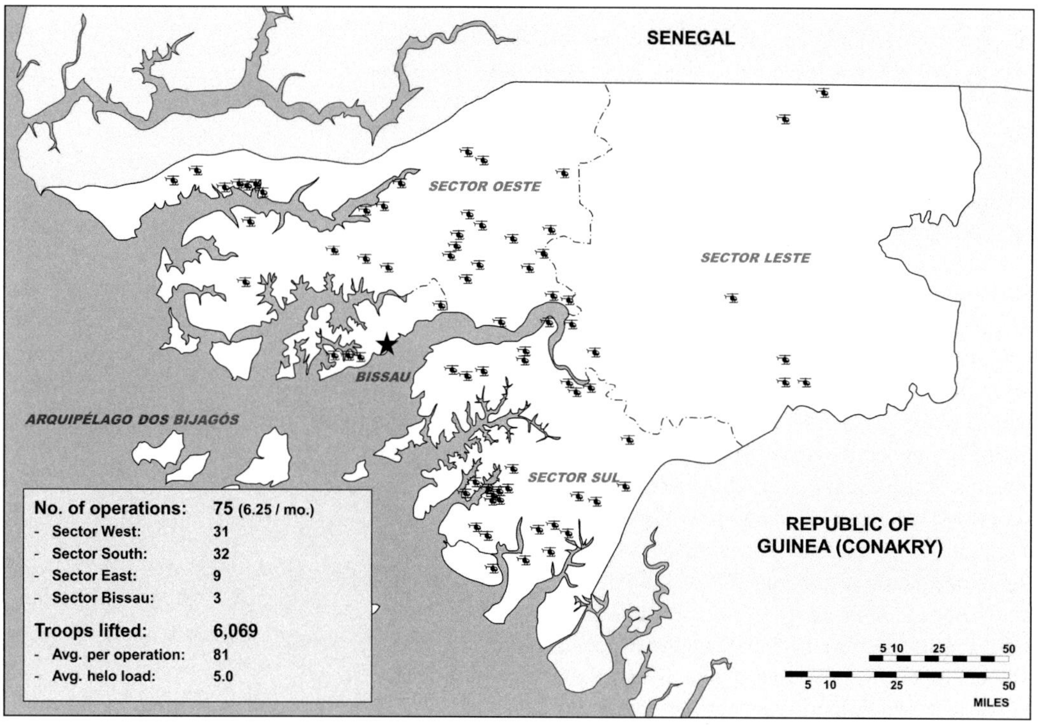

Portuguese heliborne operations, 1972. (Matthew M. Hurley based on COMZAVERDEGUINÉ SITREP Circunstanciados Nos.01/72 through 01/72, 2 January 1972 to 31 December 1972, ADN/SGDN/2REP/096.)

The ZACVG's offensive operations saw an increased emphasis on southern Guinea, due in part to the PAIGC's continued exploitation of its alleged 'liberated' areas there, especially the increasingly restive Cantanhez Peninsula. Spínola felt that 'it was absolutely necessary to demonstrate that Portuguese troops could exercise complete dominion over the Cantanhez Peninsula,' particularly in light of Portugal's failures to do so elsewhere in southern Guinea.[117] At the end of the year this imperative culminated with *Operação Grande Empress* (Operation Grand Enterprise), Portugal's most ambitious offensive operation in the province since 1964's *Operação Tridente*.

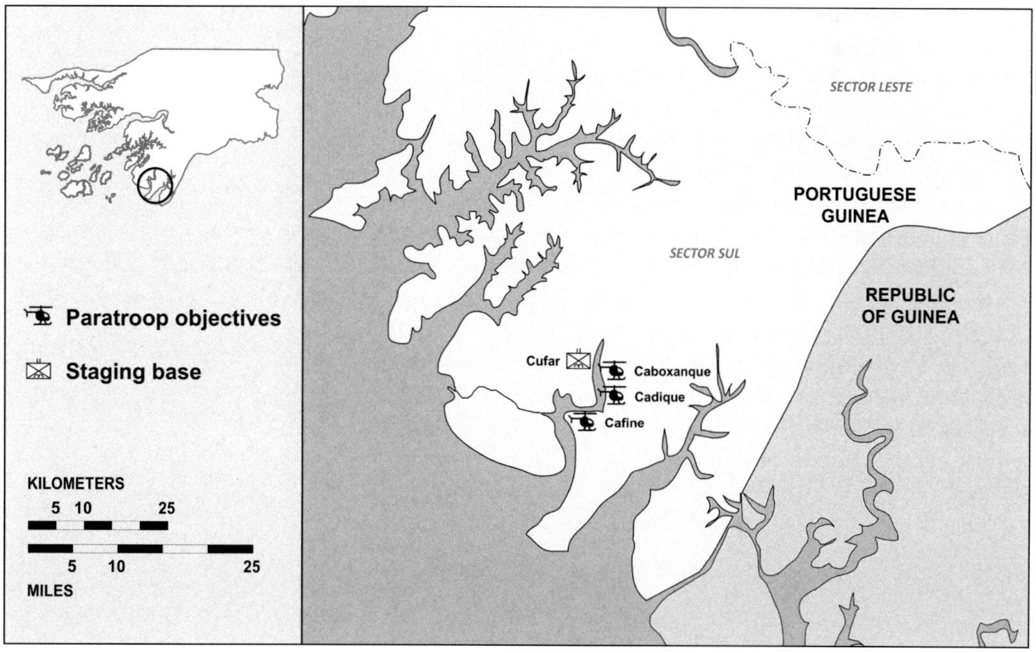

Operação Grande Empresa area of operations. (Matthew M. Hurley)

Frustrated in his attempts to outmanoeuvre the PAIGC, neutralise the Republic of Guinea, or negotiate a settlement through Senegal, Spínola now sought a local military success to regain some degree of initiative from the insurgents. He was offered a lucrative opportunity by *Major* Maura Cahiers, BCP 12's chief of operations and intelligence, who identified the PAIGC's most important base in its Cantanhez *zonas libertadas*. With his proposal for *Operação Grande Empress*, Cahiers presented Spínola with an opportunity to destroy the insurgent complex, reoccupy the peninsula, and 'recover the population under enemy control' through civil works, psychological measures, and their 'reordering' into *aldeamentos*. Directive 19/72 (29 November 1972) assigned two paratroop companies and a Special Marine Detachment to the initial assault; these forces would then occupy the villages of Caboxanque, Cadique and Cafine, on the southern bank of the Cumbijã River, engaging and destroying enemy forces there and en route. Once those objectives had been met, a follow-on force of one cavalry and three infantry companies, supported by field artillery platoons, would arrive by river landing craft to establish a network of garrisons on the peninsula and 'develop, with the greatest intensity, construction work and reordering in those areas.'[118]

On 11 December, the day before the assault, seven Noratlas flights ferried 191 paratroops from BA12 to their forward staging base at Cufar. The following morning six G.91s, flying two missions apiece, conducted a preparatory bombardment of PAIGC positions while 10 Alouette IIIs carrying 50 paratroops proceeded to their landing zones. Stiff resistance compelled the commitment of 50 additional paratroops, but by the day's end Portuguese forces had overwhelmed the opposition and occupied the villages of Caboxanque, Cadique and Cafine.[119] Then began the longer-term tasks of regional pacification and re-integration, aided by the killing or capture of several key local PAIGC commanders and officials. Portuguese forces built new villages, roads, livestock shelters, and medical posts while dealing directly with traditional authorities to determine immediate needs. Their efforts resulted in some success – most Cantanhez inhabitants at least tolerated Portuguese efforts, and many actively aided their cause, leading to the near-eradication of the PAIGC's regional leadership and infrastructure. Throughout the nine months of *Operação Grande Empresa*, FAP assets and personnel provided continual reconnaissance, airlift, medical evacuation, and fire support to participating surface units, but Spínola's forces were soon obliged to respond to more urgent developments elsewhere. Rather than remaining as guarantors of Portuguese sovereignty in Cantanhez, the paratroops and follow-on Army units were withdrawn by mid-summer, and with their departure 'the region was no longer ours.'[120]

At the end of 1972, however, Portuguese forces could be pleased with their progress in Cantanhez. But Spínola, in command of the entire war effort, remained pessimistic. 'The rising increase in the enemy's activity and potential, as well as the increasing external support it has received, allows us to forecast a worsening military situation,' he reported at the beginning of 1973.[121] As a result, Portugal in Guinea faced the growing prospect of 'a sudden politico-military deterioration,' most likely in the form of large-scale, conventional rebel assaults against Lisbon's flagging army. The war for Guinea, Spínola warned, was set to progress to 'the next level,' and he feared Portugal would be hard-pressed to prevail.[122]

PAIGC leaders, on the other hand, began 1973 with a palpable optimism. The insurgent party had recently paraded a high-profile U.N. delegation through its *zonas libertadas* and publicly announced its intention to unilaterally declare formal independence within the year.[123] In his New Year's communiqué Amílcar Cabral also praised the 'great defeats and very important losses' inflicted on Portuguese forces during 1972, but admitted that 'the enemy, having more planes and helicopters supplied to it by its NATO allies, has significantly increased the bombing and terrorist attacks against our liberated regions.' Aviation alone allowed Portugal to 'create difficult situations for us' in PAIGC dominated areas as well as contested terrain, and the FAP's impunity weakened insurgent claims of legitimate political authority. Urging his forces to 'strike harder blows against the colonialist enemy,' Cabral promised them 'even more powerful weapons and other means of war' in 1973. 'We are going to more effectively utilise the means we have, and that we will have, to deal decisive and deadly blows to the Portuguese colonialist criminal aggressors,' he warned.[124] For the Portuguese Air Force contingent in Guinea, those words would prove prophetic.

Appendix I
ZACVG Assigned Aircraft, 1961–1972

Table 14: ZACVG Assigned Aircraft, 1961–1972 (peak values)[1]

	1961	1962	1963	1964	1965	1966	1967	1968	1969	1970	1971	1972
F-86 Sabre	8	7	7	6								
G.91-R4						8	8	8	11	12	12	12
T-6 Texan/ Harvard	4	6	8	8	19	20	19	20	16	16	14	11
P2V-5 Neptune*	1	2	2	2	2					1	1	1
B-26 Invader**											2	
C-47 Dakota	1	2	3	2	3	3	3	3	4	3	2	2
Noratlas											2	2
Auster D.5	2	6	5	6								
Broussard			1									
Dornier Do-27			4	7	10	10	10	12	13	18	17	14
Alouette II			3	3	4							
Alouette III					3	9	12	11	15	19	18	20
Total	16	23	33	34	41	50	52	54	59	69	68	62

* One P2V-5 on regular rotation to AT1 (Sal Island) from February 1970 to July 1973[2]

** Two B-26s at BA12 for operational evaluation from March to June 1971[3]

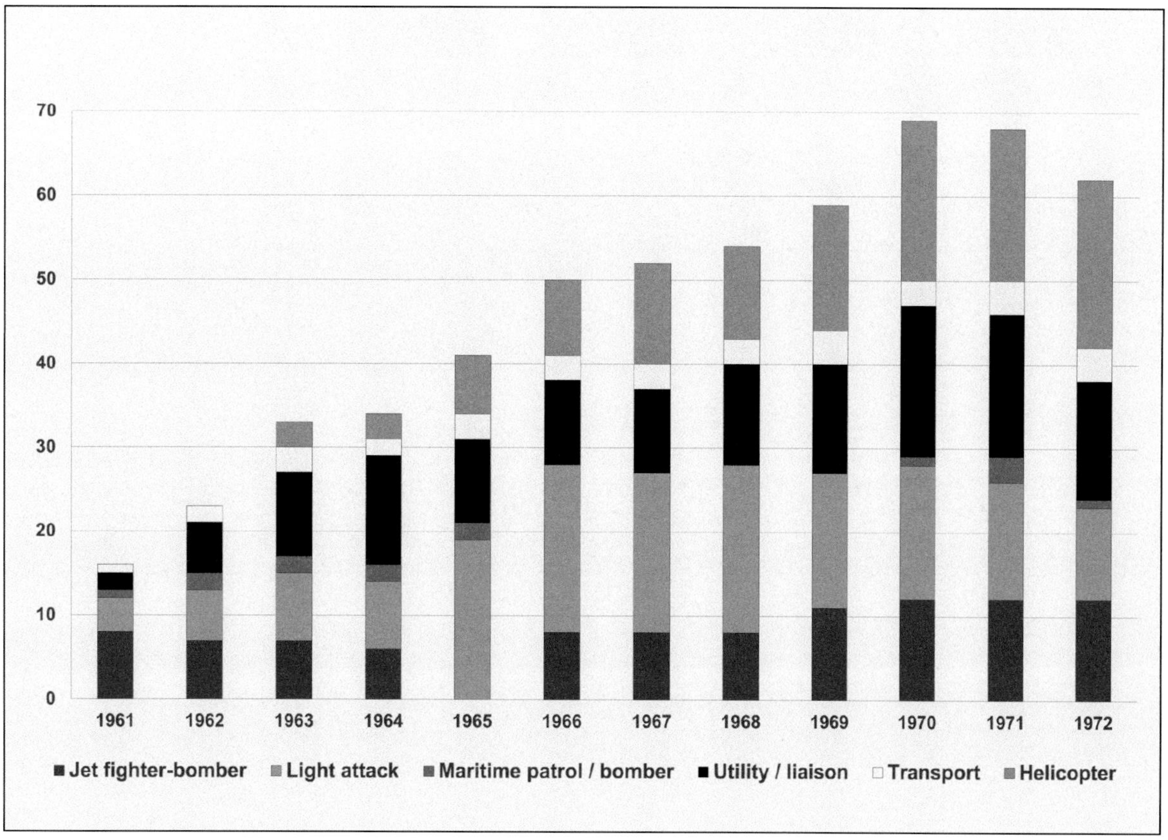

Appendix II
ZACVG Sortie Tables

Table 15: Sorties by Aircraft Type, 1968–1972[1]					
	1968	**1969**	**1970**	**1971**	**1972**
G.91	1,363	1,128	1,381	1,532	1,283
T-6	1,909	1,357	1,358	1,446	1,084
Do-27	2,854	3,105	3,974	4,114	3,956
Alouette III	1,958	3,951	2,955	3,321	3,283
C-47	702	778	605	395	452
Noratlas			39	457	595
B-26				55	
Total	8,786	10,319	10,132	11,320	10,643

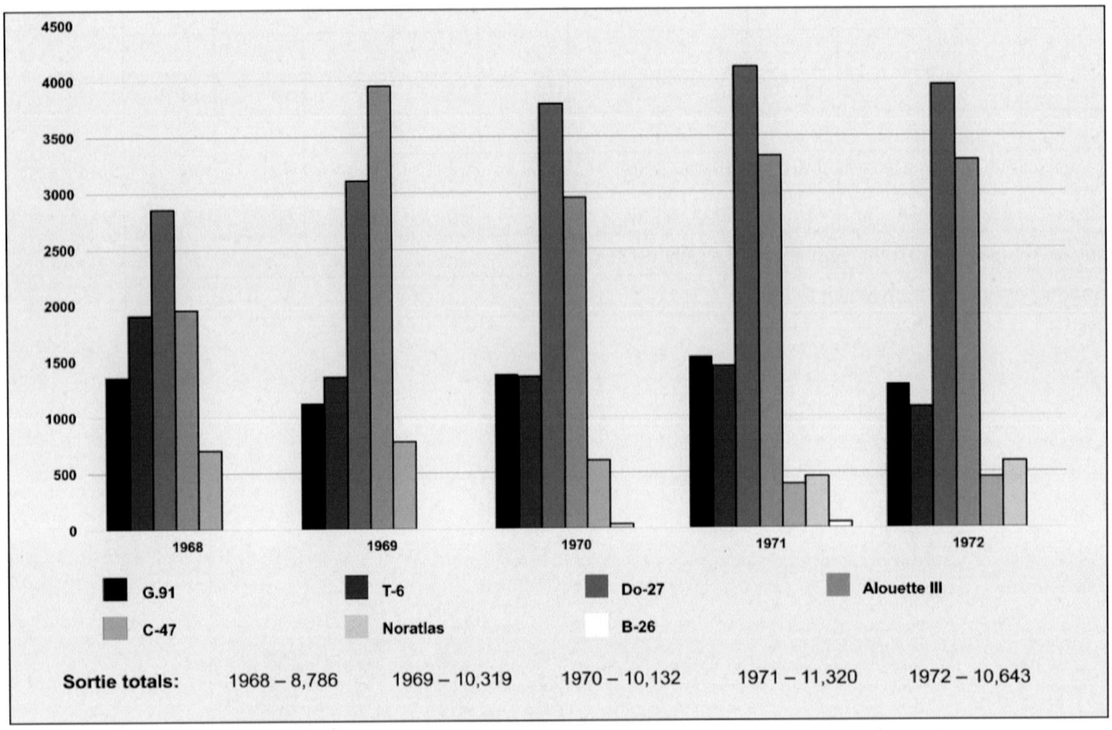

Table 16: Sorties by Mission Category, 1968–1972

	1968	1969	1970	1971	1972
Independent attack	1,789	1,301	2,297	2,458	1,761
Air support	1,572	1,129	732	1,040	1,066
Reconnaissance	301	585	368	278	278
Assault/combat airlift	1,145	2,346	1,084	754	1,064
General transport	1,934	2,327	3,085	3,120	2,814
MEDEVAC	1,498	1,800	1,687	2,119	2,487
Command and control	325	445	566	451	486
Other	222	386	313	1,100	687
Total	8,786	10,319	10,312	11,320	10,653

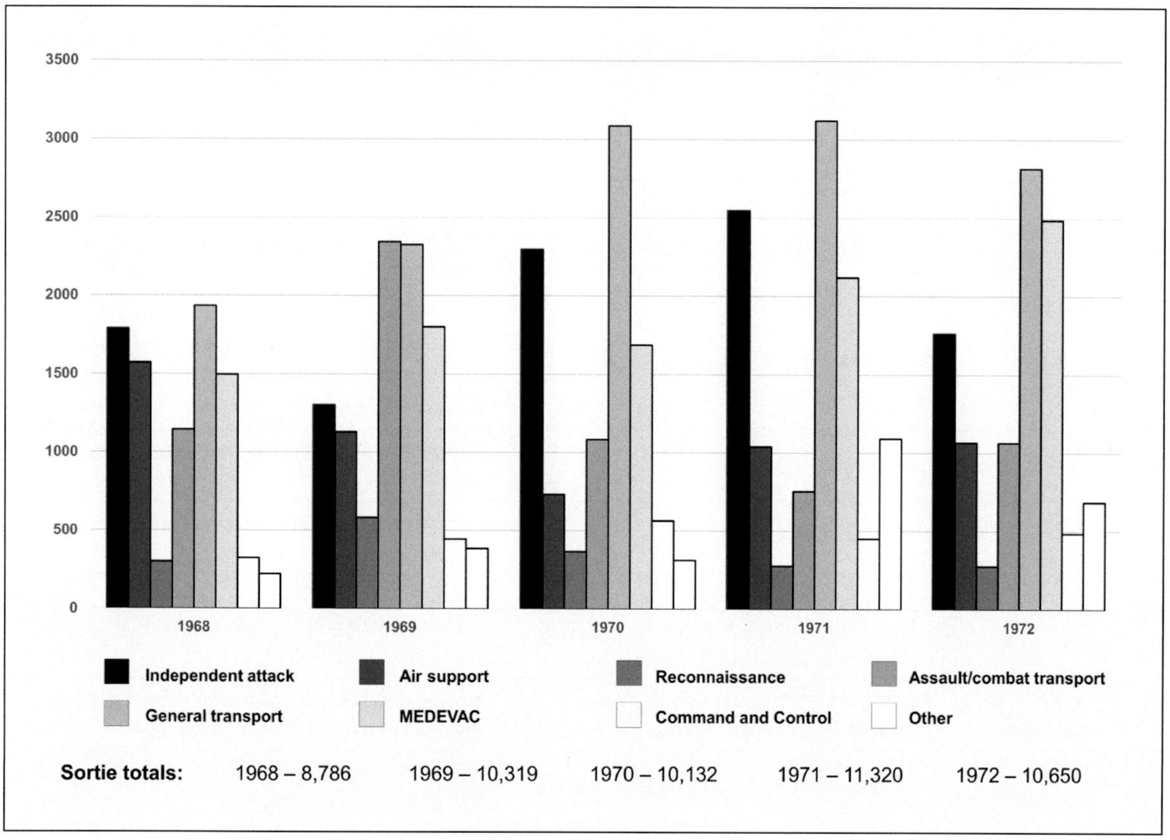

Appendix III
ZACVG Losses and PAIGC Claims, 1962–1972

Table 17: Acknowledged/Confirmed FAP Losses, 1962–1972[1]

Incident number	Date	Aircraft (reg. no.)	Identified crew / passengers	Notes
1	29 May 1962	T-6G (FAP 1677)	Tenente José Cabaço Neves Furriel Manuel Soares de Matos	Entered a spin during a low-altitude recce IVO Mina; both killed
2	17 August 1962	F-86F (FAP 5314)	Tenente Amílcar José Barbosa	Exploded after landing mishap; pilot escaped
3	22 May 1963	T-6G (FAP 1711)	Furriel Eduardo Nuno Rico Casals	Crashed after collision (see below); pilot killed
4	22 May 1963	T-6G	Furriel António Lourenço de Sousa Lobato	Crashed after midair collision IVO P. Tombali with T-6G (FAP 1711); pilot captured, POW
5	31 May 1963	F-86F (FAP 5322)	Capitão Fausto Valla	Damaged by bomb fragment IVO Bedanda, crashed over Rio Geba; pilot ejected
6	4 September 1963	Auster (FAP 3546)	Alferes José Madureira Nobre Alferes Eduardo Constantino Spínola de Freitas Sargento-Chefe José Pinheiro Garcia	Collided with a palm tree after departing Bissalanca; all killed
7	12 October 1963	Broussard	unknown/not reported	Written off after mishap on Uno Island; NFI
8	14 October 1963	T-6G (FAP 1694)	Capitão João Cardoso de Carvalho Rebelo Valente	Crashed at Bisslanca after low-altitude manoeuvre; pilot killed
9	21 January 1964	T-6 (FAP 1708)	Alferes João Manuel dos Santos Pité	Shot down between Caiar / Cauane, (Op. Tridente); pilot killed
10	26 March 1964	AL II (FAP 9202)	Furriel Alexandre Manuel Ramalho Matos Cabo Fernando Ferreira Martins	Damaged beyond repair in accident 2km south of BA12, written off 7 April 1964; 2 mechanics killed by detached gear assembly or rotors
11	31 July 1964	F-86F	unknown/not reported	Runway fire due to undercarriage collapse; written off
12	21 October 1964	T-6G (FAP 1717)	Furriel José de Sousa Rola Teixeira	Probable AA fire IVO Mansoa during MEDEVAC escort; pilot killed
13	3 December 1964	Auster (FAP 3515)	Tenente Austrelindo Gaspar Dias Furriel André Miranda Farinha Cabo Humberto Manuel Olguim Silva	Stalled after takeoff from Cabedú, crashed; all killed
14	21 July 1966	Do-27 (FAP 3485)	Alferes José Américo Baptista de Sousa Alferes Manuel Fernando Ramada Lima Leite	Strayed into Senegal, crashed offshore; crew detained in Dakar until 4 August 1966
15	22 February 1967	G.91-R4 (FAP 5407)	Major Armando Augusto dos Santos Moreira	Aircraft damaged by bomb detonation after attack IVO Gã Pedro; pilot ejected
16	15 June 1968	T-6/Harvard (FAP 1791)	unknown/not reported	Crashed IVO Madina do Boé; recovered and scrapped
17	28 July 1968	G.91-R4 (FAP 5411)	Tenente Coronel Francisco da Costa Gomes (G.O. 1201 commander)	Shot down by AA fire north of Guileje
18	12 July 1969	Alouette III (FAP 9295)	Capitão António Figueiredo Rodrigues Cabo António Carlos de Oliveira Machado	Struck ground antennae on return to Bafatá; 2 killed
19	4 December 1969	T-6 (FAP 1795)	Furriel Alberto Soares Moutinho	Crashed on takeoff from Canquelifá; pilot killed
20	25 July 1970	Alouette III (FAP 9338)	Furriel Francisco Lopes Manso + 5	Crashed in bad weather IVO Ilha de Jeta; all killed, including 4 Portuguese Assembly members
21	15 December 1971	T-6G (FAP 1756)	Alferes Humberto Narciso de Oliveira Braga Simões	Entered dive/spin on bomb run IVO Ponta Luís Dias; pilot killed

Table 17: Acknowledged/Confirmed FAP Losses, 1962–1972[1]				
Incident number	Date	Aircraft (reg. no.)	Identified crew / passengers	Notes
22	11 May 1972	Do-27 (FAP 3447)	Furriel Carlos Filipe Noronha Cabo José Luis Valoura	Stalled on takeoff from Pirada and crashed; 2 killed
23	12 August 1972	Do-27 (FAP 3492)	Alferes Víctor Manuel Caldeira António Rui de Sousa Madeira	Unrecoverable post-TO spin IVO Bambadinca; 2 killed

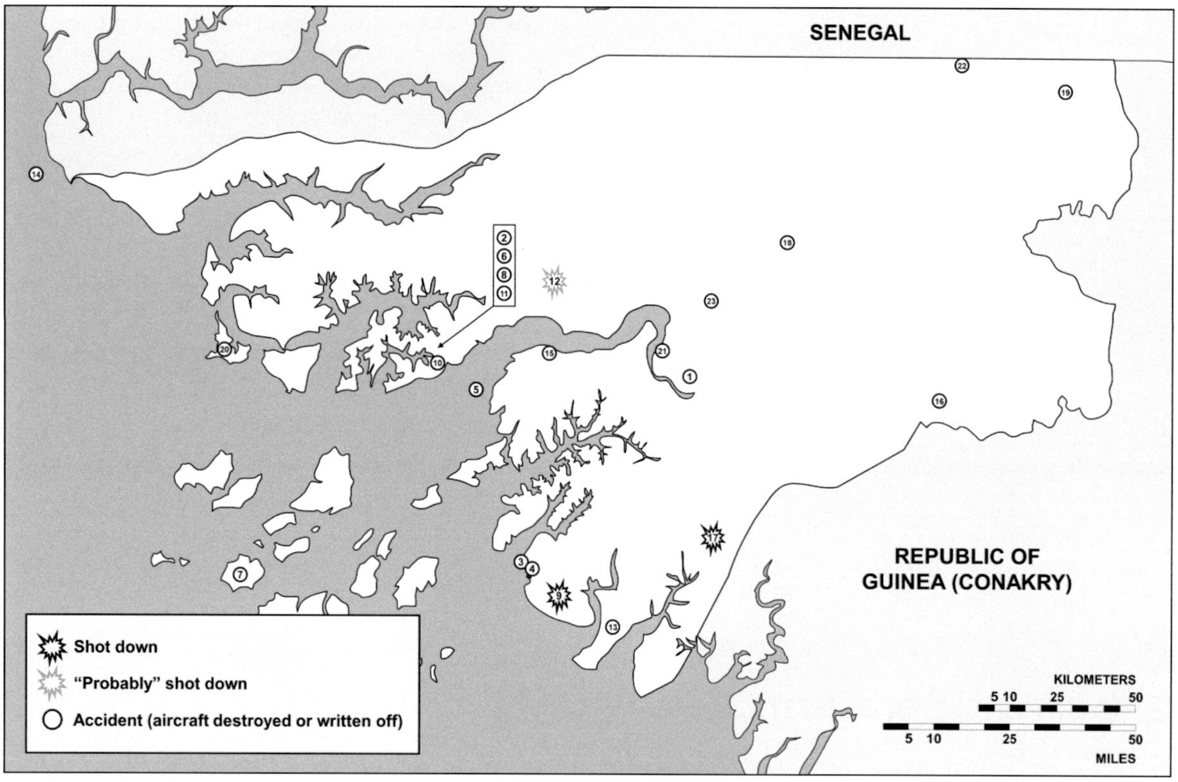

Numbers indicate location of events described in Table 17. (Map by Matthew M. Hurley)

Table 18: PAIGC Claims Compared to Acknowledged FAP Losses[2]		
Year	PAIGC claims	Acknowledged by Portugal
1962	–	2 accidents
1963	10 shot down	6 accidents
1964	4 shot down	1 shot down 1 'probably' shot down 3 accidents
1965	1 shot down	–
1966	3 shot down	1 accident
1967	4 shot down	1 accident
1968	3 shot down 2 destroyed during raid on BA12	1 shot down 1 loss to unknown causes
1969	2 shot down	2 accidents
1970	4 shot down 1 destroyed during raid on Cabedú	1 accident
1971	4 shot down 4 destroyed during raid on Nova Lamego	1 accident
1972	2 shot down 1 x destroyed during raid on Bafatá	2 accidents
Totals	37 shot down 8 destroyed on the ground	2 shot down 1 'probably' shot down 20 accidents

Table 19: Airfield Attacks Claimed by the PAIGC, 1965–1972[3]			
Date	**Location**	**Method**	**Claimed results**
4 October 1965	Olossato	unknown	'Good results'
24 November 1965	Mansoa	ambush	'Destroyed an enemy car and caused a large number of deaths and injuries'
17 November 1966	Cufar	mortar fire	'Facility rendered 'unusable to aviation''
19 February 1968	Bissalanca	rocket and mortar fire	'Destroyed the airport's control tower, two aircraft and three hangars, and caused other losses in material and casualties' (ZACVG admitted 'insignificant material damage,' 'two dead and 12 wounded in a militia group' encamped there)
13 November 1969	Cufar	ambush	Diversionary operation supporting PAIGC attack in Matos Arroba
November 1970	Cabedú	unknown	'T-6 destroyed'
1971	Bafatá	infantry assault	'Destroyed the airport control tower'
3–4 April 1971	Nova Lamego	sappers	'Destroyed three helicopters, an airplane, the control tower and other facilities of the base'
9 March 1972	Bissalanca	'bazooka' fire	'Our fighters attacked the main buildings and hangars causing significant destruction in the facilities'
September/October 1972	Bafatá	explosives	'A bomb destroyed one airplane, killing its crew'
In total, the PAIGC claimed to have conducted 58 airfield raids from 1965–71; this figure included 22 alleged attacks against forward airstrips by 1967.[4] Most were almost certainly ancillary to raids or shelling against the host barracks, and ZACVG SITREPs reflect only the 1968 attack against BA12.			

Appendix IV
ZACVG Heliborne Operations, 1967–1972

Table 20: ZACVG Heliborne Operations, 1967–1972[1]					
Month and Year	**Operation name**	**Objective area (Sector)**	**Helo flights***	**Troops lifted****	**Air support*****
May 1967	*Lara* *Tarantula* *Jerez* *Ver Para Crer*	Cambodian/Churl (W) Cambodian/ Churl (W) Matter/Tiling (W) Pache/Bula (W)	5 20 20 6	25 100 60 31	G, T T, H G, T, H T, H
June 1967	*Boom Successor* *Xampanhe* *Marabunta* *Ypanema*	Jol (W) São Domingos/Jegue (W) Pelundo (W) Oio (W)	42 5 26 11	168 30 152 30	G, T, H G, T, H, D G, T, H G, T, H
July 1967	*Nocal* *Obué*	Bula (W) Pelundo/Braque (W)	12 18	55 91	H G, T, H
August 1967	*Rapto* *Johnnie Walker* *Xangai* *Wenus*	Bula (W) Biribão (W) Gã Saude (S) Binta/Morés (W)	4 5 4 9	23 25 20 49	T, H G, T, H T, H G, T, H
September 1967	*Winchester Cathedral* *Corsico* *Volúpia* *Gavião*	Morés (W) Mansoa (W) Faquina Mandinga (W) Ganjogude/Maqué (W)	5 15 5 10	25 85 25 50	T, H G, H G, T, H G, T, H

Table 20: ZACVG Heliborne Operations, 1967–1972 *(continued)*

October 1967	*Milhafre*	Tiligi (W)	12	58	G, T
	West Side	Insumeté (W)	15	75	G, T, H
	Falção	Selim/Contuba (W)	24	120	T, H
	Veronica	Bula (W)	15	75	G, T, H
	Àguia	Bula (W)	10	50	G, T, H
	Gladiador	Bula (W)	24	120	T, H
	Insistir	Sinchã Jobel (E)	10	50	T, H
November 1967	*Wendome*	Bedanda (S)	6	30	G, T, H
	Cratera	Binta (W)	5	25	G, T, H
	Barracuda II	Gã Formoso (W)	24	115	G, T, H
	Garraio	Xime (E)	20	100	T, H
December 1967	*Mercúrio I*	Pobreza (S)	20	100	G, T, H
	Gineah I	Pobreza (S)	15	75	G, T, H
	Yungfrau	Canjambari (W)	10	50	G, T, H
	Relâmpago II	Chugué (B)	5	25	G, T, H
	Trovão	Bedanda (S)	20	100	G, T, H
	Eridanus	Gambiá (B)	15	75	G, T, H
January 1968	*Vendaval*	Pericuto (S)	20	100	T, H
	Escudo Negro	Saruol/Ambum (W)	15	75	G, T, H
	Hercules	Sinchã Jobel (E)	10	50	T, H
	Vestal	Binar (W)	8	40	G, T, H
February 1968	*Ciclone I*	Caboxanque (S)	40	200	G, T, H
	Zorba	Nova Sintra/Mato Grande (S)	16	80	G, T, H
	Avestruz	Insumeté (W)	20	100	G, T, H
	Ximena	Bachile (W)	12	60	G, T, H
	Zig-Zag	Quitamo (W)	6	30	T, H
	Ciclone II	Cafine/Cafal Balanta (S)	35	175	G, T, H
March 1968	*Ciclone III*	Darsalame (S)	20	100	G, T, H
	Centauro	Cacine/Caiar (S)	30	150	G, T, H
	Boa Bisca	Tiligi/Iador (W)	12	60	G, T, H
	Tufão	Central Como (S)	40	200	G, T, H
	Tempestade	Cassumba (S)	20	100	G, T, H
	Betelgeuse	Cassebeche (S)	10	50	G, T, H
April 1968	*Caju*	Salancaur (S)	10	50	G, T, H
	Rolls Royce	Chinchim Dari (S)	10	50	G, H
	Bola de Fogo	Guileje (S)	12	60	G, T
	Garça	Encherte (W)	6	30	H
	Titão	Morés (W)	20	100	G, T, H
May 1968	*Barracuda III*	Fulacunda (S)	20	100	G, T, H
	Alnair II	Gamparà (S)	12	60	G, T, H
June 1968	*Preparação I*	Có (W)	24	120	H
	Recolha	Che Che (E)	4	20	H
	Preparação II	Có-Bula road (W)	24	120	H
	High-Life	Quitafine (S)	8	48	G, T, H
August 1968	*Jupiter*	Guileje (S)	12	60	G, T, H
September 1968	*Dragão/68*	Binta/Sambuiá (W)	12	60	G, T, H
October 1968	*Peixe Voador*	Concolim (W)	12	60	G, T, H
	Boas Vindas	Bricama (W)	35	170	G, T, H
	Turbarão	Buba Tombó (S)	8	40	G, H
November 1968	*Venus*	Cantanhez (S)	40	200	H
	Baco	Galecunde (S)	15	75	G, H
	Apolo	Jabadá (S)	20	100	G, D, H
December 1968	*Neptuno*	Peconha (W)	12	60	H

Table 20: ZACVG Heliborne Operations, 1967–1972 *(continued)*					
January 1969	*Hercules*	Tite/Fulacunda (S)	12	60	T, H
	Hermes	Gã Formoso (S)	5	25	T, H
	Grande Coheita	Binta (W)	25	115	G, T, H
February 1969	*Aquiles I*	T. Pinto/S. Domingos (W)	55	275	T, H
	Falcão	Madina do Boé (E)	3	15	G, T, H
	Crisantemo	Chéché	11	34	G, T, H
March 1969	*Minerva*	Queré (W)	24	120	H
	Aurora	Injassane (S)	24	105	T, H
	Polux	Iangué (S)	18	80	G, H
April 1969	*Argus*	Canjambari/Farim (W)	40	190	G, H
	Flora	Caboxanque (S)	20	100	T, H
	Titã	Morés (W)	20	100	G, H
May 1969	*Midas*	Cã Quebo (W)	20	100	G, T, H
	Tourada Franca	São Vicente (W)	16	80	G, H
	Saturno	Biribão (W)	20	100	G, H
	Esmerelda	Cacine (S)	8	48	H
	Aquiles II	T. Pinto/S. Domingos (W)	65	322	G, H
	Cupido	Sárà (W)	20	100	H
June 1969	*Natura*	Sárà (W)	20	100	H
	Grande Salto	Unal (S)	20	100	H
	Orfeu	Choquemone/Encherte (W)	35	175	H
	Nestor	Infaide/Insumeté (W)	36	180	G, H
July 1969	unnamed	Poidom (W)	20	95	G, H
	Safo	Talicó (W)	20	95	H
	Safo II	Padada/Chanha (E)	20	100	H
	Marduk	Jifim (E)	15	75	H
	unnamed	Ganturé (W)	32	160	H
	unnamed	Queré (W)	12	48	H
August 1969	*Demétria*	Canjambari (W)	19	92	H
	Atena	Umpabá (W)	20	98	G, H
	Taliao	Faquina Mandinga (W)	21	75	G, T
	unnamed	Colina do Norte (W)	6	30	T, H
	Nereu	Galomaro (E)	40	20	H
September 1969	unnamed	Caboiana/Churo (W)	40	186	H
	Falcão Branco	Caboiana/Churo (W)	20	100	H
	Sexto Desforço	Gã Formoso (S)	10	50	G, H
	unnamed	Jifim (E)	16	80	H
October 1969	*Pelo*	Mamboncó (W)	40	195	G, H
	unnamed	Bigene (W)	10	50	H
	Adonis	Xime (E)	32	149	G, H
	Siamesa	Bigene/Ginta (W)	48	238	H
	Aresta	Caboiana (W)	30	150	H
November 1969	*Casa Volanta*	Sárà/Morés (W)	40	200	G, H
	Circe	Sancorlá (E)	7	35	H
	Jovis	Guileje (S)	35	140	H
December 1969	*Teuto*	Faquina (W)	10	50	G, H
	Moreia Branca	Guileje (S)	20	100	H
	Calamar Branco	Cangalai/Bedanda (S)	20	99	H
	unnamed	Mansoa (W)	10	50	H
	Jovem Zagal I	Guileje (S)	70	325	H
January 1970	*Crocodilo Negro*	Porto Balana (S)	20	100	G, T, H
	unnamed	Mansoa/Porto Gole (W)	12	40	P
	Rinoceronte Negro	Biambe (W)	20	100	G, H

Table 20: ZACVG Heliborne Operations, 1967–1972 *(continued)*

February 1970	*Tulipa Vermelha*	Queré (W)	10	50	H
	Perdiz Negra	Cubisseco (B)	40	200	G, H
	Raposa Negra	Sárà (W)	20	100	G, T, H
March 1970	*Rato Verde*	Sárà (W)	29	134	H
	Carmencita	Salamina (S)	6	26	G, H
	Orquidea Verde	Belí/Madina do Boé (E)	5	25	G
	Pavão Verde	Bária (S)	14	70	G, H
	Pica Pau Verde	Nafo (W)	7	35	G, H
	Tigre Verde	Belel/Madina Banjara (W)	14	40	G, H
	Osga Verde	Gã Júlio (S)	10	50	G, H
April 1970	*Orquidea Branca*	Guileje (S)	15	72	G, T, H
	Leão Verde	Cantanhez (S)	15	73	G, H
May 1970	*Raposa sem Covil*	Forreá (S)	10	50	G, H
	Serpente Dourada	Bissássema (S)	15	75	N/R
	Jaguar Vermeleo	Oio/Morés (W)	32	160	G, T, H
June 1970	*Lobo Bravo*	Caboiana/Churo (W)	20	98	N/R
July 1970	*Lobo Bravo II*	N/R	N/R	N/R	N/R
	Real Cavaleiro	N/R	N/R	N/R	H
	Simpatia	N/R	N/R	N/R	N/R
August 1970	unnamed	Tite (S)	10	50	H
September 1970	unnamed	Bigene (W)	10	50	N/R
	Canário	Faquina (W)	12	54	H
	Rola Cinzeta	São João (S)	55	275	G, H
	Lobo Bravo IV	Teixeira Pinto (W)	55	275	H
	Rato Cinzento	Tite (S)	5	25	G, H
October 1970	*Chacal*	Dungal (W)	22	110	H
	Nenufar	Brufa (W)	12	60	H
	Mata Batida	Teixeira Pinto (W)	5	25	H
	Relâmpago Gigante	Tecanhe/Barme/Balem (W)	22	110	H
	unnamed	Bigene (W)	24	116	H
	Canguru	Lamel corridor (S)	48	201	G, T, H
November 1970	*Rouxinol*	Bojol Beafada (S)	10	50	G, T, H
	Nespera	Injassane (S)	8	40	T, H
	Pelicano	Cabunta/Cantanhez (S)	10	50	G, T, H
	Serpente Branca	Madina Fula (W)	12	52	H
December 1970	unnamed	Mansabá/Farim (W)	10	50	N/R
	Hera Branca	Mansabá (W)	24	117	H
	Hidra Branca	Mansabá/Binta (W)	24	146	H
January 1971	*Urubu Negro*	Binta (W)	40	204	H
	Pardal	Guileje (S)	14	64	G, H
February 1971	unnamed	Mansabá (W)	48	240	N/R
	unnamed	Mansoa (W)	5	24	N/R
	unnamed	Bedanda (S)	12	60	N/R
	Cotovia	Guidage/Dungal (W)	20	100	G, H
	Selva Negra	Mansabá (W)	18	80	G, T, H
March 1971	*Desejada Oportunidade*	Tite/Jabadá (S)	17	85	G, H
	Narisco	Buduco (W)	7	28	T, H
	Perneta	Cafal Nalu (S)	20	100	G, H, B
April 1971	*Vitória*	Texeira Pinto (W)	20	100	G, H
	Rola	Sambaso/Lenguel (S)	10	52	G, H
	Sapo	Ganduá Nalu (S)	10	52	G, H
	Pomba	Santa Clara (S)	20	100	G, T, H
	Papagaio	Salancaur (S)	40	200	G, T, H

Table 20: ZACVG Heliborne Operations, 1967–1972 *(continued)*

May 1971	unnamed	Missirá (W)	15	75	N/R
	Relva Cortada	Bigene (W)	20	100	G, H
	Tordo Vermelha	P. Luís Dias/P.do Inglês (E)	30	149	G, T, H
June 1971	*Busca*	Queré (W)	6	25	H
	Flamingo	Changalana (W)	6	30	G, T, H
	Larga Agora	Tiligi (W)	80	400	G, T, H
	Sardão Dourado	Quinara/Fulacunda (S)	40	200	G, T, H
July 1971	*Martelada*	Brandão/Buduco (S)	22	108	G, H
	Osga Azul	Tiligi (W)	15	75	G, H
	Rusga Grande I	Burné (W)	10	46	G, H
	Picapau	Tombali region (S)	20	100	T, H
August 1971	*Papoila*	Tombali region (S)	6	30	T, H
	Quartzo Azul	Cubisseco (B)	20	100	G, H
	Caroch	Sinchã Djassi (E)	20	100	G, H
	Xisto	Mansabá (W)	12	60	G, H
	Nenufar	Injassane (S)	6	30	G, H
	Osga Azul II	Tiligi (W)	10	50	H
September 1971	unnamed	Boé (E)	4	16	T, H
	Lontra	Caboiana (W)	12	60	G, T, H
	Com Raça I	Caboiana (W)	30	150	G, H
	Com Raça II	Caboiana (W)	20	100	G, H
	Diana	São Domingos (W)	3	15	G, H
	Coiote	Morés (W)	6	30	G, T, H
October 1971	*Cleópatra*	Incassol (S)	2	9	G, H
	Dragão Feroz	Corubal (E)	14	70	G, H
	Sap Cinzento	Cubisseco (B)	14	70	G, T, H
	Com Raça III	Caboiana (W)	29	145	G, T, H
	Diamante Pardo	Bula/Binar (W)	5	25	N/R
	Julieta	Injassane (S)	5	25	N/R
	Ulmeiro	Farim (W)	16	85	H
	Pérola Preta	Tiligi/Binta/Bigene (W)	6	28	H
November 1971	*Com Raça IV*	Caboiana (W)	5	25	G, H
	Camélia	Maninhã (W)	4	13	G, H
	Canguru	Jabiá (E)	5	25	G, H
	Satélite Dourado I	Injassane (S)	21	104	G, T, H
	Pássaro	Intusso/Cachôbar (S)	6	30	G
	Satélite Dourado II	Injassane (S)	26	146	G, T, H
	Pérola Amarela	Gã Formoso (S)	40	201	T, H
	Bufalo	Maqué (W)	7	35	G, H
December 1971	*Safira Solitária*	Morés (W)	35	169	G, H
	unnamed	Padada (E)	10	50	H
	unnamed	São Domingos (W)	10	50	N/R
January 1972	*Dragão Dourado*	Tiligi (W)	30	150	G, T, H
	Ursula	Sárà (W)	8	40	G, H
	Sebastião	Cametonco (S)	7	32	H
	Ulanova	Suarecunda (W)	8	40	G, H
	Grande Vela	Caboiana (W)	32	160	G, H
	Topázio Forte	Quinara (S)	24	120	H
February 1972	unnamed	Porto Balana (S)	8	38	G, H
	Pérola Perdida	Morés (W)	5	25	H, D
	Mocho Verde	Enxalé/Sansanto (W)	50	250	G, T, H
	Satélite Dourado II	Gampará (S)	40	196	H
	Olga	Aidará Beafada (S)	6	29	G, H, D
	Trampolim Mágico	Xime/Xitole (E)	18	90	G, H, D

Table 20: ZACVG Heliborne Operations, 1967–1972 *(continued)*

March 1972		Fulacunda/Gampará (S)	10	50	G, T, H
	Pato Azul	Salancaur Fula (S)	6	25	G, H
	Periquito	Caboiana (W)	8	40	G, H
	Represália Gigante				
	Rubi Vigoroso	Pobreza (S)	3	15	G, H
	Noca	Guebambol (S)	18	108	G, T, H
	Muralha Químerica	Unal/Guileje (S)	48	240	G, H, D
	Pérola Invicta				
		Boé (E)	20	100	G, T, H, D
April 1972	*Topázio Maior*	Boé (E)	3	15	G, T, H, D
	Flecha Prateada	Cantanhez (S)	3	15	H
	Odete	Cubisseco (B)	6	24	G, T, H
	Novo Ciclone	Caboiana/Churo (W)	14	27	G, H
	Milhafre Dourado	Tiligi/Oio (W)	6	30	G, H
	Zagaia	Pirada (E)	5	30	G, H
May 1972	*Marco 74*	Pirada (E)	15	75	G, H
	Onca	Injassane (S)	10	50	G, T, H
	Zawenda	Pirada/Paunca (E)	6	30	G, H
	Milhafre Verde	Sárà (W)	42	208	G, T, H
	Esmeralda Encantada	Canjambari/Banjara (W)	36	180	H
June 1972	unnamed	Teixeira Pinto (W)	6	30	N/R
	Ofélia	Forreá (S)	10	45	H
	Não Ceder	Cabioana/Churo (W)	30	148	H
July 1972	*Garlopa*	Ponta Varela (E)	10	50	G, H
	Palanca	Timbó (S)	9	45	H
	Salamandra	Faja (W)	6	24	G, H
	Formiga	Mantém/Sárà (W)	20	100	G, T, H
August 1972	unnamed	Mansoa (W)	25	126	N/R
	Fadista I	Dando/Malafo/Damé (W)	6	30	H
	Romy	Cubisseco (B)	2	12	H, D
	Doninha	São Domingos (W)	20	100	G, H
	Felosa	Cantanhez (S)	18	90	G, H
	Novo Ciclo	Caboiana/Churo (W)	30	150	G, H
	Pacaça	Cantanhez (S)	6	30	H
	Nadia	Injassane (S)	6	30	N/R
September 1972	*Barata*	Inquida/Umpabá (W)	13	66	G, T, H
	unnamed	Madina Xaquili (E)	10	50	H
	unnamed	Catió (S)	8	40	H
	Águia Errante	Injassane (S)	12	60	G, H
	Olinda	Nafo (W)	3	15	G, H
	unnamed	Catió (S)	16	80	N/R
	Ofélia	Timbó (S)	10	50	G, H
October 1972	*Cavalo Ladino*	Cubonge/Inchula (W)	10	60	G, H
	Bela Madona	Quinara (S)	16	80	H, D
	Hipopótamo	Cubisseco (B)	12	60	G, H
	Rosário	Timbó (S)	8	40	G, T, H
	Rena	Faja (W)	16	80	G, H, D
	Jagudi	Pobreza (S)	16	80	G, H
	Falcão Amarelo	Tigili (W)	14	71	G, H

Table 20: ZACVG Heliborne Operations, 1967–1972 (*continued*)

November 1972	*Hipopótamo*	Quinara (S)	18	99	G, H
	Palanca	Cantanhez (S)	16	80	G, H
	Rosário II	Timbó (S)	8	40	G, T, H
	Safira Encarnada	Choquemone (W)	24	132	H
	Perdiz	Cangalai (S)	11	55	G, H
	Jacuba	São Domingos (W)	18	93	H
	Barbarela	Iador (W)	16	80	T, H
	Jamanta	Churo (W)	14	72	H, D
	Urso Encarnado	Cangalai/Timbó (S)	15	60	G, H
	Mariana	Boé (E)	3	17	H
December 1972	*Grande Empresa*****	Cantanhez (S)	90	453	G, T, H
	Cavalo Alado	Cachamba/Uangane (S)	17	95	H
	Otília	Budom/n. of Chugué (W)	6	30	H
	Empura Tudo	Caboiana/Churo (W)	14	79	H
	Rubi Maior	IVO Ponta Matar (W)	32	160	H
	Dragão Bravo	Santa Clara/Iem (S)	50	260	H

*Outbound/assault sorties only, no return or redeployment flights.

**Usually paratroops, commandos, or marines; rarely, infantry or other 'conventional' ground forces.

*** G = G.91; T = T-6; H = heli-canhão; B = B-26; D = armed Do-27; N/R = not reported.

****Activity up to 31 December 1972; *Grande Empresa* follow-on operations continue through August 1973.

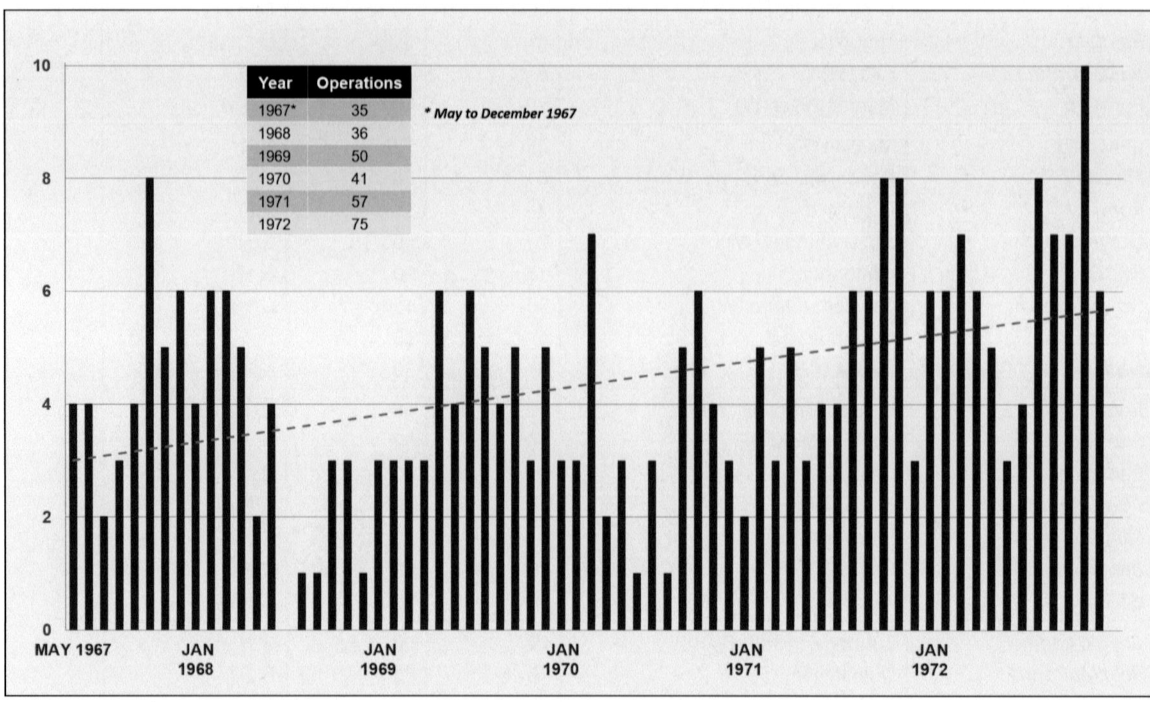

Appendix V
Independent ZACVG strike operations, 1967–1972

(including counter-AD operations)

Table 21: ZACVG Strike Operations, 1967–1972

Month/Year	Operation	Sector	Sorties				
			G.91	T-6	armed Al-III	armed Do-27	B-26
August 1967	*Teimosia*	West	4	6	1		
September 1967	*Tigre*	South	3				
October 1967	*Violeta*	South	14				
	Relâmpago	South	3				
November 1967	*Alfinetada*	South	3				
January 1968	*Faísca*	South	19				
	Fogacho I	South	7				
	Fogacho II	South	7				
	Dá-lhe Agora	South	14	12			
February 1968	*Crepúsculo*	South	4	3			
	Martelada	South	10				
	Martelada II	South	9				
March 1968	*Martelada III*	South	4				
April 1968	*Alfinetada II*	East	4				
November 1968	*Trovão*	South	12	4	1		
March 1969	*Vulcano*	South	20				
May 1969	*Diamante*	South	22				
January 1970	*Cravo Azul*	South	12				
February 1970	*Rosa Branca*	West	20	10			
	Rosa Cinza	West	16	38			
	Moreosa	West	12	16			
	Insumetido	West	8	8			
March 1970	*Moreosa II*	West	12	12			

Table 21: ZACVG Strike Operations, 1967–1972 *(continued)*

May 1970	*Piador*	West	24	16			
	Talião I	South	6				
	Talião II	West	38	19			
	Diamante Azul	South	8				
June 1970	*Abstracta I*	South, West		8			
	Abstracta II	West	54	26			
	Pérola Azul	South	24				
July 1970	*Abstracta III*	West	26	32			
	Contra Ataque I-II	South	22	6	1		
	Abstracta IV	East, West	12	18			
August 1970	*Morte Lenta*	West	8	12			
	Boa Gente	West	20	28			
September 1970	*Boa Gente II-III*	West	30	44			
	Alvo Marcado	South, West	59	56			
October 1970	*Malga Quente*	West	39	31	4		
	Partir Pedra	West	15	24			
November 1970	*Buraco Velho*	West	87	112			
December 1970	*Buraco Velho II*	South	32	68		1	
	Boa Esperança	N/R	56	39			
January 1971	*Buraco Velho III*	N/R	13	15			
	Pontada Rija	N/R	40	35			
	Contrato Verbal	N/R	28	20			
February 1971	*Bruto Lencastre*	N/R	38	52			
	Buraco Velho IV	N/R	35	24			
	Bruto Lencastre II	N/R	10	9			
March 1971	*Buraco Velho V*	N/R	7	16			2
	Boa Noite	N/R	16	25			2
	Quimera	N/R	16	11			1
	Hidra Sedenta	N/R	9	9			3

Table 21: ZACVG Strike Operations, 1967–1972 *(continued)*

April 1971	*Bater Ferro*	N/R	21	18			
	Boa Noite II	N/R	12	9			
	Água Mole	N/R	21	14		1	
	Desforço Natural	N/R	21	35			
	Piriquito	N/R	7	7			
May 1971	*Exército Popular*	N/R	7	7			
	Suspiro	N/R	8	11			1
	Bem Querer	N/R	28	19			
	Bota Fora	N/R	17	13			
	Exército Popular II	N/R	47	25			5
June 1971	*Safari*	N/R	8	7			2
	Águia Branca	N/R	8	7			2
	Barraca	N/R	7	7			
	Desforço Natural III	N/R	8	7			2
	Dará Sarilho	West	6	6			
	Armadilha	West	7	5			
	Exército Popular III	South	6	5			
July 1971	*Bem Querer II*	West	17	40			
	Ricochete	South	10	10			
	Chuva Miuda	South	31	22			
August 1971	*BemQuerer III*	N/R	44	28			
	Cirinéus Magníficos	South	14	8			
	Capacetes Laranja	West	36	32			
September 1971	*Batucada Real*	West	36	30			
	Amanhã Mais	West	20	13			
October 1971	*Resgate*	South	8	6			
	Áquia Errante	South	56	44			
	Mau Maria	West	25	23			
November 1971	*Abre Alas*	East, West	18	32		1	
	Rato Vivo	South	17	36			

Table 21: ZACVG Strike Operations, 1967–1972 *(continued)*							
December 1971	*Boa Malha*	South	9	10			
	Zig-Zag	West	28	14			
	Lua Nova	South	14	18			
	Bomba Nova	West	6				
	Com Garra	South	6	16			
January 1972	*Frente Popular*	East	16	26			
	Ilha Solitária	South	7	5			
	Bola Branca	West	10	10			
February 1972	*Manda Chuva*	South	25	14			
March 1972	*Maria Morena*	West	12	18			
	Tatuagem Terrivel	West	14	16			
	Pastel Folhado	South	11	10			
April 1972	*Vulcão Vigoroso*	West	47	34		1	
	Baga Baga	West	15	12		1	
May 1972	*Anda Pássaro*	West	19	14			
	Dardo Nocivo	South	28	10			
June 1972	*Chupa Chupa*	West	42	36			
	Cavalo Cansado	West	38	28			
July 1972	*Búfalo Feroz*	South	9	8			
	Vinho Espumoso	South	10				
August 1972	*Grande Ponto*	West		30			
	Arre Jerico	West	24	20			
	Cidade Maldita	South	25	30			
	Água Régia	West	18	20			
September 1972	*Jovial*	West		4			
	Apache Cansado	South	14	12			
	Jantar Volante	West	18	12			

Table 21: ZACVG Strike Operations, 1967–1972 *(continued)*

October 1972	*Biquini Dourado*	South	12	14			
	Cara Linda	West	16	6			
	Bela Sedutora	West	13	16			
	Boneca Querida	South	4	14			
	Ave Rara	West	26	24			
	Boa Laracha II	West	13	14			
November 1972	*Alce Veloz*	West	12	17			
	Ana Karina	South	18	20			
	Javali Feroz	South	10	4			
	Noite Dia	South	34	14			
December 1972	*Manobra Cureal*	South	34	9			
	Planta Tropical	South	15				
	Cavalgada Maluca	South	10				
	Cacada Marota	South	10				

Appendix VI
Portuguese Air Force Mission Codes[1]

Fire support (*apoio de fogo*)

ATIP – *Ataque Independente Preprado* (pre-planned independent attack): 'Actions taken without the necessity of coordination with the fires and movements of the surface forces, consisting of attacks against predetermined surface targets, and which may be prepared in advance. Allows careful planning for major employment of resources in accordance with the objective, and the absence of safety constraints due to the proximity of surface forces. It is the attack action in which aerial fires can provide the greatest results.'

ATID – *Ataque Independente Dirigido* (directed independent attack): 'Independent attack activity that strikes indicated surface targets marked in space or time by the activity of other aerial assets (PCV – *Posto de Comando Volante*) or by technical means of observers on the ground.'

ATIR – *Ataque Independente em Reconhecimento* (armed reconnaissance): 'Independent attack activity in which aerial assets search for surface targets to subsequently attack. This activity is naturally less productive than prepared attacks, and is reserved for targets of opportunity, especially moving targets.'

AESC – *Ataque em Escolta* (aerial escort): 'Only executed to protect aircraft that are particularly vulnerable to anti-aircraft fire.'

ATAP – *Ataque Apoio Próximo* (close air support): 'Ground attack executed at the request and in immediate benefit of surface forces and in their implied proximity, therefore, a strict coordination with the fires and movement of the surface forces.'

ATAC – *Ataque Acompanhamento* (armed overwatch): 'Attack in missions accompanying the surface forces. Although it is possible to consider it a particular case of ATAP, it is a distinct action because of its additional characteristics of orientation and information from the supported forces, and the frequency with which it is requested and utilised.'

Reconnaissance

RVIS – *Reconhecimento Visual* (visual reconnaissance): 'Reconnaissance over terrain in general or coastal waters, in which the search for news is made by the pilot or observer without the assistance of other means besides their own perception and visual capacities.'

RVIS-MAR – *Reconhecimento Visual, Marítimo* (maritime reconnaissance): 'Reconnaissance in which searches are made over the sea, in which not only may the visual capacity of the crew be used, but also the aircraft's electronic means.'

RVIS-SAR – *Reconhecimento Visual – Busca e Salvamento* (Search and Rescue): self-explanatory.

RFOT – *Reconhecimento Fotográfico* (photographic reconnaissance): self-explanatory.

RELE – *Reconhecimento Electrónico* (electronic reconnaissance): radar and radio interception.

Transport

TGER – *Transporte Geral* (general airlift): 'General administrative logistical transport activity (of personnel, material, et cetera).'

TGER-LCA – *Transporte Geral, Lancamento de Carga* (airdrop operations): 'Cargo dropped by parachute or in freefall for the supply of friendly elements.'

TMAN – *Transporte de Manobra* (tactical airlift): 'All transport associated with operations in progress.'

TMAN-ASS or TASS – *Transporte para Assalto* (air assault): 'Transport of troops, generally by helicopter, for assault.'

TMAN-LCA – *Transporte de Manobra, Lançamento de Carga* (tactical airdrop): 'Cargo dropped by parachute or freefall, generally for engaged friendly forces.'

TMAN-LPA – *Transporte de Manobra, Lançamento de Pára-quedistas* (airborne operations): 'Troops dropped by parachute.'

TEVS – *Transporte de Evacuação Sanitário* (medical evacuation): self-explanatory.

Miscellaneous (*diversos*)

DACO – *Acompanhamento* (overwatch): 'Support action for surface forces in movement, which consists of the presence of aircraft over the supported forces during the mission…possibly leading, ultimately, to the execution of fires against enemy surface elements that act against the surface forces or the aircraft themselves.'

DLIC – *Ligação* (liaison): 'Activities that consist of the establishment or reestablishment of contact or communications with elements of friendly forces, whose exact situation is important to know and cannot be by other means.'

DCON – *Controlo Volante* (airborne command post): 'Guidance, coordination or command of surface, aerial, or joint actions, by an aircraft in flight in the active area. Includes the adjustment of artillery fire.'

DESP – *Especiais* (special): 'Aerial actions that, for their rarity, peculiar nature, or necessity for secrecy, do not fit the previous definitions or should not be given a more explicit designation. If it is found to be convenient and appropriate, the letter 'D' can be replaced by the letter indicating the general type of action in question, e.g. TESP, RESP, AESP, et cetera'

Bibliography

Archives and special Collections – physical

Arquivo Histórico Militar, Lisbon, Portugal
Arquivo da Defesa Nacional, Paço de Arcos, Portugal
Arquivo Histórico da Força Aérea, Alfragide, Portugal
Arquivo Histórico da Presidência da República, Lisbon, Portugal
Guinea-Bissau Collection, The Hoover Institution, Stanford University, CA
Ronald H. Chilcote Collection, University of California, Riverside, CA
U.S. Air Force Historical Research Agency, Maxwell Air Force Base, AL
U.S. Army Heritage and Education Center, Carlisle, PA

Archives and special Collections – virtual

Associação Tchiweka de Documentação, www.tchiweka.org
Central Intelligence Agency, www.cia.gov/readingroom/home
Defense Technical Information Center, discover.dtic.mil
Fundação Mário Soares e Maria Barroso Arquivo e Biblioteca, www.fmsoares.pt/aeb/arquivo.
John F. Kennedy Presidential Museum and Library, www.jfklibrary.org/archives
North Atlantic Treaty Organisation Archives Online, www.archives.nato.int/nato-archives-online
Richard Nixon Presidential Library and Museum, www.nixonlibrary.gov
U.S. Declassified Documents Online, www.gale.com/c/us-declassified-documents-online
U.S. Department of State, foia.state.gov
U.S. National Archives and Records Administration, aad.archives.gov/aad/index.jsp
United Nations Digital Library, digitallibrary.un.org

Published Books

Abecasis, José Krus, *Bordo de Ataque: Memórias de uma Caderneta de voo e um Contributo Para a História*, vol. II (Coimbra: Coimbra Editora, 1985)
Afonso, Aniceto and Carlos de Matos Gomes, *Os Anos da Guerra Colonial, 1961.1975.* (Matosinhos, Portugal: Quid Novi, 2010)
Ângelo, Fernando Cavaleiro, *Os Falcões do Biafra: O Envolvimento Secreto de Portugal na Guerra Civil da Nigéria, 1967–1970* (Lisbon: Casa das Letras, 2019)
Apostolo, Giorgio, *The Fiat G.91.* Profile Publications No.119 (London: Profile Publications, 1966)
Bacelar, Sérgio Augusto Margarido Lima, *A Guerra em África, 1961–1974: Estratégias Adoptadas pelas Forças Armadas* (Porto: Ligo dos Amigos do Museu Militar do Porto, 2000)
Bispo, António de Jesus, 'Aviação na Guiné – Início das Operações Militares' in *Olhares sobre Guiné e Cabo Verde* (Linda-a-Velha and Porto, Portugal: DG Edições and Caminhos Romanos, 2012)
Bispo, António de Jesus, 'Doctrine, Capacities, Technology and Operation Environment on the Employment of the Air Power: The Case of Guerrilla Warfare,' in *Airpower in 20th Century: Doctrines and Employment – National Experiences.* (Den Haag: International Commission of Military History, 2011)
Brandão, José, *Cronologia da Guerra Colonial: Angola-Guiné-Moçambique 1961–1974* (Lisbon: Prefácio, 2008)
Cabeleira, José, *Trajecto de uma Vida entre o Mar e o Ar* (Edição de autor, 2004)
Cabral, Amílcar, *Our People Are our Mountains: Amílcar Cabral on the Guinean Revolution* (London: Committee for Freedom in Mozambique, Angola and Guinea, 1972)
Cabral, Amílcar, *Unity and Struggle: Speeches and Writings* (New York: Monthly Review Press, 1979)
Cabral, Luís, 'Prender Spínola' in José Freire Antunes (ed.) *A Guerra de África (1961–1974), I volume* (Lisbon: Temas e Debates, 1996)
Cabral, Luís, *Crónica da Libertação* (Lisbon: O Jornal, 1984)
Cabrita, Felícia, *Massacres em África,* 3rd edition (Lisbon: A esfera dos livros, 2011)
Caetano, Marcello, *Depoimento* (Rio de Janeiro: Distribuidora Record, 1974)
Caio, Horácio, *Portuguese Guinea: 9 Days in March* (Lisbon: Overseas Ministry, 1970)
Calvão, Alpoim. 'Ataque a Conakry,' in José Freire Antunes (ed.) *A Guerra de África (1961–1974), II volume* (Lisbon: Temas e Debates, 1996)
Carvalho, Norberto Tavares de, *De campo em campo: Conversas com o Comandante do PAIGC Bobo Keita*, 2nd Edition (Porto: Edição de Autor, 2020)
Carvalho, Otelo Saraiva de, *Alvorada em Abril* (Amadora, Portugal: Livraria Bertrand, 1977)
Castanho Paes, José Manuel, 'A Marinha na Guiné e Cabo Verde: Navios, Fuzileiros e Autoridade Maritima' in *Olhares sobre Guiné e Cabo Verde*, pp.189–259 (Linda-a-Velha and Porto, Portugal: DG Edições and Caminhos Romanos, 2012)
Catarino, Manual, *As Grandes Operações da Guerra Colonial, 1961–1974, VI: Operação Tridente – Ocupação de Caiar, Como e Catunco, Guiné, 1964* (Lisbon: Correio da Manhã, 2009)
Catarino, Manuel, *As Grandes Operações da Guerra Colonial 1961–1974, II: Guiné – Operação Irã, Maio 1965; Operação Hermínia, Março 1966* (Lisbon: Cofina Media, 2010)
Catarino, Manuel, *As Grandes Operações da Guerra Colonial, 1961–1974, VII: Pára-quedistas Encurralados em Cassebeche, Guiné 1969* (Lisbon: Correio da Manhã, 2009)
Catarino, Manuel, *As Grandes Operações da Guerra Colonial, 1961–1974, VIII: Captura do Capitão Peralta, Guiné 1969 e 1972* (Lisbon: *Correio da Manhã*, 2009)
Catarino, Manuel, *As Grandes Operações da Guerra Colonial, 1961–1974, XI: Ataque a Conacri, Guiné-Bissau 1970* (Lisbon: Correio da Manhã, 2009)
Catarino, Manuel, *As Grandes Operações da Guerra Colonial, 1961–1974, XIII: Viagem Secreta de Spínola ao Senegal, 1972* (Lisbon: Correio da Manhã, 2009)
Chabal, Patrick, *Amílcar Cabral: Revolutionary Leadership and People's War* (Trenton, NJ: Africa World Press, 2003)
Chaliland, Gérard, *Armed Struggle in Africa: With the Guerrillas in 'Portuguese' Guinea* (New York: Monthly Review Press, 1969)
Chicago Committee for the Liberation of Angola, Mozambique and Guinea, *Sun of Our Freedom: The Independence of Guinea-Bissau* (Chicago: Salsedo Press, 1974)
Clayton, Anthony, *Frontiersmen: Warfare in Africa since 1950* (London: Routledge, 2004)
Comissão para o Estudo das Campanhas de África, *Resenha Histórico-Militar das Campanhas de África (1961–1974), 1 Volume: Enquadramento Geral* (Lisbon: Estado-Maior do Exército, 1988)

Comissão para o Estudo das Campanhas de África, *Resenha Histórico-Militar das Campanhas de África (1961–1974), 6 Volume, Aspectos da Actividade Operational, Tomo II - Guiné, Livro I* (Lisbon: Estado-Maior do Exército, 2014)

Comissão para o Estudo das Campanhas de África, *Resenha Histórico-Militar das Campanhas de África (1961–1974), 6 Volume, Aspectos da Actividade Operational, Tomo II - Guiné, Livro II* (Lisbon: Estado-Maior do Exército, 2015)

Comissão para o Estudo das Campanhas de África, *Resenha Histórico-Militar das Campanhas de África (1961–1974), 14 Volume – Comandos* (Lisbon: Estado-Maior do Exército, 2009)

Corpo docente do Instituto Universitário Militar, *Glossário de termosmilitares.* (Lisbon: Instituto Universitário Militar e Academia das Ciências de Lisboa, 2020)

Cullen, Tony, and Christopher F. Foss (eds), *Jane's Land-Based Air Defence, 1992–1993.* (London: Jane's Information Group, 1992)

Cunha, J. Silva, *Ainda o 25 de Abril* (Lisbon: Centro do Livro Brasileiro, 1984.)

Davidson, Basil, *The Liberation of Guiné: Aspects of an African Revolution* (New York: Penguin Books, 1969)

Davis, Jennifer, *Triumph over Colonialism: The Republic of Guinea-Bissau* (New York: The Africa Fund, 1974)

Dhada, Mustafah, *Warriors at Work: How Guinea-Bissau Was Really Set Free.* (Boulder: University Press of Colorado, 1993)

Diogo Neto, Manual, 'Voo em Três Frentes' in José Freire Antunes (ed.) *A Guerra de África (1961–1974),* I volume (Lisbon: Temas e Debates, 1996)

Draper, Michael I., *Shadows: Airlift and Airwar in Biafra and Nigeria 1967–1970.* (Aldershot: Hikoki Publications, 2002)

Ferreira, José Lemos, 'No céu da Guiné' in José Freire Antunes, *A Guerra de África (1961–1974),* II volume (Lisbon: Temas e Debates, 1996)

Figueiredo, Luís Palma de, *História das Esquadras de Helicópteros da Força Aérea Portuguesa.* (Porto: Fronteira do Caos, 2018)

Fonseca, Ana Mónica, *A Força das Armas: Apoio da República Federal da Alemanha ao Estado Novo (1958–1968)* (Lisbon: Ministério dos Negócios Estrangeiros, 2007)

Fraga, Luís Alves de, A Força Aérea na Guerra em África: Angola, Guiné e Moçambique 1961–1975 (Lisbon: Prefácio, 2004)

Galvão, Alpoim, 'Ataque a Conakry' in José Freire Antunes (ed.), *A Guerra de África (1961–1974),* II volume (Lisbon: Temas e Debates, 1996)

Gleijeses, Piero, *Conflicting Missions: Havana, Washington, and Africa, 1959–1976.* (Chapel Hill: The University of North Carolina Press, 2002)

Gordon, Yefim and Dmitriy Komissarov, *The Il-28 Beagle Light Attack Bomber.* (Shrewsbury: Airlife, 2002)

Gunston, Bill (ed.), *Jane's Aero-Engines* (London: Jane's Information Group, 1996)

Hallion, Richard P. (ed.), *Silver Wings, Golden Valor: The USAF Remembers Korea* (Washington, DC: Air Force History and Museums Program, 2006)

Hernández, Humberto Trujillo, *El Grito del Baobab* (Havana: Editorial de Ciências Sociales, 2008)

Higham, Robert D. S., *100 Years of Air Power and Aviation* (College Station: Texas A&M University Press, 2003)

Howland, Nina Davis (ed.), *Foreign Relations of the United States, 1964–1968, volume XXIV, Africa.* (Washington, DC: United States Government Printing Office, 1999)

Hurley, Matthew M. and José Matos, *Sanctuary Lost: The Air War for Portuguese Guinea, vol. I – Outbreak and Escalation (1961–1966).* (Warwick: Helion & Co., 2022).

International Institute for Strategic Studies, *The Military Balance 1960: The Communist Bloc and the Free World* (London: The Institute for Strategic Studies, 1959)

International Institute for Strategic Studies, *The Military Balance 1968–1969* (London: The Institute for Strategic Studies, 1968)

International Institute for Strategic Studies, *The Military Balance 1970–1971* (London: The Institute for Strategic Studies, 1970)

Katagiri, Noriyuki, *Adapting to Win: How Insurgents Fight and Defeat Foreign States in War.* (Philadelphia: University of Pennsylvania Press, 2015)

Knaack, Marcelle Size, *Encyclopedia of U.S. Air Force Aircraft and Missile Systems, volume II: Post-World War II Fighters 1945–1973* (Washington, DC: Office of Air Force History, 1978)

Lopes, Mário Canongia and José Manuel Rodrigues Costa, *Os Aviões da Cruz de Cristo: 75 Anos da Aviação Militar em Portugal* (Lisbon: Dinalivro, 1989)

Marinho, António Luís, *Operação Mar Verde: Um documento para a história* (Lisbon: Temas e Debates, Lisboa, 2006)

Matos, José and Luís Barroso, *Nos Meandros da Guerra: O Estado Novo e a África do Sul na defesa da Guiné* (Lisbon: Caleidoscópio, 2020)

Matos, José, *Mar Verde: The Portuguese Amphibious Assault on Conakry, 1970.* (Warwick: Helion & Co., 2021)

Meneses, Filipe, *Salazar: A Political Biography* (New York: Enigma Books, 2009)

Miranda, Jorge Manuel Brochado de, *Acidentes Mortais em Aeronaves, 1917–2016: Aviaçao Naval, Aeronáutica Militar, Força Aérea Portuguesa* (Alfragide, Portugal: Arquivo Histórico da Força Aérea, 2016)

Moore, John (ed.), *Jane's Fighting Ships 1980–81* (London: Jane's Publishing, 1980)

Morgado, Nuno Alexandre Ferrer, et al, 'A atuação do Marechal Spínola no Teatro De Operações da Guiné-Bissau, entre 1968 e 1973, enquanto Comandante-Chefe das Forças Armadas e Governador Geral' in *A Campanha Militar Terrestre no Teatro de Operações da Guiné-Bissau (1963–1974): estudo da aplicação da força por funções de combate.* (Lisbon: Instituto Universitário Militar, December 2018)

Nico, José Francisco, *A Batalha do Quitafine: A Contraguerrilha Antiaérea na Guiné e a Fantasia das 'areas libertadas'* (Lisbon: edição do autor, 2020)

O'Halloran, James C. (ed.), *Jane's Land-Based Air Defence 2005–2006* (London: Jane's Information Group, 2005)

Olds, Robin, with Christina Olds and Ed Rasimus, *Fighter Pilot: The Memoirs of Legendary Ace Robin Olds* (New York: St. Martin's Press, 2010)

Oliveira, Händel de, Rui Nunes, and J. Villas Monteiro, *Os Últimos Governadores do Império.* (Lisbon: Edições Neptuno, 1994)

Oramas, Oscar, *Amílcar Cabral: para além do seu tempo* (Lisbon: Hugin, 1998)

Paes, José Castanho, et al, 'A Marinha na Guiné e Cabo Verde: Navios, Fuzileiros e Autoridade Maritima' in Manuel Barão da Cunha and José Castanho Paes (eds), *Olhares sobre Guiné e Cabo Verde* (Linda-a-Velha and Porto: DG Edições and Caminhos Romanos, 2012)

Rodrigues, António Martins, 'Aviação na Guiné – A Parte Final' in *Olhares sobre Guiné e Cabo Verde* (Linda-a-Velha and Porto: DG Edições and Caminhos Romanos, 2012)

Rodrigues, Luís Nuno, 'For a Better Guinea! Winning Hearts and Minds in Portuguese Guinea' in Philip E. Muehlenbeck (ed.) *Race,*

Ethnicity, and the Cold War: A Global Perspective, (Nashville: Vanderbilt University Press, 2012)

Rodrigues, Luís Nuno, *Spínola* (Lisbon: A Esfera dos Livros, 2010)

Santos, Manuel dos, 'Disparar os Strela' in José Freire Antunes (ed.) *A Guerra de África (1961–1974), I volume* (Lisbon: Temas e Debates, 1996)

Silva, Tomás George Conceição, 'The Portuguese Air Force in the African Wars of 1961–1974' in John P. Cann (ed.), *Memories of Portugal's African Wars, 1961–1974: Proceedings of a Conference, King's College London, 10 June 1997* (Quantico: Marine Corps University Foundation, 1998)

Spínola, António de, *País sem Rumo: Contributo para a História de uma Revolução* (Lisbon: SCIRE, 1978)

Taylor, John W. R. (ed.), *Jane's All the World's Aircraft 1965–1966* (London: Jane's Publishing, 1965)

Taylor, John W. R. (ed.), *Jane's All the World's Aircraft 1972–1973.* (London: Jane's Publishing, 1972)

Telepneva, Natalia, *Cold War Liberation: The Soviet Union and the Collapse of the Portuguese Empire in Africa, 1961–1975.* (Chapel Hill: The University of North Carolina Press, 2022)

Thompson, Scott, Douglas A-26 and B-26 Invader (Marlborough: The Crowood Press, 2002)

Vaz, Nuno Mira, *Guiné 1968 e 1973: Soldados uma vez, Sempre Soldados!* (Lisbon: Tribuna da História, 2003)

Venter, Al J., *Portugal's Guerrilla War: The Campaign for Africa.* (Cape Town: John Malherbe Pty Ltd., 1973)

Venter, Al J., *The Chopper Boys: Helicopter Warfare in Africa* (London: Greenhill Books, 1994)

Journals

Abecasis, José Duarte Krus, 'Dois Relatos de Guerra – Guiné Portuguesa' in *Revista Militar 70*, no.2483 (December 2008)

Arbuckle, Thomas, 'Rhodesian Bush War Strategies and Tactics: An Assessment,' *RUSI Journal* 124, no.4 (1979)

Borges, João Jorge Botelho Vieira, 'A Academia Militar e a Guerra de África: A formação dos quadros 1960 1974' in *Revista Militar* no.2493 (October 2009).

Cabral, Amílcar, 'Guinea: The Power of Arms' in *Tricontinental*, May-June 1969. In Joint Publications Research Service, 'Translations on Africa no. 823,' JPRS 48980, 6 October 1969.

Cabral, Amílcar, 'A Brief Report on the Situation of the Struggle (January-August 1971)' *Ufahamu: A Journal of African Studies* 2, no.3 (1972)

Cabral, Amílcar, 'A Report to Our Friends' in *Africa Today* 20, no.1 (Winter 1973).

Cabral, Luís, 'Portuguese Guinea Called United Front Against Imperialism' *Tricontinental* 15 (November-December 1969). In Joint Publications Research Service, 'Translations on Africa no.867', JPRS 49903, 20 February 1970

Cann, John P., 'Lessons in Airpower Projection: Indochina and Algeria' in *Small Wars & Insurgencies* 24, no.1 (2013)

Cann, John P., 'The Imperial Airline' in *Revista Militar* nos 2521/2522 (February-March 2012).

Cardina, Miguel and Susana Martins, 'Evading the War: Deserters and Draft Evaders from the Portuguese Army during the Colonial War' in *E-Journal of Portuguese History 17, no.1 (June 2019).*

Comissão da História das Transmissões, 'As Transmissões Miliares na Guerra Colonial' in *Revista Militar* 49, nos 2513/2514 (June-July 2011).

Correia, José Manuel, "Rotina' de Guerra: Os F-86F Sabre' na Guiné, 2a Parte'in *Mais Alto* 43, no. 358 (November-December 2005)

Correia, José Manuel, 'Os Fiat G.91 ao Ataque na Guiné: Operação Barracuda' in *Mais Alto* 45, no.367 (May-June 2007)

Correia, José Manuel, 'Fiat G.91 na Guiné 1966–68: Os dois primeiros anos de combate, 1a Parte.' *Mais Alto* 50, no. 398 (July-August 2012)

Correia, José Manuel, 'Fiat G.91 na Guiné 1966–68: Os dois primeiros anos de combate, 2a Parte' in *Mais Alto* 50, no.399 (September-October 2012)

Costa, António José Pereira da, 'Testemunho do Coronel Art Pereira da Costa' in *Boletim da Artilharia Antiaérea* II, no.3 (October 2003)

Cruz, Alfredo. 'Os 50 anos do Alouette III na Força Aérea Portuguesa: Uma perspectiva histórica,' in *Mais Alto* 51, no.404 (July-August 2013)

Dhada, Mustafa, 'The Liberation War in Guinea-Bissau Reconsidered' in *The Journal of Military History* 62, no.3 (July 1998).

Dhada, Mustafah, 'Guinea-Bissau's Diplomacy and Liberation Struggle' in *Portuguese Studies Review* IV, no.1 (Spring-Summer 1995)

Dias, João Paulo Véstia, 'A Evolução dos Materiais de Artilharia Antiaérea em Portugal: da Génese à Actualidade' in *Revista de Artilharia* nos 1016–1018 (April-June 2010)

Diniz, Mário and Luís Proença, 'P2V-5 Neptune No. 4711: Muito Mais do que um Avião de Luta Anti-Submarina, 2a Parte' in *Mais Alto* 50, no.398 (July-August 2012).

Diniz, Mário and Luís Proença, 'AL III: História Breve de uma Vida Longa, 1963–2013' in *Mais Alto* 51, no.404 (July-August 2013).

Diogo Neto, Manuel, '*Operação Vulcano*: Cassebeche, 7 de Março de 1969' in *Mais Alto* 27, no.257 (January-February 1989)

Diogo Neto, Manuel, 'A Força Aérea em África (1961/1974)' in *Mais Alto* 32, no.228 (March-April 1994)

Dunnell, Ben and José Matos, 'Meteor Down' in *Aeroplane* 48, no.11 (November 2020)

Felgas, Hélio, 'A luta na Guiné' in *Revista Militar* 22, no.4 (April 1970)

Fernandes, Gil and John Marcum, 'The Azores over Africa' in *Africa Today* 19, no.1 (Winter 1972)

Ferreira, Eduardo de Sousa, 'Amílcar Cabral: Theory of Revolution and Background to His Assassination' in *Ufahamu: A Journal of African Studies* 3, no.3 (1973)

Ferreira, Rui Alberto Fidalgo, 'Uma Perspectiva da Logística da Força Aérea Durante as Operações em África Entre 1961 e 1974' in *Revista Militar* 62, no.12 (December 2010)

'Fiat G.91: First-Generation NATO Strike Fighter' in Flight, 23 May 1958

Gleijeses, Piero, 'Cuba's First Venture in Africa: Algeria, 1961–1965' in *Journal of Latin American Studies* 28, no.1 (February 1996)

Henriksen, Thomas H, 'Portugal's Changing Fortunes in Africa' in *Current History* 64, no.379 (March 1973)

Henriksen, Thomas H., 'Some Notes on the National Liberation Wars in Angola, Mozambique, and Guinea-Bissau' in *Military Affairs* 41, no.1 (February 1977)

Lopes, Mario Canongia, 'Portugal's Ginas' in *Air Enthusiast* 36 (May-August 1988)

Lousada, Abílio Pires, Luís Falcão Escorrega, and António Cordeiro Menezes. 'Fernando Cavaliero e a Operação Tridente' in *Jornal do Exército* 52, no.602 (January 2011)

MacQueen, Norrie, 'Portugal's First Domino: 'Pluricontinentalism' and Colonial War in Guiné-Bissau, 1963–1974' in *Contemporary European History* 8, no.2 (July 1999)

Martins, Arménio Duarte, 'Cotovia E Falcão' in *Mais Alto* 36, no.311 (February-March 1998)

Matos, José. 'A Guerra das Antiaéreas na Guiné (1965/1970)' in *Revista Militar* no.2601 (October 2018)

Matos, José, 'A História Secreta dos Mirage Portugueses, 1a Parte' in *Mais Alto* 50, no.400 (November-December 2012)

Matos, José, 'A História Secreta dos Mirage Portugueses, 2a Parte' in *Mais Alto* 51, no.401 (January-February 2013)

Matos, José, 'A saga do Sabre 6' in *Mais Alto* 49, no.394 (November/ December 2011) and no.395 (January/February 2012)

Matos, José, 'Into Africa' in *Aeroplane* 48, no.11 (November 2020)

Matos, José, 'O Projecto Feierabend e a compra do Fiat G.91, 1a Parte' in *Mais Alto* 50, no.397 (May-June 2012)

Matos, José, 'O projecto Feierabend e a Compra do Fiat G.91, 2a Parte' in *Mais Alto* 50, no.398 (July-August 2012)

Matos, José, 'O Caso dos Bombardeiros Canberra e as relações luso-britâncias Durante a Guerra Colonial' in *Revista Militar* 80, nos 2597–2598 (June-July 2018)

Mimoso e Carvalho, António. 'O Fiat G91: Contributo Para a Defesa da África e Resposta à Guerra Fria, 1965–1993' in *Mais Alto* 53, no.418 (November-December 2015)

Mira, José Cardoso, 'Sidewinder: 50 Anos de Operação de Mísseis na Força Aérea Portuguesa' in *Mais Alto* 51, no. 403 (May-June 2013)

Miranda, José M. Brochado de, 'El Empleodel Arma aérea en la Lucha Antiguerrilla' in *Revista de Aeronautica y Astronauticano.* 715 (July-August 2002)

Monteiro, Rui Tavares, 'Recordando os Noratlas' in *Mais Alto* 30, no.279 (September-October 1992)

Moore, Zelbert, 'Cuba in Africa 1960–1985' in *Afro-Hispanic Review* 5, nos 1–3 (January, May, and September 1986)

Munkelt, José, '707: Ordem para voar, II – preparação, formação e operação' in *Mais Alto* 47, no.379 (May-June 2009)

Nico, José Francisco, 'Pedaços das nossas vidas I – Intercepçao de um helicóptero em 10 de Setembro de 1967' in *Mais Alto* 44, no.359 (January/February 2006)

Nico, José Francisco, 'Pedaços das nossas vidas III – O rosto do Inimigo' in *Mais Alto* 44, no.363 (September-October 2006).

'O Aeroporto military de Bissau foi atacado pelas Nossas Forças' in *PAIGC Libertaçã*ono 87 (February 1968)

Omaka, Arua Oko, 'Through the Imperial Lens: The Role of Portugal in the Nigeria-Biafra War' in *Journal of Global South Studies* 36, no.1 (Spring 2019).

Partido Africano da Independência da Guiné e Cabo Verde, 'As Operações Militares no Decurso do mês de Novembro' in *PAIGC Libertaçã*ono. 72 (November 1966).

Rudebeck, Lars, 'Political Mobilisation for Development in Guinea-Bissau' in *Journal of Modern African Studies* 10, no.1 (May 1972)

Seibert, Gerhard, 'São Tomé and the Biafran War (1967–1970)' in *The International Journal of African Historical Studies* 51, no.2 (October 2018)

Spencer, David E.and Miguel Machado, 'The Unknown War: Portuguese Paratroops in Africa, 1961–74' in *Military Illustrated Past & Present* no.47 (April 1992)

Stone, Glyn, 'Britain and Portuguese Africa, 1961–1965' in *Journal of Imperial and Commonwealth History* 28, no.3 (2000)

Unknown, 'Guinea to Declare Independence' in *Pakistan Forum* 3, no.4 (January 1973)

Unknown, 'Mobile and Agile: The Fiat G.91 – West Germany's and NATO's Choice' in Flight, 3 April 1959

Unknown, 'The Biafran Airlift' in *Flight International*, 21 March 1968.

Unknown, 'Tropas Pára-quedistas Portuguesas' in *Boina Verde* no.158 (July-September 1991)

Valdés, Jorge Risquet, 'The Deep Roots of Cuba's Internationalism' in *Tricontinental* 38 (May 2005)

Venter, Al J., 'Portugal's Forgotten War' in *Air Enthusiast* 2, no.2 (February 1972)

Venter, Al J., 'Portugal's War in Guiné-Bissau' in *Munger Africana Library Notes* 19 (April 1973)

'World's Air Forces: Guinea-Republic' in *Flight International* 124, no.3874 (6 August 1983)

Newspapers, newsletters, and wire services

'Africans Report Forcing Withdrawal of Portuguese' in *The New York Times*, 21 April 1964

'Avião Militar Incendiado na Guiné' in *Diário de Lisboa*, 1 August 1964

Castanheira, José Pedro, 'A Mais Espetacular Ação de Sabotagem dos Tempos da Ditadura' in *Expresso*, 16 April 2016

'Chinese to Help Build Mali-to-Guinea Railroad' in *The New York Times*, 30 May 1968

'Desertion Grows in Portugal' in *The Observer*, 15 February 1970

Faria, Dutra, 'Governor Tells of Independence Party Activity' in *ABC-Diario de Angola*, 7 December 1969. In Joint Publications Research Service, 'Translations on Africa no.867,' JPRS 49903 (20 February 1970)

'Fight for Life in Guinea-Bissao' in *France Nouvelle*, 19 November 1969. In Joint Publications Research Service, 'Translations on Africa no.860,' JPRS 49761 (5 February 1970)

'Fighting in Guinea Spurs African Unity' in *The New York Times*, 28 November 1970

'Guinea Again Asks Arms to Fight Foe: Touré Appeals for Planes – U.N. Mission Arrives' in *The New York Times*, 26 November 1970

'Guinea Seeks Planes to Fight Raiders' in *The Times*, 26 November 1970

Machado, Pedro., 'Liberation Movement Discussed by Guerrilla Leader' in *Etumba* (Brazzaville), 11 September 1971. In Joint Publications Research Service, 'Translations on Africa no.1081,' JPRS 54466 (11 November 1971)

Marques, José Carlos., 'O Abraço dos Antigos Inimigos' in *Correio de Manhã*, 8 March 2008

Mota, Santana., 'Governor Says Conditions Exist for Success of Portuguese Cause' in *Voz da Guiné*, 28 July 1973. In Joint Publications Research Service, 'Translations on Africa no.1375,' JPRS 60168 (1 October 1973)

Nico, José Francisco., 'Pedaços das nossas vidas VI – Um ataque com 'olhos azuls'' in *ABC Portugais-Français* 2, no.37 (29 August 2015).

'Portugal Censured in U.N. over Senegal' in *The New York Times*, 10 December 1969

'Portugal Increases Budget 10 Per Cent; Criticism by Economists' in *The New York Times*, 28 December 1967

Presidência da República, 'Decreto no.48 597' in *Diário do Governo*, I série, no.229 (27 September 1968)

Presidência do Conselho e Ministério do Ultramar., 'Portaria no.22 260' in *Diário do Governo*, I série, no.244 (20 October 1966)

Secretaria de Estado da Aeronáutica, 'Portaria no.21 259'in *Diário do Governo*, I série, no.96 (1 May 1965)

'Sidewinder Upsets Peiping' in *The New York Times*, 1 October 1958

Szulc, Tad, 'Craft from Lisbon Fly Men and Arms to African Rebels' in *The New York Times*, 5 November 1967

Davidson, Basil., 'Unknown War in Portuguese West Africa' in *The Times*, 10 November 1967.

'Token Force En Route' in *The New York Times*, 28 November 1970

Studies, Reports, and Manuals

'Alouette III – équipements facultatifs' Paris: Sud Aviation, March 1961

Branquinho, Luís Filipe Ricardo, 'Características de actuação das tropas pára-quedistas nas guerras de África (1961–1974)' Lisbon: Academia Militar, August 2011

Cagle, Mary T., *History of the Redeye Weapons System*. Redstone Arsenal, AL: U.S. Army Missile Command Historical Division, May 1974

Davis, Morris, et al., 'Factors Affecting the Role and Employment of Peacekeeping Forces in Africa South of the Sahara' Contract no. MDA908-82-C-0174. Urbana: University of Illinois, 1982.

Durch, William J., 'The Cuban Military in Africa and the Middle East: From Algeria to Angola' Professional Paperno 201. Arlington, VA: Center for Naval Analysis, September 1977

Freire, João Sérgio, 'Portugal na Guerra do Biafra: a Diplomacia do Estado Novo em África, 1967–69' Graduate thesis, Lisbon: Universidade Autónoma de Lisboa, 2016

'French SA-316B Alouette III' Aberdeen Proving Ground, MD: U.S. Army Intelligence and Security Command, Foreign Material Intelligence Battalion, July 1990

'G91-R4 Flight Manual' T.O. NATO 1RF-G91-R4-1NATO 1. Turin, Italy: Fiat Aviazione, 20 May 1961

'Identification Guide, Part One: Weapons and Equipment, East European Communist Armies, Volume II – Artillery' Pamphlet No.30-60-1. Vaihingen-Stuttgart, Germany: HQ U.S. Army Europe and Seventh Army, 15 January 1973

O Exército na guerra subversiva. Lisbon: Estado-Maior do Exército, 1963. (Translated by Department of the Army/Assistant Chief of Staff for Intelligence, Translation no.I-5216, August 1964)

'Standard Aircraft Characteristics: F-86F -25 thru -40 Sabre.' Los Angeles: U.S. Air Force and North American Aviation, 1 October 1956

'Survivability Guide for U.S. Army Aircraft, Volume I – Small Arms Ballistic Protection,' Technical Report 71-41A. Ft Eustis, VA: U.S. Army Air Mobility Research and Development Laboratory, November 1971

Worldwide Equipment Guide, Volume 2: Airspace and Air Defense Systems. Ft Leavenworth, KS: U.S. Army Training and Doctrine Command G-2, December 2011

Communications with the Authors

Fernando de Jesus Vasquez to José Matos, email, 31 July 2011

Oliveira Couto to José Matos, email, 2013

José Francisco Nico to José Matos, email, 6 March 2013

Egídio Lopes to Matthew M. Hurley and José Matos, email, 22 July 2013

Websites

Aviation Safety Network, aviation-safety.net

Luís Graça e Camaradas da Guiné, blogueforanadaevaotres.blogspot.com

Stockholm International Peace Research Institute (SIPRI), sipri.org

NOTES

Military Ranks and Positions

1 Military Agency for Standardisation, STANAG 2116, MIS (Edition 5) – NATO Codes for Grades of Military Personnel (Brussels: North Atlantic Treaty Organisation, 1996), passim.; Força Aérea Portuguesa, 'Postos e Distintivos,' 2022, www.emfa.pt/p-201-postos-e-distintivos.

Chapter 1

1 José Krus Abecasis, *Bordo de Ataque: Memórias de Uma Caderneta de Voo e um Vontributo Para a História,* volume II (Coimbra: Coimbra Editora, 1985), p. 459.

2 Cf Matthew M. Hurley and José Matos, *Sanctuary Lost: The Air War for Portuguese Guinea, Vol. I – Outbreak and Escalation (1961–1966)* (Warwick: Helion & Company, 2022), passim.

3 Estado Maior do Exército, Gabinete do Chefe, 'Relatório da missão chefiada pelo Chefe do Estado Maior do Exército à Guiné, Abril 1966,' 13 July 1966, FO/007/B/16 (Cx. 289/5), Arquivo Histórico Militar, Lisbon (hereafter AHM).

4 Formally the *Comando-Chefe das Forças Armadas da Guiné* (Commander-in-Chief of the Armed Forces of Guinea, or CCFAG).

5 Alternatively spelled Schulz. Confusingly, both spellings are used in Portuguese media and official publications.

6 Comando-Chefe das Forças Armadas da Guiné, 'Relatório da Situação,'July 1966, SGDN/1REP/092/0309/013, Arquivo da Defesa Nacional, Paço de Arcos, Portugal (hereafter ADN).

7 Comando Territorial Independente da Guiné (CTIG), 2a Repartição (2REP), 'SUPINTREP No. 12: O Inimigo em 1966,' April 1967, SGDN/2REP/088/0363/009, ADN.

8 Oscar Oramas, *Amílcar Cabral: para além do seu tempo* (Lisbon: Hugin, 1998), p. 71.

9 So designated following 1951 amendments to the Portuguese Constitution, superseding the former label 'colonies.' 'Lei no. 2045,' Titulo VII, *Diário do Governo I Série*, no. 117 (11 June 1951), p. 409.

10 Lloyd Garrison, 'Battle Widening in Lisbon Enclave,' *The New York Times*, 8 September 1963, p. 21; Tony Hodges, 'Five Years of Independence,' *Africa Report* 24, no.1 (January-February 1979), p. 4.

11 Manuel Nicolau de Abreu Castelo Branco, letter, to Governador da Guiné, 1966, SGDN/2REP/0411/008, ADN.The 'Overseas (or *Ultramar*) War' was the collective term used by Portuguese to identify the simultaneous conflicts raging in Portuguese Guinea (1963–74), Angola (1961–75), and Mozambique (1964–75).

12 Comissão para o Estudo das Campanhas de África (CECA), *Resenha Histórico-Militar das Campanhas de África (1961–1974), 1 Volume: Enquadramento Geral* (Lisbon: Estado-Maior do Exército, 1988), pp. 260–261.

13 *Secratario-Geral da Defesa Nacional*, or SGDN.

14 Secretário Adjunto da Defesa Nacional (SADN), 'Defesa da Guiné,' 8 October 1966, SGDN/1REP/092/0309/013, ADN.

15 Brigadier Fernando Louro de Sousa, 'Exposição pelo Comandante-Chefe das Forças Armadas da Guiné no Conselho Superior Militar,' September 1963, SGDN/1REP/092/0306/004, ADN; Luís Alves de Fraga, *A Força Aérea na Guerra em África: Angola, Guiné e Moçambique 1961–1975* (Lisbon: Prefácio, 2004), p. 121.

16 Comando da Zona Aérea de Cabo Verde e Guiné (CZACVG), 'Memorial para S. Exª O Governador,' 14 July 1966, SGDN/1REP/092/0309/013, ADN.

17 Secretariado-Geral da Defesa Nacional (SGDN), 'Necessidades da FAP na Guiné – pedido de meios de reforço,' Informação No. 88/62, 17 March 1965, SGDN/1REP/105/0345/002, ADN; CZACVG,'Memorial para S. Exa.O Governador,' 14 July 1966, SGDN/1REP/092/0309/013, ADN; SADN, 'Deficiências e necessidades da zona aérea de Cabo Verde e Guiné,' 31 March 1967, SGDN/1REP/092/0309/015, ADN.

18 The FAP received only 43 percent of required maintenance funding for 1966, a figure that improved to only 47 percent the following year; fiscal outlays for the purchase of spare parts represented only 42 percent and 67 percent of need during those two years, respectively.

19 José Francisco Nico, *A batalha do Quitafine: A contraguerrilha antiaérea na Guiné e a fantasia das 'areas libertadas'* (Lisbon: edição do autor, 2020), pp. 124, 126; Secretário de Estado da Aeronáutica (SEA), letter, to Ministro da Defesa Nacional (MDN), 26 December 1968, GABMIN/007/0035/050, ADN.

20 SEA letter to MDN, 26 December 1968, GABMIN/007/0035/050, ADN.

21 Secretaria de Estado da Aeronáutica, 'Portaria No. 21 259,'*Diário do Governo, I Série*, no. 96 (1 May 1965), p. 619.

22 CZACVG, 'Deficiências e necessidades mais graves e urgentes da Zona Aérea de Cabo Verde e Guiné,' 17 February 1967;SADN, 'Deficiências e necessidades da zona aérea de Cabo Verde e Guiné,' 31 March 1967; and SGDN, 1a Repartição (1REP), 'Verbete do Chefe da 1a Repartição do SGDN para Chefe do Gabinete do MDN,' 31 March 1967, SGDN/1REP/092/0309/015, ADN.

23 António José Pereira da Costa, 'Testemunho do Coronel Art Pereira da Costa,'*Boletim da Artilharia Antiaérea* II, no. 3 (October 2003), p. 108.

24 'Missão do CEM do Comando da 1a RA à Zona Aérea de Cabo Verde e Guiné entre 5 e 23 Agosto 1963: Relatório,' 1963, SGDN/1REP/077/0270/002, ADN; 'Exposição pelo Comandante-Chefe das Forças Armadas da Guiné no Conselho Superior Militar,' September 1963, SGDN/1REP/092/0306/004, ADN; CZCVAG, 'Necessidades em pilotos da B.A.12,' 31 March 1967, SGDN/1REP/092/0309/015, ADN.

25 SADN, 'Pilotos para a Provincia da Guiné,' 31 March 1967, SGDN/1REP/092/0309/015, ADN.

26 SGDN, Informação No. 88/62, 'Necessidades da FAP na Guiné – pedido de meios de reforço,' 17 March 1965, SGDN/1REP/105/0345/002, ADN; Mário Canongia Lopes and José Manuel Rodrigues Costa, *Os Aviões da Cruz de Cristo: 75 Anos da Aviação Militar em Portugal* (Lisbon: Dinalivro, 1989), p. 171; Aniceto Afonso and Carlos de Matos Gomes, *Os anos da Guerra Colonial, 1961.1975* (Matosinhos, Portugal: QuidNovi, 2010), pp. 323 & 325.

27 Sérgio Augusto Margarido Lima Bacelar, *A Guerra em África, 1961–1974: Estratégias Adoptadas pelas Forças Armadas* (Porto: Ligo dos Amigos do Museu Militar do Porto, 2000), p. 53; SADN, 'Defesa da Guiné,' 8 October 1966, SGDN/1REP/092/0309/013, ADN; 'Relatório da Visita à Guiné: 11.5.63/18.5.63,' 1963, SGDN/1REP/061/0231/063, ADN; CECA, *Resenha Histórico-Militar das Campanhas de África (1961–1974), 14 Volume – Comandos* (Lisbon: Estado-Maior do Exército, 2009), p. 440. In terms of land area, Portuguese Guinea was slightly larger than Belgium, and only three percent of Angola's territory.

28 Abecasis, *Bordo de ataque*, Vol. II, p. 466.

29 CTIG, 'Relatório de Posse do Comando do CTIG de 31 de Outubro de 1966,' in CECA, *Resenha Histórico-Militar das Campanhas de África (1961–1974), 6 Volume, Aspectos da Actividade Operational, Tomo II – Guiné, Livro I* (Lisbon: Estado-Maior do Exército, 2014), pp. 484–485.

30 Estado Maior do Exército, 13 July 1966, FO/007/B/16 (Cx. 289/5), AHM. By 1964, however, the FAP had already begun operating the Noratlas in Angola; see Rui Tavares Monteiro, 'Recordandoos Noratlas,' *Mais Alto* 30, no.279 (September-October 1992), p. 12.

31 Abecasis, *Bordo de Ataque*, volume II, p. 472.

32 SADN, 'Deficiências e necessidades da zona aérea de Cabo Verde e Guiné,' 31 March 1967, SGDN/1REP/092/0309/015, ADN.

33 Mario Canongia Lopes, 'Portugal's Ginas,' *Air Enthusiast* 36 (May-August 1988), p. 66.

34 At the time, the UK maintained its own arms embargo against Portugal over the latter's African wars. Despite the embargo, London had shown some willingness to sell the bombers if they were explicitly barred from African service. Portugal eventually gave up on the deal because of these restrictions as well as issues of cost. Glyn Stone, 'Britain and Portuguese Africa, 1961–1965' in *The Journal of Imperial and Commonwealth History* 28, no.3 (2000), pp. 180–184; José Matos, 'O caso dos bombardeiros

Canberra e as relações luso-britâncias durante a guerra colonial' in *Revista Militar* 80, nos. 2597–2598 (June-July 2018), pp. 583–593.

35 U.S. Mission to the U.N. (USUN), telegram, to U.S. Secretary of State, 'U.S. Supplied Arms in Portuguese Territories,' 1 August 1963, John F. Kennedy National Security Files 1961–1963: Western Europe, Box 154, John F. Kennedy Presidential Museum and Library, Boston, MA.

36 Lopes and Costa, pp. 111–112.

37 Fraga, p. 83; COMZAVERDEGUINÉ, SITREPs circunstanciados nos. 10/71 through 25/71, 10 March to 26 June 1971, SGDN/2REP/096, ADN.

38 Abecasis, *Bordo de ataque*, Vol. II, . 456.

39 Richard P. Hallion, ed., *Silver Wings, Golden Valor: The USAF Remembers Korea* (Washington, DC: Air Force History and Museums Program, 2006), p. 75.

40 CCFAG letter to SGDN, 4 July 1964, GABMIN/007/0031/021, ADN.

41 SADN, 'Deficiências e necessidades da zona aérea de Cabo Verde e Guiné,' 31 March 1967, SGDN/1REP/092/0309/015, ADN; Estado Maior do Exército, Gabinete do Chefe, memorandum, 13 July 1966, FO/007/B/16 (Cx. 289/5), AHM.

42 SADN, 'Defesa da Guiné,' 8 October 1966, SGDN/1REP/092/0309/013, ADN.

43 Minister of Defence (Canada), letter, to Minister of National Defence (Portugal), 9 August 1965, GABMIN/007/0031/021, ADN.

44 At the time, Portugal repeatedly proclaimed that its overseas possessions were integral components of the Portuguese state, not mere colonies or territories, and they consistently claimed that the insurgencies in Africa resulted from 'foreign aggression'. Consequently, the assurance to restrict the aircrafts' use to the defence of Portugal was ambiguous at best.

45 Minister of National Defence (Portugal), letter, to Minister of National Defence (Canada), 3 September 1965, GABMIN/007/0031/021, ADN; António Mimoso e Carvalho, 'O Fiat G91: Contributo para a defesa da África e resposta à Guerra Fria, 1965–1993,' *Mais Alto* 53, no. 418 (November-December 2015), p. 8; José Matos, 'A saga do Sabre 6,' *Mais Alto* no. 394 and 395 (November/December 2011 and January/February 2012), passim.

46 SGDN, 'Necessidades da FAP na Guiné – pedido de meios de reforço,' Informação no. 88/62, 17 March 1965, SGDN/1REP/105/0345/002, ADN.

47 Hurley and Matos, p. 51.

48 Ana Mónica Fonseca, *A Força das Armas: Apoio da República Federal da Alemanha ao Estado Novo (1958–1968)* (Lisbon: Ministério dos Negócios Estrangeiros, 2007), pp. 161–169; José Matos, 'O projecto Feierabend e a compra do Fiat G.91, 1a parte,' *Mais Alto 50*, no. 397 (May-June 2012), pp. 37-40. Dornier Flugzeugwerke, which designed and built the Do-27, also manufactured the G.91 as part of a production sharing arrangement with Fiat Aviazione.

49 José Manuel Correia, 'Fiat G.91 na Guiné 1966–68: Os dois primeiros anos de combate, 1a Parte,' *Mais Alto* 50, no. 398 (July-August 2012), p. 32; Mimoso e Carvalho, p. 8. Portugal bought the 40 aircraft for DM 17.5 million, or approximately $110,000 each in 1966 US dollars (roughly $1,030,000 per aircraft in 2023 dollars).

50 EMFA, 3a Repartição (3REP), 'Relatório da missão à Alemanha relativa ao projecto Feierbend,' 11 March 1966, CMLA/025/0057/019, ADN; José Cabeleira, *Trajecto de uma Vida entre o Mar e o Ar* (Edição de autor, 2004), p. 251.

51 Abecasis, *Bordo de ataque*, Vol. II, p. 524.

52 FAP registration numbers for the second quartet of ZACVG assigned G.91s were 5403, 5407, 5417, and 5418. CZACVG, 'Actividade Operacional dos G-91,' 25 March 1967, Guiné 1964–1974/FiatCollection, Processo 430.121, Arquivo Histórico da Força Aérea, Alfragide, Portugal (hereafter 'AHFA'); Correia, 'Fiat G.91 na Guiné 1966–68, 1a Parte,' pp. 33–34.

53 Fiat Aviazione, 'G91-R4 Flight Manual,' T.O. NATO 1RF-G91-R4-1NATO 1, 20 May 1961, p. 1–1; Giorgio Apostolo, *The Fiat G.91* (London: Profile Publications no.119, 1966), pp. 2–4; 'Fiat G.91: First-Generation NATO Strike Fighter' in *Flight*, 23 May 1958, p. 696; 'Mobile and Agile: The Fiat G.91 – West Germany's and NATO's Choice' in *Flight*, 3 April 1959, p. 462.

54 Correia, 'Fiat G.91 na Guiné 1966–68, 1a Parte,' p. 31.

55 *Jane's All the World's Aircraft 1965–1966* (London: Jane's Publishing, 1965), p. 93; *Jane's Aero-Engines* (Coulsdon: Jane's Information Group, 1996), pp. 330–331; Manuel Diogo Neto, 'A Força Aérea em África (1961/1974)' in *Mais Alto* no. 228 (March-April 1994), p. 12.

56 Fraga, p. 117. For more general descriptions of the psychological effects of air power, see Irving L. Janis, *Air War and Emotional Stress: Psychological Studies of Bombing and Civilian Defense* (New York: McGraw-Hill, 1951).

57 Fraga, p. 115.

58 Fraga, pp. 115–116.

59 EMFA/3REP, 'Relatório da missão à Alemanha relativa ao projecto Feierbend,' 11 March 1966, CMLA/025/0057/019, ADN; SGDN/1REP, 'Planeamento de Operação do Fiat G-91,' 20 November 1967, SGDN/1REP/105/0345/003, ADN.

60 Diogo Neto, 'A Força Aérea em África,'p. 12; Correia, 'Fiat G.91 na Guiné 1966–68, 1a Parte,'p. 31.

61 Manuel Diogo Neto, 'Voo em Três Frentes,' in *A Guerra de África (1961–1974), Vol. I*, ed. José Freire Antunes (Lisbon: Temas e Debates, 1996), pp. 311–312. The FAP did in fact receive and operate 30mm-equipped G.91-R3s, but only beginning in 1976, two years after the end of the war in Portuguese Guinea; the last were retired in 1993.

62 Delegação Portuguesa à Comissão Mista Luso-Alemã (CMLA) to MDN, 'Contrato de compra de 40 aviões G-91,' 29 June 1966, CMLA/025/0057/019, ADN.

63 Mimoso e Carvalho, p. 9.

64 Ministério da Defesa Nacional, 'Projecto Feierabend,' 4 June 1966, CMLA/025/0057/019, ADN; Delegação Portuguesa à CMLA to Minister of Defence, 'Contrato de compra de 40 aviões G-91,' 29 June 1966, CMLA/025/0057/019, ADN; José Matos, 'O Projecto Feierabend e a compra do Fiat G.91, 2a Parte'in *Mais Alto* 50, no. 398 (July-August 2012), p. 28.

65 CZACVG, 'Actividade Operacional dos G-91,' 25 March 1967, Guiné 1964–1974/FiatCollection, Processo 430.121, AHFA.

66 Ofício da Direcção do Serviço de Material da Força Aérea to Presidente da Delegação Portuguesa à CMLA, 'Turboreactores 'Orpheus' 803D11,' 19 March 1966, CMLA/025/0058/025, ADN; Mimoso e Carvalho, p. 9; José Manuel Correia, 'Os Fiat G.91 ao Ataque na Guiné: Operação Barracuda' in *Mais Alto* 45, no.367 (May-June 2007), p. 23.

67 CZACVG, 'Actividade Operacional dos G-91,' 25 March 1967, Guiné 1964–1974/Fiat Collection, Processo 430.121, AHFA; Mimoso e Carvalho, p. 9; Correia, 'Os Fiat G.91 ao Ataque na Guiné: Operação Barracuda,' p. 23.

68 FAP studies forecast an average 2,000lbs of JP-4 required for each G.91 sortie, while braking chutes were necessary for landing on surfaces shorter than 2,000 feet. EMFA/3REP, 'Relatório da missão à Alemanha relativa ao projecto Feierbend,' 11 March 1966, CMLA/025/0057/019, ADN; SADN, 'Deficiências e necessidades da zona aérea de Cabo Verde e Guiné,' 31 March 1967, SGDN/1REP/092/0309/015, ADN; Correia, 'Os Fiat G.91 ao Ataque na Guiné: Operação Barracuda,' p. 23; Mimoso e Carvalho, p. 9.

69 Correia, 'Fiat G.91 na Guiné 1966–68, 1a Parte,'p. 34.

70 Lopes, pp. 66–67.

71 CZACVG, 'Actividade Operacional dos G-91,' 25 March 1967, Guiné 1964–1974/FiatCollection, Processo 430.121, AHFA.

72 Nico, *A Batalha do Quitafine*, pp. 151–152.

73 Correia, 'Fiat G.91 na Guiné 1966–68, 1a Parte,' p. 34.

74 José FranciscoNico, 'Pedaços das nossas vidas III – O rosto do Inimigo' in *Mais Alto* 44, no.363 (September-October 2006), pp. 22–23.

75 Ofício no. 2977/C/67 do CCFAG para o SGDN, 'PAIGC – Amílcar Cabral,' 19 October 1967, SGDN/1REP/092/0309/014, ADN.

76 The FAP registration numbers for the initial six helicopters were 9272, 9273, 9274, 9275, 9276 and 9277; FAP 9278, 9279 and 9280 arrived in the second shipment; see Mário Diniz and Luís Proença, 'AL III: História Breve de uma Vida Longa, 1963–2013' in *Mais Alto* 51, no.404 (July-August 2013), p. 21.

Some authors have mistakenly placed the first Alouette III arrivals (6) in Guinea in November 1966, with reinforcements (3) first provided in March 1967. However, contemporaneous Portuguese records clearly indicate this fleet of nine aircraft was at BA12-Bissalanca before October 1966. See SADN, 'Defesa da Guiné,' 8 October 1966, SGDN/1REP/092/0309/013, ADN.

77 Foreign Material Intelligence Battalion, 'French SA-316B Alouette III' (Aberdeen Proving Ground, MD: U.S. Army Intelligence and Security Command, July 1990), p. 38; John P. Cann, 'Lessons in Airpower Projection: Indochina and Algeria' in *Small Wars & Insurgencies* 24, no.1 (2013), pp. 124–125.

78 *Jane's All the World's Aircraft 1972–73* (London: Jane's Publishing, 1972), p. 43; Nico, *A Batalha do Quitafine*, p. 228.

79 Manuel Catarino, *As Grandes Operações da Guerra Colonial 1961–1974, II: Guiné –Operação Irã, Maio 1965; Operação Hermínia, Março 1966* (Lisbon: Cofina Media, 2010), pp. 24–25; Alfredo Cruz, 'Os 50 anos do Alouette III na Força Aérea Portuguesa: Uma perspectiva histórica' in *Mais Alto* no. 404 (July-August 2013), p. 11; Al J. Venter, *The Chopper Boys: Helicopter Warfare in Africa* (London: Greenhill Books, 1994), p. 97.

80 *Jane's All the World's Aircraft 1965–1966* (London: Jane's Publishing, 1965), p. 62.

81 *Jane's All the World's Aircraft 1972–73* (London: Jane's Publishing, 1972), p. 43.

82 *Jane's All the World's Aircraft 1965–1966* (London: Jane's Publishing, 1965), pp. 188–189.

83 The 'Guinea Independent Territorial Command,' the senior Portuguese Army echelon in Guinea.

84 Afonso and Gomes, *Os anos da Guerra Colonial*, pp. 323, 325.

85 CECA, *Resenha Histórico-Militar das Campanhas de África, 6 Volume, Tomo II - Guiné, Livro I* (hereafter 6-II-I), pp. 390, 393–394, 397.

86 Headquarters 1 Cavalry Division (Airmobile), 'Combat After-Action Report: Operation Masher 25 Jan–3 Feb 66, Operation White Wing 4 Feb–6 Mar 66,' 28 April 1966, pp. 13–14; Captain Charles S. Sykes Jr., *Interim Report of Operations of the 1st Cavalry Division (Airmobile) July 1, 1965, to December 311966* (Albuquerque, NM: 1 Cavalry Division Association, 1967), p. 31.

87 Literally 'hand strike' (i.e., a 'jab' or 'slap'), Portuguese military doctrine defines a *golpe de mão* as an 'attack intended to temporarily conquer an area in order to obtain information, confuse an opponent, capture personnel or equipment, or destroy a capability.' The activity closely corresponds to the definition of 'raid' in U.S. and NATO doctrine. For 'golpe de mão,' see *Glossário de termos militares* (Lisbon: Instituto Universitário Militar e Academia das Ciências de Lisboa, 2020), p. 151; for 'raid,' see Office of the Chairman of the Joint Chiefs of Staff, Joint Publication 3-0, *Joint Operations* (Washington, DC: The Joint Staff, amended 22 October 2018), p. xxi.

88 Rui Alberto Fidalgo Ferreira, 'Uma Perspectiva da Logística da Força Aérea Durante as Operações em África Entre 1961 e 1974' in *Revista Militar* 62, no.12 (December 2010), www.revistamilitar.pt/artigo/619.

89 Ministério do Exército, 'Relatório da Missão a Argélia, 10 de Março – 20 de Abril 1959,'1959, GABMIN/050/0235/007, ADN.

90 'Exposição feita pelo Comandante-Chefe das Forças Armadas na Guiné no CSM,' 4 September 1963, SGDN/1REP/092/0306/004, ADN; Luís Palma de Figueiredo, *História das Esquadras de Helicópteros da Força Aérea Portuguesa* (Porto: Fronteira do Caos, 2018), pp. 16–27, 49; Fraga, p. 105.

91 Fraga, p. 117.

92 António de Jesus Bispo, 'Aviação na Guiné – início das operações militares,' in *Olhares Sobre Guiné e Cabo Verde* (Linda-a-Velha and Porto, Portugal: DG Edições and Caminhos Romanos, 2012), p. 279.

93 Bispo, 'Aviação na Guiné – início das operações militares,' p. 279.

94 CECA, *Resenha Histórico-Militar das Campanhas de África, 6-II-I*, p. 397.

95 Arménio Duarte Martins, 'Cotovia E Falcão' in *Mais Alto* 36, no. 311 (February-March 1998), pp. 8–9; Diniz and Proença, 'AL III: História Breve de uma Vida Longa,'pp. 36–37.

96 Information related to José Matos by General Fernando de Jesus Vasquez, email, 31 July 2011.

97 'Alouette III – équipements facultatifs' (Paris: Sud Aviation, March 1961), p.c-5. French forces had earlier employed cannon-armed Sikorsky H-34 Choctaw helicopters, nicknamed 'Pirates,' in Algeria; see Stephen Rookes, 'Pirates, Mammoths, Flying Bananas, and Skylarks: Helicopter Envelopment Operations in the Small Wars of Algeria, Angola, and Rhodesia, 1954–1979' in *Nacelles* no.12 (Spring 2022), www.interfas.univ-tlse2.fr/nacelles/index.php?id=1681.

98 Diniz and Proença, 'AL III: História Breve de uma Vida Longa,' p. 21; Martins, 'Cotovia E Falcão,' pp. 8–9; Diogo Neto, 'A Força Aérea em África,' p. 13.

99 José M. Brochado de Miranda, 'El empleodel arma aérea en la lucha antiguerrilla' in *Revista de Aeronautica y Astronautica no.*715 (July-August 2002), p. 597.

100 Abecasis, *Bordo de Ataque*, vol. II, p. 513.

101 Cruz, 'Os 50 anos do Alouette III na Força Aérea Portuguesa,' p. 12.

102 COMZAVERDEGUINÉ, SITREP circunstanciados nos. 01/67 through 49/68, 10 May 1967 – 25 December 1968, SGDN/2REP/096, ADN.

103 Cruz, 'Os 50 anos do Alouette III na Força Aérea Portuguesa,' p. 12.

104 Secretaria de Estado da Aeronáutica, 'Portaria no. 21 259,' p. 619.

105 Comando da Zona Aérea de Cabo Verde e Guiné, Base Aérea no. 12, 'Organogramas,' October 1968, AHFA; Fraga. 'Tudo alcança' roughly translates to 'it reaches everything' in English.

106 Fraga, p. 116.

107 Presidência do Conselho e Ministério do Ultramar, 'Portaria no. 22 260,' *Diário do Governo, I Série*, no. 244 (20 October 1966), pp. 1723–1724; 'Tropas Pára-quedistas Portuguesas,' *Boina Verde* no. 158 (July-September 1991), p. 58; Luís Filipe Ricardo Branquinho, 'Características de actuação das tropas pára-quedistas nas guerras de África (1961–1974)' (Lisbon: Academia Militar, August 2011), pp. 28–29.

108 David E. Spencer and Miguel Machado, 'The Unknown War: Portuguese Paratroops in Africa, 1961–74' in *Military Illustrated Past & Present* no.47 (April 1992), p. 25.

109 José Duarte Krus Abecasis, 'Dois relatos de guerra – Guiné Portuguesa,' *Revista Militar* 70, no. 2483 (December 2008), https: //www.revistamilitar.pt/artigo/360.

110 Abecasis, *Bordo de Ataque*, vol. II, p. 445.

111 Secretaria de Estado da Aeronáutica, 'Portaria no.21 259,' p. 620.

112 Nico, *A Batalha do Quitafine*, p. 277fn.

113 Fraga, p. 107.

114 Nico, *A Batalha do Quitafine*, p. 277fn.

115 Serviço de Instrução da Força Aérea, 'Manual do Apoio Aéreo na Contra-Guerrilha,' 17 February 1972, 2a Região Aérea Manuais Collection, AHFA; Abecasis, *Bordo de ataque*, vol. II, p. 467 fn.

116 Comissão da História das Transmissões, 'As transmissões miliares na guerra colonial' in *Revista Militar* 73, nos. 2513/2514 (June-July 2011), www.revistamilitar.pt/revista/2513; Nico, *A Batalha do Quitafine*, p. 35n. While other types of radios were used, Portugal's primary surface force radios were the AN/PRC-10 and AVP-1, while FAP tactical aircraft generally carried the AN/ARC-44.

117 Coreia, 'Os Fiat G.91 ao ataque na Guiné: Operação Barracuda,' pp. 23–24.

118 António de Jesus Bispo, 'Doctrine, Capacities, Technology and Operation Environment on the Employment of the Air Power: The Case of Guerrilla Warfare,' in *Airpower in the 20th Century: Doctrines and Employment – National Experiences* (The Hague: International Commission of Military History, 2011), pp. 241–242.

Chapter 2

1 PAIGC (Amílcar Cabral), 'Mensagem a todos os responsáveis, militantes e combatentes de todos as frentes de lut do nosso grande Partido,' 2 January 1968, Pasta 09701.002.014, Fundação Mário Soares Arquivo e Biblioteca, Lisbon (hereafter FMS).

2 PAIGC, 'Esclarecimento para a reorganização do Partido, da população e das Forças Armadas, de acordo com as decisões do nosso I Congresso),' February 1964, Pasta 04340.003.007, FMS; Amílcar Cabral, *Unity and Struggle: Speeches and Writings* (New York: Monthly Review Press, 1979) p. 179.

3 Amílcar Cabral, 'Sobre o trabalho dos membros do Comando Geral das F.A.R.P. em cada Inter-região,' 9 May 1966, Pasta 10192.001.011, FMS; COMCHEFE Guiné, 'SUPINTREP no. 35 (evolução da actividade e da situação do IN no TO referente a 1970),' Anexo H, 20 April 1971, SGDN/2REP/088/0364/024, ADN.

4 'Relatório da missão chefiada pelo Chefe do Estado Maior do Exército à Guiné, 1966,' FO/007/B/16 – Cx. 289/5, AHM; CECA, *Resenha Histórico-Militar das Campanhas de África*, 6-II-I, pp. 297 & 362.

5 SGDN, 'Visita do Ministro da Defesa Nacional á Guiné: Memorando, Reunião no Comando-Chefe da Guiné,' 12 February 1967, SGDN/1REP/092/0309/015, ADN.

6 Amílcar Cabral, 'Directivas – Nov 65,'cited in CTIG/2REP, 'SUPINTREP no. 12: O Inimigo em 1966,' April 1967, SGDN/2REP/088/0363/009, ADN.

7 CTIG/2REP, 'SUPINTREP 16: Estudo do Inimigo,' 15 October 1968, SGDN/2REP/088/0363/012, ADN.

8 'Relatório da missão chefiada pelo Chefe do Estado Maior do Exército à Guiné, 1966,' FO/007/B/16 – Cx. 289/5, AHM; 'Exposição do Chefe de Divisão de Informações,' in SGDN, 'Reunião no Comando-Chefe da Guiné,' 12 February 1967, SGDN/1REP/092/0309/015, ADN; CECA, *Resenha Histórico-Militar das Campanhas de África*, 6-II-I, pp. 297 & 362.

9 SADN, 'Defesa da Guiné,' 8 October 1966, SGDN/1REP/092/0309/013, ADN.

10 'A nossa vida e a nossa luta,' *PAIGC Libertação* no. 67 (June 1966), pp. 5–6.

11 Estado Maior do Exército, Gabinete do Chefe, 13 July 1966, FO/007/B/43/368/2/relCEME, AHM. The following February, the CCFAG's military intelligence department further cautioned against 'The possibility of a sudden and massive attack on any of our border positions, given that it could take place in very short terms that would make it very difficult for the reserves to arrive in a timely manner and, if successful, would represent a severe blow to our prestige with the populations and for the morale of our troops.' See SGDN, 'Exposição do Chefe de Divisão de Informações,' 12 February 1967, SGDN/1REP/092/0309/015, ADN.

12 CTIG/2REP, 'SUPINTREP no. 12: O Inimigo em 1966,' SGDN/2REP/088/0363/009, ADN.

13 Sometimes called *regiões libertadas* (liberated regions) or *áreas libertadas* (liberated areas) in PAIGC and sympathetic publications.

14 Basil Davidson, *The Liberation of Guiné: Aspects of an African Revolution* (London: Penguin Books, 1969), p. 117. The Portuguese, on the other hand, characterised them as 'zones of the Province where the guerillas exercised pressure on certain small villages and scattered groups of people which, not having a permanent military and administrative presence, could not deny food and refuge to the guerillas without risking brutal reprisals. This kind of control is similar to that which hijackers on a plane exercise over its crew and passengers.' Ministério dos Negócios Estrangeiros, Direcção-Geral dos Negócios Políticos, memorandum to CEMGFA with attached report (untitled), 16 May 1973, SGDN/2REP/018/0062/009, ADN.

15 Chicago Committee for the Liberation of Angola, Mozambique and Guinea, *Sun of Our Freedom: The Independence of Guinea-Bissau* (Chicago: Salsedo Press, 1974), p. 10. Ultimately the PAIGC established a network of popularly elected *comités de tabanca* (village committees), *tribunais populares* (people's courts) and *armazens do povo* (people's stores) to facilitate the sale or barter of indigenous crops and goods; see Lars Rudebeck, 'Political Mobilisation for Development in Guinea-Bissau' in *The Journal of Modern African Studies* 10, no.1 (May 1972), pp. 4 & 9.

16 Amílcar Cabral, *Our People Are Our Mountains: Amílcar Cabral on the Guinean Revolution* (London: Committee for Freedom in Mozambique, Angola & Guiné, 1972), p. 7.

17 Thomas H. Henriksen, 'Some Notes on the National Liberation Wars in Angola, Mozambique, and Guinea-Bissau' in *Military Affairs* 41, no.1 (February 1977), p. 33.

18 Luís Nuno Rodrigues, *Spínola* (Lisbon: A Esfera dos Livros, 2010), p. 95.

19 Estado Maior do Exército, Gabinete do Chefe, 13 July 1966, FO/007/B/43/368/2/relCEME, AHM.

20 Davidson, *The Liberation of Guiné*, pp. 105–106.

21 Rodrigues, *Spínola*, p. 95. According to an analysis sympathetic to African liberation causes, continued FARP successes in the field had compelled the Portuguese to 'change their military tactics and take to the air in a desperate attempt to stave off defeat' by 1967. Jennifer Davis, *Triumph over Colonialism: The Republic of Guinea-Bissau* (New York: The Africa Fund, 1974), p. 8.

22 SGDN, 'Exposição do Chefe de Divisão de Informações,' 12 February 1967, SGDN/1REP/092/0309/015, ADN.

23 PAIGC (Amílcar Cabral), 'Sobre a situação da luta e as suas perspectivas,' November 1965, Pasta 04602.039, FMS.

24 During those two years the ZACVG reported a total of 262 surface-to-air fire (SAFIRE) incidents over Portuguese Guinea, 163 of them in *Sector Sul*. COMCHEFE Guiné, 'SUPINTREP no. 35,' Anexo H, SGDN/2REP/088/0364/024, ADN.

25 See Hurley and Matos, pp. 492–494.

26 We use the non-doctrinal term 'counter-air defence' instead of the better-known label 'Suppression of Enemy Air Defences,' or SEAD, because the latter is almost universally associated with air defence networks employing radar and missiles. The FAP's operations in Guinea were more akin to traditional 'flak-busting' missions of the Second World War or the Korean War.

27 Alternatively spelled 'Kitafine'.

28 António Martins Rodrigues, 'Aviação na Guiné – A Parte Final,' in *Olhares sobre Guiné e Cabo Verde* (Linda-a-Velha and Porto, Portugal: DG Edições and Caminhos Romanos, 2012), p. 287; CECA, *Resenha Histórico-Militar das Campanhas de África*, 6-II-I, pp. 423–424.

29 Abecasis, *Bordo de Ataque*, vol. II, pp. 555–556.

30 Abecasis, *Bordo de Ataque*, vol. II, pp. 555–556; Fraga, p. 110.

31 COMCHEFE Guiné, 'SUPINTREP no.35,' Anexo H, SGDN/2REP/088/0364/024, ADN.

32 PAIGC (Amílcar Cabral), 'Ordem de Missão,' 20 March 1967, Pasta 04606.045.105, MS; Relatório Tecnico de Informações do QG/CTIG/2REP, 'PERINTREP No.1,' January 1966, cited in Nico, *A Batalha do Quitafine*, pp. 73–74.

33 The PAIGC referred to its ZPU anti-aircraft weapons as 'Vladimir', after their Soviet designer S. V. Vladimirov.

34 The single-barrelled ZPU-1, for example, weighed over 400lb and required four to operate.

35 Nico, *A batalha do Quitafine*, p. 86.

36 'Identification Guide, Part One: Weapons and Equipment, East European Communist Armies, volume II – Artillery,' USAREUR PAM No. 30-60-1 (Headquarters U.S. Army Europe and Seventh Army, 15 January 1973), pp. 182, 186, 204; 'Survivability Guide for U.S. Army Aircraft, Volume I – Small Arms Ballistic Protection,' Technical Report 71-41A (Ft Eustis, VA: U.S. Army Air Mobility Research and Development Laboratory, November 1971), p. 346; *Jane's Land-Based Air Defence 1992–1993* (London: Jane's Information Group, 1992), passim; U.S. Army Training and Doctrine Command, *Worldwide Equipment Guide, volume 2: Airspace and Air Defense Systems* (Ft Leavenworth, KS: U.S. Army TRADOC G-2, December 2011), p. 6–45.

37 In bullfighting, an *estoque* is the matador's sword; more generally, estoc refers to any sharply pointed thrusting sword.

38 Abecasis, *Bordo de Ataque*, vol. II, pp. 556–557.

39 Fraga, p. 110; Lopes, p. 67; Abecasis, *Bordo de Ataque*, vol. II, p. 556.

40 Fraga, p. 110.

41 Abecasis, *Bordo de Ataque*, vol. II, p. 557.

42 Fraga, p. 110.

43 Abecasis, *Bordo de Ataque*, vol. II, p. 558.

44 Correia, 'Fiat G.91 na Guiné 1966–68, 1a Parte,' p. 34.

45 Fraga, pp. 110–111; Abecasis, *Bordo de Ataque*, vol. II, pp. 558–559; Lopes, p. 67. Another source maintains that FAP 5401 was forced to eject its wing pylons and external fuel due to a hung bomb; see Correia, 'Fiat G.91 na Guiné 1966–68, 1a Parte,' p. 34.

46 Abecasis, *Bordo de Ataque*, vol. II, pp. 560–562; Fraga, p. 111.

47 Abecasis, *Bordo de Ataque*, vol. II, p. 561.

48 Correia, 'Fiat G.91 na Guiné 1966–68, 1a Parte,' p. 35.

49 Abecasis, *Bordo de Ataque*, vol. II, p. 576.

50 CZACVG, 'Relatório da Operação Samurai,' 17 de Novembro de 1966, SGDN/1REP/105/0349/018, ADN.

51 The ZACVG commander dubbed the operation 'Samurai' to deliberately evoke the martial values of the traditional Japanese military nobility; as

Abecasis summarised it, 'A samurai does not surrender or retreat.' *Bordo de Ataque* vol. II, p. 578.

52 Fraga, pp. 113–114.

53 Lopes, p. 67; Abecasis, *Bordo de Ataque*, vol. II, p. 578.

54 Abecasis, *Bordo de Ataque* vol. II, pp. 578–579.

55 Abecasis, *Bordo de Ataque*, vol. II, pp. 581–583.

56 TEVS (*Transporte de Evacuação Sanitário*) in FAP nomenclature.

57 CZACVG, 'Relatório da Operação 'Samurai', realizada de 13 de Novembro a 19 de Novembro de 1966,' 23 November 1966, SGDN/1REP/105/0349/018, ADN; Abecasis, *Bordo de Ataque*, vol. II, pp. 577–588.

58 Abecasis, *Bordo de Ataque*, vol. II, pp. 577–578; Lopes, p. 67.

59 Fraga, p. 114; Abecasis, *Bordo de Ataque*, vol. II, p. 579.

60 CZACVG, 'Relatório da Operação Samurai,' SGDN/1REP/105/0349/018, ADN.

61 CZACVG, 'Relatório da Operação Samurai,' SGDN/1REP/105/0349/018, ADN; Abecasis, *Bordo de Ataque* vol. II, pp. 577–579 & 584–585.

62 Abecasis, *Bordo de Ataque*, Vol. II, p. 585.

63 CZACVG, 'Relatório da Operação 'Samurai', SGDN/1REP/105/0349/018, ADN; Abecasis, *Bordo de Ataque*, Vol. II, pp. 585, 588, 592–593. The airborne forces were divided into three independent groups; each grupo was further subdivided into five teams of six personnel each. Additional medical, religious, and command personnel completed the tally of 97.

64 CZACVG, 'Relatório da Operação Samurai', SGDN/1REP/105/0349/018, ADN; Abecasis, *Bordo de Ataque*, vol. II, p. 114.

65 Abecasis, 'Dois Relatos de Guerra – Guiné Portuguesa,' www.revistamilitar.pt/artigo/360; Fraga, p. 114; Abecasis, *Bordo de Ataque*, vol. II, p. 602.

66 CZACVG, 'Relatório da Operação Samurai,' SGDN/1REP/105/0349/018, ADN.

67 CZACVG, 'Relatório da Operação 'Samurai',' SGDN/1REP/105/0349/018, ADN.

68 Abecasis, *Bordo de Ataque*, vol. II, pp. 608–609; Fraga, p. 114.

69 Abecasis, *Bordo de Ataque*, vol. II, p. 609; Lopes, p. 67.

70 Fraga, p. 114; Abecasis, *Bordo de Ataque* vol. II, pp. 609–610.

71 Abecasis, *Bordo de Ataque*, vol. II, pp. 609–610.

72 Abecasis, *Bordo de Ataque*, vol. II, p. 611.

73 Abecasis, *Bordo de Ataque*, vol. II, p. 612.

74 José Matos, 'A Guerra das Antiaéreas na Guiné (1965/1970)' in *Revista Militar* no.2601 (October 2018), www.revistamilitar.pt/artigo/1355.

Chapter 3

1 Comandante Egídio Lopes to the authors, email, 22 July 2013.

2 CCFAG, 'Directiva no. 26/C do Comandante-Chefe, de 1 de Dezembro,' 1 December 1966, in CECA, *Resenha Histórico-Militar das Campanhas de África*, 6-II-I, pp. 420–421.

3 CECA, *Resenha Histórico-Militar das Campanhas de África*, 6-II-I, p. 420.

4 SGDN/2REP, 'Exposição da situação operacional na Provincia da Guiné (Jan 61 / Mar 64), feita ao Curso de Altos Comandos, no IAEM, em 2 de Maio de 1964,'May 1964, SGDN/1REP/092/0307/007, ADN.

5 Zelbert Moore, 'Cuba in Africa 1960–1985,' in *Afro-Hispanic Review* 5, nos. 1–3 (January, May, and September 1986), p. 31; William J. Durch, 'The Cuban Military in Africa and the Middle East: From Algeria to Angola,' Professional Paper no. 201 (Arlington, VA: Center for Naval Analysis, September 1977), pp. 1, 14.

6 Piero Gleijeses, 'Cuba's First Venture in Africa: Algeria, 1961–1965,' in *Journal of Latin American Studies* 28, no.1 (February 1996), p. 188–189; Durch, pp. 14, 18.

7 Piero Gleijeses, *Conflicting Missions: Havana, Washington, and Africa, 1959–1976* (Chapel Hill, NC: The University of North Carolina Press, 2002), p. 185.

8 Manuel dos Santos, 'Disparar os 'Strela'' in *A Guerra de África (1961–1974), Vol. I*, ed. José Freire Antunes (Lisbon: Temas e Debates, 1996), p. 724; Jorge RisquetValdés, 'The DeepRoots of Cuba's Internationalism,' in *Tricontinental* 38 (May 2005), http: //www.tricontinental.cubaweb.cu/REVISTA/texto22ingl.html (site discontinued).

9 Oramas, *Amílcar Cabral*, p. 81.

10 José Carlos Marques, 'O abraço dos antigos inimigos,' *Correio de manhã*, 8 March 2008, macua.blogs.com/moambique_para_todos/files/o_abrao_dos_antigos_inimigos.doc. In early 1967, however, Portuguese military intelligence estimated 500 Cubans serving at that one time; see SGDN/2REP, 'Cubanos ao serviço do PAIGC,' 22 February 1967, SGDN/2REP/106/0411/007, ADN.

11 Central Intelligence Agency (CIA), 'Cuban Meddling in Africa: Special Report – WeeklyReview,' 24 March 1967, U.S. Declassified Documents Online, www.gale.com/c/us-declassified-documents-online (hereafter DDO); PAIGC, 'Lista de distribuição dos técnicos Cubanos,' 1967, Pasta 07056.001.003, FMS.

12 Amílcar Cabral, 'Decisão,' 8 December 1967, Pasta 04606.045.144, FMS.

13 Cited in Afonso and Gomes, *Os anos da Guerra Colonial*, p. 397.

14 Manuel Catarino, *As Grandes Operações da Guerra Colonial, 1961–1974, VIII: Captura do capitão Peralta, Guiné 1969 e 1972* (Lisbon: Correio da Manhã, 2009), pp. 4–5. Capt. Peralta was later repatriated to Cuba as part of a U.S. brokered deal that traded his freedom for the release of an American intelligence officer detained in Havana. See also Captain Peralta's process in SGDN/2REP/106/0415/022, ADN.

15 CCFAG, 'O Problema Militar da Guiné: Seu estudo e proposta de solução,' October 1968, CEMGFA/017/0034/006, ADN; SGDN/2REP, 'Apoio à subversão em África: Penetração comunista, 1a Parte – China Continental,' 1965, SGDN/2REP/021/0091/001, ADN; Hélio Felgas, 'A luta na Guiné,'*Revista Militar* 22, no.4 (April 1970), pp. 219–237; Mustafah Dhada, 'Guinea-Bissau 's Diplomacy and Liberation Struggle,' in *Portuguese Studies Review* IV, no. 1 (Spring-Summer 1995), p. 30.

16 Natalia Telepneva, *Cold War Liberation: The Soviet Union and the Collapse of the Portuguese Empire in Africa, 1961 – 1975* (Chapel Hill, NC: The University of North Carolina Press, 2022), pp. 110–111.

17 CCFAG, 'O Problema Militar da Guiné,' CEMGFA/017/0034/006, ADN.Senegal had previously supported the rival *Frente de Luta pela Independência Nacional da Guiné* movement in Portuguese Guinea.

18 'Vamos abater cada dia um maior número de aviões inimigos,' *PAIGC Libertação* no. 65 (April 1966), p. 1.

19 Nico, *A Batalha do Quitafine*, pp. 87–89, 140–141; Correia, 'Fiat G.91 na Guiné 1966–68, 1a Parte,' p. 36.

20 Nico, *A Batalha do Quitafine*, pp. 140–141; see also Rodrigues, 'Aviação na Guiné – A Parte Final,' p. 287. In this, the PAIGC's intent was compatible with modern concepts regarding anti-access/area denial strategies.

21 Correia, 'Fiat G.91 na Guiné 1966–68, 1a Parte,' p. 34; Diogo Neto, 'Voo em Três Frentes,'p. 321.

22 Diogo Neto, 'Voo em Três Frentes,' p. 321; Nico, *A Batalha do Quitafine*, p. 169.

23 PAIGC, 'Informações a obter em Bissau ou outras fontes,' no date, Pasta 07068.098.001, FMS; SGDN/1REP, 'Planeamento da defesa da Guiné,' 1966, SGDN/1REP/092/0309/013, ADN. General Nico also suspected 'the gunners would be warned of the G-91 formations taking off.' Nico, *A Batalha do Quitafine*, p. 156.

24 José Manuel Correia, 'Fiat G.91 na Guiné 1966–68, 2a Parte: Os dois primeiros anos de combate,' in *Mais Alto* 50, no.399 (September-October 2012), p. 31.

25 Correia, 'Fiat G.91 na Guiné 1966–68, 2a Parte,' p. 31.

26 Batalhão de Caçadores Páraquedistas 12, 'Ordem de Operações no.1/67, 'Operação Barracuda',' 5 February 1967, SGDN/1REP/102/0326/011, ADN.

27 CZACVG, 'Relatório da Ordem de Operaçãos no. 1/67 'Operação Barracuda',' 10 February 1967, SGDN/1REP/102/0326/011, ADN.

28 Correia, 'Fiat G.91 na Guiné 1966–68, 2a Parte,' p. 31.

29 CZACVG, 'Relatório da Ordem de Operaçãos no. 1/67 'Operação Barracuda',' 10 February 1967, SGDN/1REP/102/0326/011, ADN.

30 CZACVG, 'Relatório da Ordem de Operaçãos no. 1/67 'Operação Barracuda',' 10 February 1967, SGDN/1REP/102/0326/011, ADN; Correia, 'Fiat G.91 na Guiné 1966–68, 2a Parte,'p. 26.

31 Photo interpreters at the CCEF in Bissalanca reportedly found photos taken by G.91s to be so detailed, they could measure the distance between furrows left in the soil to confirm the movement of tripod-mounted AAMGs. Correia, 'Fiat G.91 na Guiné 1966–68, 2a Parte,' pp. 25–26.

32 CZACVG, 'Relatório da Ordem de Operações no. 1/67 'Operação Barracuda,' 10 February 1967, SGDN/1REP/102/0326/011, ADN; Coreia, 'Os Fiat G.91 ao ataque na Guiné: Operação Barracuda,' p. 26.

33 CCFAG Directiva no. 26/C, 1 December 1966, in CECA, *Resenha Histórico-Militar das Campanhas de África*, 6-II-I, pp. 420–435.

34 CECA, *Resenha Histórico-Militar das Campanhas de África*, 6-II-I, pp. 431–433; CECA, *Resenha Histórico-Militar das Campanhas de África (1961–1974), 6 volume, Aspectos da Actividade Operational, Tomo II – Guiné, Livro II* (Lisbon: Estado-Maior do Exército, 2015), pp. 16–23, 38, 41, 71.

35 CECA, *Resenha Histórico-Militar das Campanhas de África*, 6-II-I, pp. 432–433; CECA, *Resenha Histórico-Militar das Campanhas de África, 6 Volume, Tomo II – Guiné, Livro II* (hereafter 6-II-II), p. 23.

36 CCFAG, 'Nota no. 6829/C de 21Nov66,' in CECA, *Resenha Histórico-Militar das Campanhas de África*, 6-II-I, p. 385.

37 COMZAVERDEGUINÉ, SITREP scircunstanciados nos.31/67 through 35/67, 10 May–25 December 1967, SGDN/2REP/096, ADN; CECA, *Resenha Histórico-Militar das Campanhas de África*, 6-II-II, pp. 38–72.

38 COMZAVERDEGUINÉ, SITREP scircunstanciados nos. 31/67 through 35/67, 10 May–25 December 1967, SGDN/2REP/096, ADN; CECA, *Resenha Histórico-Militar das Campanhas de África*, 6-II-II, pp. 38–72.

39 Thomas Arbuckle, 'Rhodesian Bush War Strategies and Tactics: An Assessment,' in *RUSI Journal* 124, no 4 (1979), pp. 29–30; Anthony Clayton, *Frontiersmen: Warfare in Africa since 1950* (London: Routledge, 2004), p. 55.

40 Luís Cabral, *Crónica da Libertação* (Lisbon: O Jornal, 1984), p. 315; Luís Cabral, 'Prender Spínola,' in *A Guerra de África (1961–1974)*, vol. I, José Freire Antunes (ed.) (Lisbon: Temas e Debates, 1996), p. 539. PAIGC commander João Bernardo 'Nino' Viera also acknowledged that Portuguese helicopter operations 'had some effect' in the first period of their use, 'because the people were not accustomed to that kind of enemy activity [and] were disoriented.' Pedro Machado, 'Liberation Movement Discussed by Guerrilla Leader,' in *Etumba* (Brazzaville), 11 September 1971, in 'Translations on Africa no.1081' Joint Publications Research Service (JPRS) 54466 (11 November 1971), p. 56.

41 Oscar Oramas, *Amílcar Cabral*, pp. 71–72. Referring specifically to local superstitions and supernatural beliefs, Amílcar Cabral acknowledged that 'Our struggle is based on our culture, [but] our culture is filled with weakness in the face of nature.' Amílcar Cabral, *Unity and Struggle*, p. 59.

42 A pejorative term often used by the PAIGC, derived from the word 'Portugal.'

43 PAIGC, 'Para o desenvolvimento da nossa luta contra os helicópteros,' June 1967, Folder 04602.046, FMS.

44 PAIGC, 'Para o desenvolvimento da nossa luta contra os helicópteros,' June 1967, Folder 04602.046, FMS.

45 COMZAVERDEGUINÉ, SITREPs circunstanciados nos. 32/67, 34/67, 35/67, 13/68, and 49/68, November 1967 – December 1968, SGDN/2REP/096, ADN. Three of the damaged helicopters took small arms fire, one was hit with an unidentified weapon, the fifth suffered windscreen damage from an RPG blast. For its part the PAIGC did claim a single Portuguese helicopter 'destroyed by bazooka fire the moment it touched the ground' in September 1967, but there is no other evidence to corroborate this assertion. PAIGC (Amílcar Cabral), 'Communiqué,' 6 November 1967, Cota 0098.000.001, Associação Tchiweka de Documentação, www.tchiweka.org/documento-textual/0098000001.

46 Luís Cabral, 'Prender Spínola,' p. 539.

47 COMZAVERDEGUINÉ, 'SITREP circunstanciado no. 04/67, Período Abrangido 240000MAI67 – 310000MAI67,' 31 May 1967, SGDN/2REP/096, ADN.

48 COMZAVERDEGUINÉ, 'SITREP circunstanciado no. 20/67, Período Abrangido 130000SET67 – 200000SET67,' 20 September 1967, SGDN/2REP/096, ADN.

49 COMCHEFGUINÉ, 'Directiva Operacional no. 29/C,' 29 September 1967, SGDN/1REP/098/0319/001, ADN.

50 COMZAVERDEGUINÉ, 'SITREP circunstanciado no. 23/67, Período Abrangido 040000OUT67 – 110000OUT67,' 11 October 1967, SGDN/2REP/096, ADN. For a more thorough account of this incident see Nico, *A Batalha do Quitafine*, pp. 170–175. On 9 October a British journalist witnessed one of the FAP's attacks and confirmed the destruction of 'a four-barrelled 14mm cannon.' Basil Davidson,' Unknown War in Portuguese West Africa,' in *The Times*, 10 November 1967, p. 9.

51 United Nations (U.N.), 'Letter Dated 13 October 1967 from the Chargé d'Affairs of the Republic of Guinea Addressed to the President of the Security Council,' S/8193, 13 October 1967; Suzanne Cronje, 'Portuguese Guinea Hit Hard by African Rebels,' in *The Washington Post, Times Herald*, 22 February 1968, K1. Between May 1966 and June 1969, Portugal's simultaneous war in Angola allegedly resulted in at least 25 cross-border air raids into neighbouring Zambia; see Permanent Representative of Zambia, letter, to the President of the United Nations Security Council, 15 July 1969, https: //digitallibrary.un.org/record/580377/files/S_PV-1488-EN.pdf.

52 COMZAVERDEGUINÉ, 'SITREP circunstanciado no. 26/67, Período Abrangido 250000OUT67 – 010000NOV67,' 25 October 1967, and 'SITREP circunstanciado no. 31/67, Período Abrangido 220000NOV67 – 290000NOV67,' COMZAVERDEGUINÉ, 29 November 1967, SGDN/2REP/096, ADN.

53 COMZAVERDEGUINÉ, SITREPs circunstanciados nos. 28/67 (15 November 1967), 32/67 (5 December 1967), 03/68 (10 January 1968), and 04/68 (24 January 1968), ADN/SGDN/2REP/096.

54 Nico, *A Batalha do Quitafine*, pp. 141–146.

55 SGDN to EMFA, Ofício no. 3170/B, 'Guiné – Necessidade em aviões,' 13 September 1967, SGDN/1REP/092/0309/014, ADN; Nico, *A batalha do Quitafine*, pp. 160–161.

56 Nico, *A Batalha do Quitafine*, p. 160.

57 The average number of operational G.91s during this period was 4.33 aircraft, based on analysis of COMZAVERDEGUINÉ, SITREPs Circumstantiates nos. 01/68 through 18/68, 2 January–1 May 1968, SGDN/2REP/096, ADN.

58 Nico, 'Pedaços das Nossas Vidas III,' pp. 22–23.

59 Diogo Neto, 'Voo em Três Frentes,'p. 321.

60 Nico, *A Batalha do Quitafine*, pp. 160–162.

61 Nico, *A Batalha do Quitafine*, p. 148.

62 Cited in Nico, *A Batalha do Quitafine*, pp. 161.

63 COMZAVERDEGUINÉ, 'SITREP circunstanciado no. 01/68, Período Abrangido 270000DEZ67 – 020000JAN68,' 2 January 1968, SGDN/2REP/096, ADN; Correia, 'Fiat G.91 na Guiné 1966–68, 2a Parte,' p. 34.

64 Correia, 'Fiat G.91 na Guiné 1966–68, 2a Parte,'p. 34.

65 Correia, 'Fiat G.91 na Guiné 1966–68, 2a Parte,' p. 34.

66 Nico, *A Batalha do Quitafine*, pp. 187–188.

67 COMZAVERDEGUINÉ, 'SITREP circunstanciado no. 01/68, Período Abrangido 270000DEZ67 – 020000JAN68,' 2 January 1968, SGDN/2REP/096, ADN; Correia, 'Fiat G.91 na Guiné 1966–68, 2a Parte,' p. 34.

68 COMZAVERDEGUINÉ, 'SITREP circunstanciado no. 07/68, Período Abrangido 060000FEV68 – 130000FEV68,' 13 February 1968, SGDN/2REP/096, ADN.

69 Nico, *A Batalha do Quitafine*, p. 287.

70 COMZAVERDEGUINÉ, 'SITREP circunstanciado no. 08/68, Período Abrangido 140000FEV68 – 200000FEV68,' 20 February 1968, SGDN/2REP/096, ADN; Director Geral dos Negócios Políticos do Ministério dos Negócios Estrangeiros, 'Acção dos Terroristas Contra a Base Aérea 12 (Bissalanca),' 19 April 1968, SGDN/2REP/106/0413/017, ADN.

71 'O Aeroporto military de Bissau foi atacado pelas Nossas Forças,' in *PAIGC Libertação* no. 87 (February 1968), p. 1; 'Comunicado do Bureau Político do PAIGC sobre o ataque ao Aeroporto de Bissalanca,' March 1968, Pasta 04602.048, FMS. Although Cabral declared that 'For us, the best way to face the Portuguese planes is to destroy them in the fields, not fighting against them in the air,' this was the only recorded PAIGC/FARP attack against Bissalanca. Some small-scale raids against forward airstrips

were also recorded, usually incidental to larger assaults against adjacent army garrisons. Amílcar Cabral, 'A Report to Our Friends,' in *Africa Today* 20, no.1 (Winter 1973), p. 11.

72 Some of their confederates within Bissau were quickly arrested by Portuguese security services, however. Afonso and Gomes, *Os anos da Guerra Colonial*, p. 438.

73 Amílcar Cabral, *Unity and Struggle*, p. 233.

74 Most of the claimed attacks were almost certainly ancillary to raids or shelling against the host barracks, and ZACVG SITREPs reflect only the February 1968 attack against BA12.' As operações militares no decurso do mês de Novembro,' in *PAIGC Libertação*no 72 (November 1966), p. 3; Mustafah Dhada, *Warriors at Work: How Guinea-Bissau Was Really Set Free* (Boulder: University Press of Colorado, 1993), p. 171; Robert D. S. Higham, *100 Years of Air Power and Aviation* (College Station: Texas A&M University Press, 2003), p. 292.

75 COMZAVERDEGUINÉ, 'SITREP circunstanciado no. 11/68, Período Abrangido 060000MAR68 – 120000MAR68,' 12 March 1968, SGDN/2REP/096/0384/011, ADN; Nico, 204.

76 Nico, *A Batalha do Quitafine*, pp. 204, 206.

77 COMCHEFE Guiné, 'SUPINTREP No. 35 (evolução da actividade e da situação do IN no TO referente a 1970),' Anexo H, 20 April 1971, SGDN/2REP/088/0364/024, ADN.

78 COMCHEFGUINÉ, 'Acta das conclusões da reunião de comandos,' 9 April 1968, SGDN/1REP/098/0319/001, ADN.

79 The PAIGC claimed a total of 12 aircraft shot down, including helicopters, and two others destroyed on the ground during this period, but offered no substantive evidence to support those assertions. See *PAIGC Libertação* nos 63 (February 1966), 72 (November 1966), 74 (January 1967), 75 (February 1967), and no.91 (June 1968); PAIGC communiqués dated 28 November 1965, 22 March 1966, and 6 November 1967; and Amílcar Cabral, 'Sur la situation de notrelutte de libérationnationale,' March 1968, www.tchiweka.org/documento-textual/0103000023.

80 Mensagem 8991, COMCHEFGUINÉ to DEFNAC, 21 July 1966, GABMIN/007/0029/004, ADN; Mensagem 9045, COMCHEFGUINÉ to MINDEFNAC, 22 July 1966, GABMIN/007/0029/004, ADN; Mensagem 9396, COMCHEFGUINÉ to DEFNAC, 4 August 1966, GABMIN/007/0029/004, ADN.

81 EMFA/3REP, 'Informação no. 84: Acidente com o avião Fiat G-91 no. 5407 em 22 Fev 67,' 19 June 1967, AHFA; Correia, 'Fiat G.91 na Guiné 1966–68, 2a Parte,' p. 32; Lopes, p. 67.

82 COMZAVERDEGUINÉ, 'SITREP circunstanciado no. 25/68, Período Abrangido 120000JUN68 – 190000JUN68,' 19 June 1968, SGDN/2REP/096, ADN; Vitor Oliveira, 'A queda do T6G no 1791 entre o Cheche e Madina de Boé, no dia 15/6/1968,' Luís Graça e Camaradas da Guiné, 16 October 2013, https: //blogueforanadaevaotres.blogspot. com/2013/10/guine-6374-p12158-fap-76-queda-do-t6g-n.html.

83 COMZAVERDEGUINÉ, SITREPs circunstanciados nos. 03/68 through 20/68, 10 January – 8 May 1968, SGDN/2REP/096, ADN; CECA, *Resenha Histórico-Militar das Campanhas de África*, 6-II-II, pp. 152–168.

84 COMZAVERDEGUINÉ, 'SITREP circunstanciado no. 03/68, Período Abrangido 100000JAN68 – 170000JAN68,' 10 January 1968, SGDN/2REP/096, ADN; COMZAVERDEGUINÉ, 'SITREP circunstanciado no. 13/68, Período Abrangido 200000MAR68 – 260000MAR68,' 26 March 1968, SGDN/2REP/096, ADN.

85 For comparison data, see COMZAVERDEGUINÉ, SITREPs circunstanciados nos. 14/67 through 35/67, 8 August – 25 December 1967, SGDN/2REP/096, ADN.

86 COMZAVERDEGUINÉ, 'SITREP circunstanciado no.02/68, Período Abrangido 030000JAN68 – 100000JAN68,' 10 January 1968, and 'SITREP circunstanciado no.03/68, Período Abrangido 100000JAN68 – 170000JAN68,' 17 January 1968, SGDN/2REP/096, ADN; Correia, 'Fiat G.91 na Guiné 1966–68, 2a Parte,' p. 34.

87 COMZAVERDEGUINÉ, 'SITREP circunstanciado no.04/68, Período Abrangido 170000JAN68 – 240000JAN68,' 24 January 1968, SGDN/2REP/096, ADN.

88 COMZAVERDEGUINÉ, 'SITREP circunstanciado no.06/68, Período Abrangido 310000JAN68 – 070000FEV68,' 13 February 1968, SGDN/2REP/096, ADN.

89 COMZAVERDEGUINÉ SITREPs circunstanciados nos 01/68 through 49/68, 2 January–25 December 1968, SGDN/2REP/096, ADN; Fraga, p. 123.

90 Mustafa Dhada, 'The Liberation War in Guinea-Bissau Reconsidered,' in *The Journal of Military History* 62, no.3 (July 1998), pp. 582–583.

91 For a discussion of insurgent concerns regarding Portuguese helicopter use specifically, see PAIGC, 'Para o desenvolvimento da nossa luta contra os helicópteros,'Folder 04602.046, FMS.

92 Amílcar Cabral, 'Guinea: The Power of Arms,' in *Tricontinental*, May-June 1969, in 'Translations on Africa no. 823,' JPRS 48980 (6 October 1969), p. 60.

93 CCFAG, 'O Problema Militar da Guiné,' CEMGFA/017/0034/006, ADN.

94 CTIG/2REP, 'SUPINTREP 14: Organização militar IN,' 31 July 1968, SGDN/2REP/088/0363/010, ADN.

95 CCFAG, 'O Problema Militar da Guiné,' CEMGFA/017/0034/006, ADN.

96 CTIG/2REP, 'SUPINTREP 14,' SGDN/2REP/088/0363/010, ADN.

97 Dhada, 'The Liberation War in Guinea-Bissau Reconsidered,' p. 581; COMCHEFGUINÉ, 'Relatório anual de Comando do CCFA da Guiné, Período do 01 JAN 71 a 31 DEC 71,' 15 March 1972, SGDN/ REP/103/0330/009, ADN.

98 CCFAG, 'O Problema Militar da Guiné,' CEMGFA/017/0034/006, ADN.

99 *PAIGC Libertação* nos.86 to 90 (January to May 1968), passim; Afonso and Gomes, *Os anos da Guerra Colonial*, pp. 437–447.

100 'Uma vergonhosa derrota para as colonialistas Portugueses,' *PAIGC Libertação*no 87 (February 1968), p. 5.

101 Manual Catarino, *As Grandes Operações da Guerra Colonial, 1961–1974, VI: Operação Tridente – Ocupação de Caiar, Como e Catunco, Guiné, 1964* (Lisbon: Correio da Manhã, 2009), p. 11.

102 A contemporaneous American diplomatic assessment concluded 'Given the current balance of forces, the prospect is for continuing protracted warfare, debilitating both sides, which is unlikely to be resolved in one direction or another.' American Embassy Dakar, airgram to U.S. Department of State, 'Portuguese Guinea: The War,' 3 January 1969, DDO.

103 Patrick Chabal, *Amílcar Cabral: Revolutionary Leadership and People's War* (Trenton, NJ: Africa World Press, 2003), pp. 92–93; Abílio Pires Lousada, Luís Falcão Escorrega, and António Cordeiro Menezes, 'Fernando Cavaleiro e a Operação Tridente,' in *Jornal do Exército* 52, no.602 (January 2011), p. 227.

104 Dhada, 'The Liberation War in Guinea-Bissau Reconsidered,' p. 582; Afonso and Gomes, *Os anos da Guerra Colonial*, p. 427.

105 CIA Directorate of Intelligence (DI), 'The Guerrilla War in Portuguese Guinea,' 20 December 1968, p. 11.

106 American Embassy Dakar, airgram, to U.S. Department of State, 'Portuguese Guinea: The War,' 3 January 1969, DDO.

107 Mustafah Dhada, *Warriors at Work: How Guinea-Bissau Was Really Set Free* (Boulder: University Press of Colorado, 1993), p. 33.

108 The 'protracted struggle' model of insurgency preferred by the PAIGC leadership broadly aligned with methods attributed to Mao Zedong, whose published works regarding revolution and guerrilla warfare have deliberately or subconsciously been adopted as 'how to' manuals by aspiring insurgents around the world. For a thorough discussion of their application in Portuguese Guinea, see 'The Maoist Model: The Guinean War of Independence (1963– 1974),' in Noriyuki Katagiri, *Adapting to Win: How Insurgents Fight and Defeat Foreign States in War* (Philadelphia: University of Pennsylvania Press, 2015), pp. 131–149.

109 Gil Fernandes and John Marcum, 'The Azores over Africa,' in *Africa Today* 19, no.1 (Winter 1972), p. 4

110 Dhada, 'The Liberation War in Guinea-Bissau Reconsidered,' pp. 583–584.

111 In 1968 Lisbon raised the government budget 10 percent to $781.7 million, of which $290.2 million was allocated to military spending. 'Portugal Increases Budget 10 Per Cent; Criticism by Economists,' in *The New York Times*, 28 December 1967, p. 6.

112 *The Military Balance 1960: The Communist Bloc and the Free World* (London: The Institute for Strategic Studies, 1959), p. 11; *The Military Balance 1968–1969* (London: The Institute for Strategic Studies, 1968), p. 27.

113 CECA, *Resenha Histórico-Militar das Campanhas de África (1961–1974), 1 Volume*, p. 258.

114 Miguel Cardina and Susana Martins, 'Evading the War: Deserters and Draft Evaders from the Portuguese Army during the Colonial War,' in *e-Journal of Portuguese History 17, no.1 (June 2019), www.brown.edu/Departments/Portuguese_Brazilian_Studies/ejph/html/issue34/html/v17n2a03.html;'* Desertion Grows in Portugal,' in *The Observer*, 15 February 1970, p. 4.

115 João Jorge Botelho Vieira Borges, 'A Academia Militar e a Guerra de África: A formação dos quadros 1960 1974,' in *Revista Militar* no.2493 (October 2009), www.revistamilitar.pt/artigo/515.

116 SGDN/2REP, 'Exposição da situação operacional na Provincia da Guiné (Jan 61/Mar 64),' SGDN/1REP/92/307/7, ADN; COMZAVERDEGUINÉ, 'SITREP circunstanciado no. 23/68, Período Abrangido 220000MAI68 – 050000JUN68,' 5 June 1968, SGDN/2REP/096, ADN; CECA, *Resenha Histórico-Militar das Campanhas de África (1961–1974), 1 Volume*, p. 259.

117 CIA/DI, 'The Guerrilla War in Portuguese Guinea,' p. 11.

118 Afonso and Gomes, *Os Anos da Guerra Colonial*, p. 449.

119 Gregory A. Daddis, *Westmoreland's War: Reassessing American Strategy in Vietnam* (New York: Oxford University Press, 2014), pp. 8–9.

120 Santos, 'Disparar os 'Strela'' p. 725.

121 American Embassy Dakar, airgram to U.S. Department of State, 'Portuguese Guinea: The War,' 3 January 1969, DDO.

122 Afonso and Gomes, *Os Anos da Guerra Colonial*, pp. 449–450. South African journalist Al J. Venter offered a different assessment of Schultz's administration, asserting that 'his hands were in effect tied by Lisbon's filibusters in many of the plans he tried to put into operation. Looking back one can only conclude that the fault was his for tolerating such a situation in the face of a steadily deteriorating military front.' Al J. Venter, 'Portugal's War in Guiné-Bissau,' in *Munger Africana Library Notes* 19 (April 1973), p. 25.

123 Afonso and Gomes, *Os Anos da Guerra Colonial*, p. 450.

Chapter 4

1 CCFAG, 'Acção da Força Aérea no T.O. da Guiné,' 10 December 1968, SGDN/1REP/098/0319002, ADN.

2 American Embassy Lisbon, airgram, to U.S. Department of State, 'Portuguese Guinea and Its Governor,' 19 October 1971, DDO.

3 Venter, 'Portugal's War in Guiné-Bissau,'p. 25.

4 Luís Nuno Rodrigues, 'For a Better Guinea! Winning Hearts and Minds in Portuguese Guinea,' in *Race, Ethnicity, and the Cold War: A Global Perspective*, Philip E. Muehlenbeck (ed.) (Nashville: Vanderbilt University Press, 2012), p. 2; American Embassy Dakar, airgram, to U.S. Department of State, 'Portuguese Guinea: The War,' 3 January 1969, DDO; American Embassy Lisbon, airgram, to U.S. Department of State, 'Portuguese Guinea and Its Governor,' 19 October 1971, DDO.

5 Rodrigues, *Spínola*, pp. 31 and 37–41.

6 Rodrigues, '*For a Better Guinea*,' p. 119; Norrie MacQueen, 'Portugal's First Domino: 'Pluricontinentalism' and Colonial War in Guiné-Bissau, 1963–1974,' *Contemporary European History* 8, no.2 (July 1999), p. 213.

7 'Händel de Oliveira, Rui Nunes, and J. Villas Monteiro, *Os Últimos Governadores do Império* (Lisbon: Edições Neptuno, 1994), pp. 63–65; António de Spínola, *País sem Rumo: Contributo para a História de uma Revolução* (Lisbon: SCIRE, 1978), pp. 22–23.

8 CCFAG, 'O Problema Militar da Guiné,' CEMGFA/017/0034/006, ADN.

9 CCFAG, 'O Problema Militar da Guiné,' CEMGFA/017/0034/006, ADN; Rodrigues, '*For a Better Guinea*,' pp. 120, 126.

10 Dutra Faria, 'Governor Tells of Independence Party Activity,' *ABC-Diario de Angola*, 7 December 1969, in 'Translations on Africa no. 867,' JPRS 49903 (20 February 1970), p. 1. See also CCFAG Directiva no.360/68, 'Campanha Psicológica de Recuperação,' 17 December 1968, DIV/2/04, AHM.

11 Santana Mota, 'Governor Says Conditions Exist for Success of Portuguese Cause' (*Voz da Guiné*, 28 July 1973, in 'Translations on Africa no. 1375,' JPRS 60168 (1 October 1973), p. 5. Such ideas were in no way novel to the Portuguese armed forces. The 1963 Portuguese Army COIN manual, *O Exercitona Guerra Subversiva*, explicitly stated that 'The struggle against subversion is a struggle for the populace and never against the populace. This is not the enemy, but the medium in which the struggle takes place.' Given this starting proposition, the manual's authors of concluded that 'The struggle against subversion cannot be carried out in full by the military forces alone; on the contrary, a convergence of efforts is necessary in all fields, political, psychological, social, economic, et cetera' Estado-Maior do Exército, *O Exército na guerra subversiva*, 1963, Department of the Army/Assistant Chief of Staff for Intelligence Translation no. I-5216, August 1964, pp. 31, 35.

12 Oliveira, Nunes, and Monteiro, pp. 63–65; Spínola, pp. 22–23.

13 CCFAG Directiva no.360/68, 'Campanha Psicológica de Recuperação,' 17 December 1968, DIV/2/04, AHM.

14 Rodrigues, '*For a Better Guinea*,' p. 126.

15 American Embassy Lisbon, airgram, to U.S. Department of State, 'Portuguese Guinea and Its Governor,' 19 October 1971, DDO; Rodrigues, '*For a Better Guinea*,'p. 128.

16 CCFAG Directiva no. 360/68, 'Campanha Psicológica de Recuperação,' 17 December 1968, DIV/2/04, AHM.

17 During the Malayan Emergency of 1948–1960, British forces established a similar system of 'New Villages;' the French in Indochina constructed 'Agrovilles' as part of their programme of 'pacification by prosperity.'

18 CCFAG, 'Directiva no. 49/68,' 16 October 1968, SGDN/1REP/098/0319, ADN.

19 CCFAG, 'Directiva de Propaganda no. 1,' 30 September 1968, DIV/2/04, AHM.

20 Faria, p. 1; see also CCFAG, 'Análise da situação na Guiné e perspectivas de evolução,' 19 November 1969, CEMGFA/017/0036/025, ADN.

21 CECA, *Resenha Histórico-Militar das Campanhas de África*, 6-II-II, p. 401.

22 'Fight for Life in Guinea-Bissao,' in *France Nouvelle*, 19 November 1969, in 'Translations on Africa no. 860,' JPRS 49761 (5 February 1970), p. 87.

23 Pedro Machado, p. 60.

24 Horácio Caio, *Portuguese Guinea: 9 Days in March* (Lisbon: Overseas Ministry, 1970), p. 41.

25 Amílcar Cabral claimed that 'Madina de Boé was a great victory. We laid siege to the Portuguese camp for almost two years… The capture of Madina completely liberated the Boé region in the Southeast of the country and created a new set of conditions for the development of the struggle.' 'Fight for Life in Guinea-Bissao,' p. 87.

26 Abecasis, *Bordo de Ataque*, Vol. II, p. 649.

27 COMCHEFGUINÉ, 'Directiva no. 58/68 de 16Dez – Ideia de manobra para o desenvolvimento operacional na época seca em 1969,' 16 December 1968, SGDN/2REP/078/0329/003, ADN.

28 CCFAG, 'Diretiva no. 57/68: Ação da Força Aérea na Guiné TO,' 10 December 1968, SGDN/1REP/098/0319/002, ADN; see also CCFAG, 'Directiva no. 31/68: Reforço Aéreo,' 11 September 1968, DIV/2/4/226/1, AHM.

29 CCFAG, 'Diretiva no. 29/69: Areas de Intervenção do Comando-Chefe,' 20 March 1969, SGDN/1REP/098/0319/003, ADN; SGDN/1REP, 'Areas de intervenção do Comando-Chefe,' Directiva 29/69 do C/C Guiné, 20 March 1969, SGDN/1REP/098/0319, ADN; Nuno Alexandre Ferrer Morgado, et al, 'A atuação do Marechal Spínola no Teatro De Operações da Guiné-Bissau, entre 1968 e 1973, enquanto Comandante-Chefe das Forças Armadas e Governador Geral,' in *A Campanha Militar Terrestre no Teatro de Operações da Guiné-Bissau (1963–1974): Estudo da Aplicação da Força por Funções de Combate* (Lisbon: Instituto Universitário Militar, December 2018), pp. 276–277.

30 CCFAG, 'Acção da Força Aérea no T.O. da Guiné,' 10 December 1968, SGDN/1REP/098/0319-002, ADN.

31 COMCHEFGUINÉ, 'Directiva no. 58/68,' SGDN/2REP/078/0329/003, ADN; Conselho Superior da Defesa Nacional, 'Relato sucinto da Sessão de 8 de Novembro de 1968,' November 1968, B/GB0205/1729/009, Arquivo Histórico da Presidência da República, Lisbon (hereafter AHPR).

32 CCFAG, 'Directivo nº. 78/69 – Ideia de manobra para o desenvolvimento operacional na 'época seca' de 1969/70,' November 1969, CEMGFA/017/0036/025, ADN; CCFAG, 'A solução do problema da Guiné,' December 1969, CEMGFA/017/0034/001, ADN.

33 COMZAVERDEGUINÉ, 'SITREP circunstanciado no. 39/68, Período Abrangido 180000SEP68 – 250000SEP68,' 25 September 1968, SGDN/2REP/096, ADN; Correia, 'Fiat G.91 na Guiné 1966–68, 2a Parte,' p. 36.

34 COMZAVERDEGUINÉ, 'SITREP circunstanciado no. 01/69, Período Abrangido 010000JAN69 – 080000JAN69,' 8 January 1969, SGDN/2REP/096, ADN. The insurgent weapons used were reported as '57mm anti-vehicle cannons,' presumably of the Soviet M1943/ZiS-2 type or a derivative.

35 COMZAVERDEGUINÉ, 'SITREP circunstanciado no.01/69, Período Abrangido 010000JAN69 – 080000JAN69,' 8 January 1969, SGDN/2REP/096, ADN.

36 For a detailed account of this engagement, see José Francisco Fernandes Nico, 'Pedaços das nossas vidas VI – Um ataque com 'olhos azuls',' in *ABC Portugais-Français* 2, no.37 (29 August 2015), pp. 21–22.

37 Nico, *A batalha do Quitafine*, pp. 214–216.

38 Tomás George Conceição Silva, 'The Portuguese Air Force in the African Wars of 1961–1974,' in *Memories of Portugal's African Wars, 1961–1974: Proceedings of a Conference, King's College London, 10 June 1997*, John P. Cann (ed.) (Quantico, VA: Marine Corps University Foundation, 1998), pp. 119–120.

39 Manuel Diogo Neto, 'Operação Vulcano: Cassebeche, 7 de Março de 1969,' in *Mais Alto* 27, no.257 (January-February 1989), p. 16. Diogo Neto, later promoted to General, briefly served as the chief of the Portuguese Air Force from April to September 1974.

40 Diogo Neto, 'Operação Vulcano,' p. 15; Silva, 'The Portuguese Air Force in the African Wars of 1961–1974,' p. 119.

41 Nico, *A Batalha do Quitafine*, p. 227; Diogo Neto, 'Operação Vulcano,' p. 16; COMZAVERDEGUINÉ, 'SITREP circunstanciado no. 10/69, Período Abrangido 030000MAR69 – 100000MAR69,' 10 March 1969, ADN/SGDN/2REP/096.

42 In English, 'Volcano.' Diogo Neto, 'Operação Vulcano,' p. 15.

43 As *General* Nico recalled, 'during *Operação Vulcano* movement across BA12's apron reached an intensity never before observed, nor would it be observed again later. Those were exciting moments we all experienced early that morning.' Nico, *A Batalha do Quitafine*, p. 228.

44 Nico, *A Batalha do Quitafine*, p. 234.

45 Diogo Neto, 'Operação Vulcano,' p. 15.

46 Silva, p. 119.

47 COMZAVERDEGUINÉ, 'SITREP circunstanciado no. 10/69, Período Abrangido 030000MAR69 – 100000MAR69,' 10 March 1969, ADN/SGDN/2REP/096; Diogo Neto, 'Operação Vulcano,'p. 16; Nico, *A Batalha do Quitafine*, pp. 227–228.

48 Diogo Neto, 'Operação Vulcano,' p. 16.

49 Diogo Neto, 'Operação Vulcano,' p. 16; Nico, *A Batalha do Quitafine*, pp. 230, 247.

50 Manuel Catarino, *As Grandes Operações da Guerra Colonial, 1961–1974, VII: Pára-quedistas encurralados em Cassebeche, Guiné 1969* (Lisbon: Correio da Manhã, 2009), p. 4; Nico, *A Batalha do Quitafine*, pp. 230–233.

51 Diogo Neto, 'Operação Vulcano,' pp. 16–17.

52 Diogo Neto, 'Operação Vulcano,' p. 17; Nico, *A Batalha do Quitafine*, pp. 234–237.

53 The remaining 15 paratroops had just previously launched in helicopters in case search and recovery were required for the pilot of the damaged G.91 as it returned to Bissalanca. Nico, *A Batalha do Quitafine*, pp. 237–238.

54 Nico, *A Batalha do Quitafine*, p. 238; Diogo Neto, 'Operação Vulcano,' p. 17.

55 Diogo Neto, 'Operação Vulcano,' p. 17.

56 Diogo Neto, 'Operação Vulcano,' p. 17; Silva, p. 119.

57 Nico, *A Batalha do Quitafine*, pp. 244, 246; Diogo Neto, 'Operação Vulcano,' p. 17.

58 Nico, *A Batalha do Quitafine*, pp. 246–247.

59 Diogo Neto, 'Operação Vulcano,' p. 18; Nico, *A Batalha do Quitafine*, p. 248.

60 Diogo Neto, 'Operação Vulcano,' p. 18.

61 Diogo Neto, 'Operação Vulcano,' p. 18; Nico, *A Batalha do Quitafine*, p. 247.

62 COMZAVERDEGUINÉ, 'SITREP circunstanciado no. 10/69, Período Abrangido 030000MAR69 – 100000MAR69,' 10 March 1969, ADN/SGDN/2REP/096.

63 Diogo Neto, 'Operação Vulcano,' p. 18.

64 COMZAVERDEGUINÉ, 'SITREP circunstanciado no. 10/69, Período Abrangido 030000MAR69 – 100000MAR69,' 10 March 1969, ADN/SGDN/2REP/096.

65 Nico, *A Batalha do Quitafine*, p. 242.

66 CTIG/2REP, 'SUPINTREP 14,' SGDN/2REP/088/0363/010, ADN.

67 Nico, *A Batalha do Quitafine*, p. 249.

68 Nico, *A Batalha do Quitafine*, p. 251.

69 COMZAVERDEGUINÉ, 'SITREP circunstanciado no. 10/69, Período Abrangido 030000MAR69 – 100000MAR69,' 10 March 1969, ADN/SGDN/2REP/096; COMZAVERDEGUINÉ, 'SITREP circunstanciado no.11/69, Período Abrangido 100000MAR69 – 170000MAR69,' 17 March 1969, ADN/SGDN/2REP/096.

70 Nico, *A Batalha do Quitafine*, p. 254.

71 Nico, *A Batalha do Quitafine*, p. 254; Diogo Neto, 'Operação Vulcano,' p. 20.

72 Diogo Neto, 'Operação Vulcano,' p. 20.

73 Silva, p. 120. Luís Cabral was later the first President of independent Guinea-Bissau.

74 CTIG, PERINTREP no.9/63, 4 August 1963, SGDN/2REP/083/0342/003, ADN.

75 Portugal deployed a Second World War-vintage AA No.4 Mk.IV radar set to the Mansoa vicinity of Western Guinea early in the war, and this equipment detected unidentified aerial activity on eight occasions during a single week in the summer of 1963. CTIG, PERINTREP no.13/63, 25 September 1963, SGDN/2REP/083/0342/003, ADN.

76 COMZAVERDEGUINÉ, 'Operação Ver Para Crer' (25 de Maio 67),' 27 May 1967, SGDN/1REP/105/0349/018, ADN.

77 COMZAVERDEGUINÉ, 'Operação Ver Para Crer' (25 de Maio 67),' 27 May 1967, SGDN/1REP/105/0349/018, ADN.; BCP 12, 'Relatório da Operação no.10/67 'Operação Ver ara Crer',' 26 May 1967, SGDN/1REP/105/0349/018, ADN.

78 SGDN/2REP, 'Relatório da Notícia: PAIGC,' 13 May 1969, SGDN/2REP/100/0392/014, ADN.

79 PAIGC, 'Ao Comite Central do Partido Africano da Independência da Guiné e Cabo Verde,' 5 June 1964, Pasta 04602.039, FMS.

80 Direcção General da Segurança (DGS), 'Meios Aérea do PAIGC,' 11 December 1969, SGDN/2REP/076, ADN; Direcção-Geral de Segurança-Guiné, 'Informação no. 1.230-CI (2): Meios Aéreos do 'PAIGC',' 11 December 1969, SGDN/1REP/105/0345/003, ADN. The 'PAIGC air base' was said to be planned for a location 12km from Koundara, to be built with the assistance of specialists from the People's Republic of China.

81 *The Military Balance 1970–1971* (London: The Institute for Strategic Studies, 1970), pp. 48–49; 'World's Air Forces: Guinea-Republic,' in *Flight International* 124, no.3874 (6 August 1983), p. 346; Stockholm International Peace Research Institute (SIPRI), 'SIPRI Arms Transfers Database,' 1960–1974, armstrade.sipri.org/armstrade/page/trade_register.php.

82 CCFAG/2REP, 'Estudo dos meios aéreos inimigos e dos países limítrofes,' November 1973, SGDN/2REP/106/0417/031, ADN. Senegal only received jet combat-capable aircraft in 1976, with the delivery of six French-built Fouga *Magister* armed trainers; see Defense Intelligence Agency, 'Military Intelligence Summary, Volume IV: Africa South of the Sahara,' DDB-2680-104-85, March 1985, www.dia.mil/FOIA/FOIA-Electronic-Reading-Room/FileId/162641/.

83 CCFAG, 'Estudo da situação operacional e logística do T.O. da Guiné e evolução prevista para 1970–1971,' January 1970, CEMGFA/017/0036/028, ADN.

84 Information provided to José Matos by Oliveira Couto and José Francisco Nico, email, 2013.

85 Memorandum, Ministério dos Negócios Estrangeiros to Chefe de Gabinete do Ministro da Defesa, 12 June 1968, GABMIN/007/0029/004,

ADN. At the time, Guinea and Mali were jointly negotiating a railway construction deal with China, explaining the mixed nationality of the plane's occupants; see 'Chinese to Help Build Mali-to-Guinea Railroad,' in *The New York Times*, 30 May 1968, p. 3.

86 Ministério dos Negócios Estrangeiros, letter, to Chefe de Gabinete do Ministro de Defesa (and attachments), 12 June 1968, GABMIN/007/0029/004, ADN; Diogo Neto, 'Voo em Três Frentes,'p. 323; 'Testemunho do Coronel Art Pereira da Costa,' p. 109.

87 José Francisco Nico, 'Pedaços das nossas vidas I – Intercepçao de um helicóptero em 10 de Setembro de 1967,' in *Mais Alto* 44, no.359 (January/ February 2006), pp. 16–27.

88 Abreu dos Santos and Diamantino P. Monteiro, 'O misterioso helicóptero interceptado pela FAP em meados dos anos 60,' Luís Graça e Camaradas da Guiné, 30 September 2009, blogueforanadaevaotres.blogspot.com/2007/09/guin-6374-p2155-paigc-o-misterioso.html.

89 Rodrigues, *Spínola*, p. 89.

90 'Testemunho do Coronel Art Pereira da Costa,'p. 108.

91 Chefe de Estado-Maior do Exército to CEMGFA, Processo P. 2.103.1.5/62, 11 January 1962, FO/29/1/351/51, AHM.

92 'Testemunho do Coronel Art Pereira da Costa,'p. 108.

93 SGDN/1REP, 'Defesa Aérea da Guiné – Possibilidades de Actuação Aérea do PAIGC,' 9 December 1969, 1a Divisão Aérea/3a Divisão EMFA/ CZACVGCollection, AHFA; João Paulo Véstia Dias, 'A Evolução dos Materiais de Artilharia Antiaérea em Portugal – da Génese à Actualidade,' in *Revista de Artilharia* nos.1016–1018 (April-June 2010), pp. 178–179.

94 CCFAG, 'Estudo da situação operacional e logística do T.O. da Guiné e evolução prevista para 1970–1971,' January 1970, CEMGFA/017/0036/028, ADN; Estado-Maior do Exército, 4a Repartição, 'Defesa antiaérea da Guiné – Reforço de 1 BatArt AA,' Informação no.197/LM-5093, 21 September 1970, FO/029/1/351/51, AHM.

95 'Testemunho do Coronel Art Pereira da Costa,' pp. 108–110.

96 EMFA/3REP, 'Informação no.104: Defesa Aérea da Guiné,' 28 April 1970, 1a Divisão Aérea/3a Divisão EMFA/CZACVGCollection, AHFA.

97 Mary T. Cagle, *History of the Redeye Weapons System* (Redstone Arsenal, AL: U.S. Army Missile Command Historical Division, May 1974), pp. 1, 5–7.

98 The prospect of acquiring 'Redeye' missiles from the U.S. would resurface in 1973–1974, as Portugal sought to capitalise on its support for Washington's resupply airlift to Israel during the October War against Egypt and Syria.

99 SEA to MDN, Ofício no.289, 19 April 1971, ADN/ GABMIN/007/0035/050.

100 José Cardoso Mira, 'Sidewinder: 50 anos de operação de mísseis na Força Aérea Portuguesa,' in *Mais Alto* 51, no. 403 (May-June 2013), p. 9. This was the same aircraft-missile combination that debuted during the 1958 air battles over the Taiwan Straits, to much official and public fanfare; see 'Sidewinder Upsets Peiping,' in *The New York Times*, 1 October 1958, p. 12.

101 CCFAG, 'Proposta de Reforço de Meios e Medidas Necessárias para a Concretização de um Plano de Contra-Subersão no T.O. da Guiné,' 1 May 1969, CEMGFA/017/0036/024, ADN.

102 The MiG-17F could out-run and outmanoeuvre the G.91 in all likely air combat scenarios and also carried heavier gun armament; even against USAF F-4 Phantoms II in Southeast Asia, the FRESCO was 'a vicious, nasty little beast.' Robin Olds, with Christina Olds and Ed Rasimus, *Fighter Pilot: The Memoirs of Legendary Ace Robin Olds* (New York: St. Martin's Press, 2010), pp. 313–314.

103 EMFA/3REP, 'Defesa Aérea da Guiné,' Informação no. 104, 28 April 1970, 1a Região Aérea Collection, Cx. 64, AHFA. For a USAF summary of AIM-9B limitations over Vietnam, see Pacific Air Forces Directorate of Tactical Evaluation, 'Project CHECO Southeast Asia Report: COMBAT SNAP (AIM-9J Southeast Asia Introduction),' 24 April 1974, pp. 9–10.

104 For example, see CZACVGletterto Chefe do Estado-Maior da Força Aérea (CEMFA), 27 November 1973, CEMGFA/017/0034/009, ADN.

105 CCFAG, 'Estudo da situação operacional e logística do T.O. da Guiné e evolução prevista para 1970–1971,' January 1970, CEMGFA/017/0036/028, ADN.

106 'Relatório da visita à Zona Aérea de Cabo Verde e Guiné (ZACVG) do Chefe da Secção de Comunicações,' undated, 1a Região Aérea Collection, Cx. 102, Processo 430.201, AHFA.

107 Secção de Radar da BA12, 'Relatório,' 23 March 1970, 1a Região Aérea Collection, Cx. 102, Processo 430.201, AHFA.

108 SGDN/1REP, 'Informaçãono. 283/62,' 12 October 1962, SGDN/1REP/092/0306/001, ADN.For AN/TPS-1D performance, see also North Atlantic Military Committee, 'Radar Operating Ranges, AN/FPS-8 and AN/TPS-1D,' 18 February 1954.

109 CCFAG, 'Estudo da situação operacional e logística do T.O. da Guiné e evolução prevista para 1970–1971,' January 1970, CEMGFA/017/0036/028, ADN.

110 SGDN/2REP, 'Defesa Aérea da Guiné,' Verbete no. 1592/RB, 16 June 1969, SGDN/1REP/089/0299/003, ADN.

111 EMFA/3REP, 'Medidas para protecção de aeronaves da BA12,' Informação no.169, 26 September 1969, 1a Região Aérea Collection, Cx. 102, Processo 430.201, AHFA.

112 EMFA/3REP, 'Defesa Aérea da Guiné,'Informação no. 104, 28 April 1970, 1a Região Aérea Collection, Cx. 64, AHFA. It should also be noted that the anti-aircraft armament then available to Portuguese forces in Guinea was largely obsolete and of little operational utility against the anticipated threat. However, Lisbon encountered great difficulty in its attempt to acquire more modern and effective air defence equipment given both fiscal constraints and the arms embargoes levied against Portugal by most weapons-producing states.

113 COMZAVERDEGUINÉ, 'SITREP circunstanciado no. 39/69, Período Abrangido 220000SET69 – 290000SET69,' 25 September 1969, SGDN/2REP/096, ADN; Nico, *A Batalha do Quitafine*, p. 266.

114 COMZAVERDEGUINÉ, 'SITREP circunstanciado no. 04/70, Período Abrangido 190000JAN70 – 260000JAN70,' 28 January 1970, SGDN/2REP/096, ADN.

115 Nico, *A Batalha do Quitafine*, pp. 268–271.

116 COMZAVERDEGUINÉ, SITREP circunstanciados nos.09/70 through 48/70, 23 February – 30 November 1970, ADN/SGDN/2REP/096.

117 COMZAVERDEGUINÉ, 'SITREP circunstanciado no.20/70, Período Abrangido 110000MAI70 – 180000MAI70,' 25 May 1970, ADN/ SGDN/2REP/096; *Jane's Land-Based Air Defence, 1992–1993*, pp. 207–209.

118 Rodrigues, 'Aviação na Guiné – A Parte Final,' p. 288.

119 Rodrigues, 'Aviação na Guiné – A Parte Final,' p. 288. From 13–16 May 1970, paratroops and Portuguese Army personnel conducted another operation also named *Diamante Azul*, a sweep through the same general area; see CECA, *Resenha Histórico-Militar das Campanhas de África*, 6-II-I, pp. 487–488.

120 COMZAVERDEGUINÉ, 'SITREP circunstanciado no.26/70, Período Abrangido 230000JUN70 – 300000JUN70,' 8 July 1970, and COMZAVERDEGUINÉ, 'SITREP circunstanciado no. 27/70, Período Abrangido 010000JUL70 – 070000JUL70,' 14 July 1970, ADN/ SGDN/2REP/096.

121 COMCHEFE Guiné, 'SUPINTREP no. 35 (evolução da actividade e da situação do IN no TO referente a 1970),' 20 April 1971, SGDN/2REP/088/0364/024, ADN; COMZAVERDEGUINÉ, SITREP circunstanciados nos. 01/69 through 53/72, 08 January 1969 – 31 December 1972, ADN/SGDN/2REP/096.

122 Amílcar Cabral, 'L'an VIII de notre lutte armée de libération nationale,' January 1970, Pasta 04602.062, FMS.

123 COMCHEFEGUINÉ, teletype message no. 2401, to DEFNAC, 28 July 1968, SGDN/2REP/104/0402/007, ADN; CZACVG, 'Perda do avião Fiat G-91 porreação AA,' 30 July 1968, SGDN/2REP/104/0402/007, ADN.

124 Diogo Neto, 'Voo em Três Frentes,'pp. 319–320; Correia, 'Fiat G.91 na Guiné 1966–68, 2a Parte,' pp. 35–36.

125 COMZAVERDEGUINÉ, SITREP circunstanciados nos. 22/68 through 53/72, 29 May 1968 – 31 December 1972, ADN/SGDN/2REP/096.

Chapter 5

1 José Lemos Ferreira, 'No céu da Guiné,' in *A Guerra de África (1961–1974)*, Vol. 2, José Freire Antunes (ed.) (Lisbon: Temas e Debates, 1996), pp. 590–591.

2 Luís Cabral, 'Portuguese Guinea Called United Front Against Imperialism,' '*Tricontinental* 15 (November-December 1969), in 'Translations on Africa no.867,' JPRS 49903 (20 February 1970), p. 72.

3 CCFAG, 'O Problema Militar da Guiné,' CEMGFA/017/0034/006, ADN; CCFAG to CEMGFA, 'Assunto: situação militar no T.O. da Guiné,' 3 January 1971, SGDN/2REP/074/0320/017, ADN; CECA, *Resenha Histórico-Militar das Campanhas de África*, 6-II-II, p. 437.

4 CEMGFA, 'Relatório sobre a situação na Guiné,' 1971, CEMGFA/017/0037/060, ADN.

5 CECA, *Resenha Histórico-Militadas Campanhas de África*, 6-II-II, pp. 297, 300.

6 CCFAG, 'SUPINTREP no.35,' Aditamento no.1, 20 April 1971, SGDN/2REP/088/0364/024, ADN; CECA, Resenha Histórico-Militar das Campanhas de África, 6-II-II, pp. 297, 300.

7 CCFAG, 'SUPINTREP no.35,' SGDN/2REP/088/0364/024, ADN.

8 CCFAG, 'Estudo da situação operacional e logística do TO da Guiné e evolução prevista para 1970–1971,' January 1970, CEMGFA/017/0036/028, ADN.

9 This was *Operação Diamante*, undertaken against suspected PAIGC concentrations in Salancaur-Bedanda area (Cantanhez peninsula) from 9–15 May 1969. The attack involved 11 pairs of G.91s, each armed with four 200 and four 50kg bombs. COMZAVERDEGUINÉ, 'SITREP circunstanciado no. 19/69, Período Abrangido 050000MAI69 – 120000MAI69,' 12 May 1969, ADN/SGDN/2REP/096.

10 COMZAVERDEGUINÉ, SITREPs circunstanciados nos.01/69 through 01/71, 08 January 1969 to 8 January 1971, ADN/SGDN/2REP/096.

11 COMZAVERDEGUINÉ, SITREPs circunstanciados nos.05/70 through 53/72, 2 February 1970 to 31 December 1972, ADN/SGDN/2REP/096.

12 COMZAVERDEGUINÉ, SITREPs circunstanciados nos.22/68 through 01/71, 29 May 1968 to 3 January 1971, ADN/SGDN/2REP/096; CECA, *Resenha Histórico-Militar das Campanhas de África*, 6-II-II, passim; CECA, *Resenha Histórico-Militar das Campanhas de África (1961–1974), 6 Volume, Aspectos da Actividade Operacional, Tomo II – Guiné, Livro III* (Lisbon: Estado-Maior do Exército, 2015), passim.

13 Venter, 'Portugal's War in Guiné-Bissau,' pp. 164–165.

14 COMZAVERDEGUINÉ, SITREP circunstanciados nos.01/68 through 01/72, 2 May 1968 to 2 January 1972, ADN/SGDN/2REP/096.

15 CCFAG, 'O Problema Militar da Guiné,' CEMGFA/017/0034/006, ADN; CCFAG, 'Proposta de Reforço de Meios e Medidas Necessárias para a Concretização de um Plano de Contra-Subversão no T.O. da Guiné,' 1 May 1969, CEMGFA/017/0036/024, ADN.

16 Rodrigues, *Spínola*, pp. 96–97. The SA330 Puma could carry 16 equipped troops as opposed to the Alouette III's nominal load of five.

17 'Exposição do Governador e Comandante Chefe das Forças Armadas da Guiné ao Conselho Superior da Defesa Nacional em 7–5–1971,' 7 May 1971, GB/GB0205/1729/057, AHPR.

18 COMZAVERDEGUINÉ, 'SITREP circunstanciado no.21/69,' 26 May 1969, SGDN/2REP/096, ADN/0384/024.

19 The Noratlas was frequently referred to as the 'Nord Atlas' or 'Nord' in contemporary Portuguese reports.

20 Monteiro, p. 12. The 1st Air Region was the FAP organisational echelon immediately above the ZACVG.

21 Fraga, p. 123.

22 Monteiro, p. 12; COMZAVERDEGUINÉ, 'SITREP circunstanciado no. 05/71, Período Abrangido 240801 – 310800JAN71,' 5 February 1971, SGDN/2REP/096, ADN.

23 Comando-Chefe das Forças Armadas da Guiné, Quartel General – Repartição de Operações, 'Normas de Empenhamento – Operações (2o volume) – Alteração Geral no. 7,' 15 March 1973, PT/ADN/SGDN/1REP/092/0306/005.

24 USUN, 'U.S.-Supplied Arms in Portuguese Territories,' 1 August 1963; Scott Thompson, *Douglas A-26 and B-26 Invader* (Marlborough: The Crowood Press, 2002), pp. 131–132.

25 COMZAVERDEGUINÉ, SITREP circunstanciados nos.10/71 through 25/71, 10 March to 26 June 1971, SGDN/2REP/094/0377, ADN; Fraga, p. 83.

26 Mário Diniz and Luís Proença, 'P2V-5 Neptune No. 4711: Muito Mais do que um Avião de Luta Anti-Submarina,' 2a Parte, in *Mais Alto* 50, no.398 (July-August 2012), pp. 39–40.

27 One foreign journalist who travelled to Bissau on a DC-6 reported 'Statistically it appeared that there is a 20 percent chance of engine failure on any FAP transport flight' employing the type. Al J. Venter, 'Portugal's Forgotten War,' in *Air Enthusiast* 2, no.2 (February 1972), p. 74.

28 National Security Council, 'National Security Memorandum 81: Implementation of Arms Embargo on South Africa and Portuguese African Territories' 17 August 1970, Richard Nixon Presidential Library and Museum, www.nixonlibrary.gov/sites/default/files/virtuallibrary/documents/nsdm/nsdm_081.pdf.

29 American Embassy Lisbon, telegram, to U.S. Secretary of State, 'Boeing 707s for Portugal,' 17 July 1970, Nixon Presidential Materials, NSC Files, Box 701, Country Files – Europe, Portugal, vol. I, National Archives, Washington DC; José Munkelt, '707: Ordem para voar, II – preparação, formação e operação,' in Mais Alto 47, no.379 (May-June 2009), pp. 23–24; Afonso and Gomes, *Os anos da Guerra Colonial*, p. 631.

30 John P. Cann, 'The Imperial Airline,' in *Revista Militar* nos.2521/2522 (February-March 2012), www.revistamilitar.pt/artigo.php?art_id=740.

31 CEMGFA, 'Projecto Para a Visita á Guiné,' 17 July 1971, CEMGFA/017/0037/060, ADN.

32 CEMFA, 'Substituição dos Do-27 e T-6 pelo milrole: considerações gerais,' 23 February 1973, CEMGFA/007/0013/005, ADN; *Jane's All the World's Aircraft 1972–73*, p. 77. For a detailed account of Portugal's attempt to acquire aircraft during this period, see José Matos and Luís Barroso, *Nos Meandros da Guerra: O Estado Novo e a África do Sul na defesa da Guiné* (Lisbon: Caleidoscópio, 2020), pp. 77–93.

33 MDN, 'Ofício 1473/GB,' 22 December 1970, GABMIN/007/0035/050, ADN;SEA to MDN, 'Helicópteros Alouette III para completamente da dotação orgânica das Unidades e substituição,' 28 December 1971, GABMIN/007/0035/050, ADN; COMZAVERDEGUINÉ, 'SITREP circunstanciado no.52/70,' 30 December 1970, SGDN/2REP/096, ADN.

34 José Pedro Castanheira, 'A mais espetacular ação de sabotagem dos tempos da ditadura,'*Expresso*, 16 April 2016, expresso.pt/multimedia/2016-04-01-A-mais-espetacular-ação-de-sabotagem-dos-tempos-da-ditadura.

35 SEA letter to MDN, 25 March 1971, GABMIN/007/0035/050, ADN.

36 Al J. Venter, *Portugal's Guerrilla War: The Campaign for Africa* (Cape Town: John Malherbe Pty Ltd, 1973), p. 192

37 CTIG/2REP, SUPINTREP no.16, 'Estudo do Inimigo,' 15 October 1968, SGDN/2REP/088/0363/012, ADN; CCFAG, 'SUPINTREP 32 do CCFAG: Ordem de batalha do PAIGC. Instrução, táctica e logística,' June 1971, SGDN/2REP/088/0364/023, ADN.

38 Alpoim Galvão, 'Ataque a Conakry,' in *A Guerra de África (1961–1974), II Vol.*, José Freire Antunes (ed.) (Lisbon: Temas e Debates, 1996), p. 509.

39 COMCHEFGUINÉ, 'Directiva no.58/68,' SGDN/2REP/078/0329/003, ADN.

40 MDN letter to Governador da Guiné, 22 December 1969, GABMIN/007/0029/004, ADN. The Defence Minister specifically directed Spínola to avoid 'fireworks over Senegal.'

41 José Lemos Ferreira, 'No Céu da Guiné,' in *A Guerra de África (1961–1974), II Vol.*, José Freire Antunes (ed.) (Lisbon: Temas e Debates, 1996), p. 590.

42 A FAP helicopter flying over Senegalese territory reportedly directed Portuguese artillery fire during the December attack. U.N. Letter dated 27 November 1969 from the Permanent Representative of Senegal addressed to the President of the Security Council, S/9513, 27 November 1969; U.N., Letter dated 8 December 1969 from the Permanent Representative of Senegal addressed to the President of the Security Council, S/9541, 8 December 1969; 'Portugal Censured in U.N. over Senegal,' in *The New York Times*, 10 December 1969, p. 17.

43 Morris Davis, et al, 'Factors Affecting the Role and Employment of Peacekeeping Forces in Africa South of the Sahara,' Contract no. MDA908-82-C-0174 (Urbana: University of Illinois, 1982), pp. 105–106.

44 United Nations Security Council (UNSC) Resolution 273, S/RES/273, 9 December 1969.

45 U.N., 'Letter dated 17 July 1970 from the Chargé d'Affairs a.i. of Senegal to the United Nations addressed to the President of the Security Council,' S/9875, 18 July 1970.

46 Eduardo de Sousa Ferreira, 'Amílcar Cabral: Theory of Revolution and Background to His Assassination,' in *Ufahamu: A Journal of African Studies* 3, no.3 (1973), pp. 56–57.

47 U.N., 'Letter Dated 12 December 1969 from the Permanent Representative of the Republic of Guinea Addressed to the President of the Security Council,' S/9554, 12 December 1969.

48 According to an American intelligence assessment of the operation, 'Seldom has a clandestine operation in West Africa received as much publicity or had its origins so thoroughly exposed.' CIA Office of National Estimates, 'Some Repercussions of the Raid on Guinea,' 31 December 1970, www.cia.gov/readingroom/docs/CIA-RDP79R00967A000300010002-6.pdf.

49 For a more complete discussion of the operation, see José Matos, *Mar Verde: The Portuguese Amphibious Assault on Conakry, 1970* (Warwick: Helion & Co., 2021). Calvão's own summarised account can be found in Alpoim Calvão, 'Ataque a Conakry,' in *A Guerra de África (1961–1974), II Vol.*, José Freire Antunes (ed.) (Lisbon: Temas e Debates, 1996).

50 COMZAVERDEGUINÉ, 'SITREP circunstanciado no.46/70, Período Abrangido 090801NOV70 – 1608000NOV70,' 19 November 1970, SGDN/2REP/096, ADN; Matos, *Mar Verde*, pp. 35–36.

51 Otelo Saraiva de Carvalho, *Alvorada em Abril* (Amadora, Portugal: Livraria Bertrand, 1977), p. 73; José Matos, 'Into Africa,' in *Aeroplane* 48, no.11 (November 2020), p. 89.

52 Manuel Catarino, *As Grandes Operações da Guerra Colonial, 1961–1974, XI: Ataque a Conacri, Guiné-Bissau 1970* (Lisbon: Correio da Manhã, 2009), p. 16. Lobato told the press he and his fellow prisoners escaped on their own during a coup attempt and spent several days making their way to Portuguese-held territory by truck and on foot. Manuel Murias, 'Portuguese Tells of Guinea Escape,' in *The Washington Post*, 6 December 1970, p. 31.

53 José Castanho Paes, et al, 'A Marinha na Guiné e Cabo Verde: Navios, Fuzileiros e Autoridade Maritima,' in Manuel Barão da Cunha and José Castanho Paes (eds), *Olhares Sobre Guiné e Cabo Verde* (Linda-a-Velha and Porto, Portugal: DG Edições and Caminhos Romanos, 2012), p. 243; Carvalho, p. 81; *The Military Balance 1970–1971*, pp. 48–49.

54 António Luís Marinho, *Operação Mar Verde: Um Documento Para a História* (Lisbon: Temas e Debates, Lisboa, 2006), pp. 132–133.

55 Humberto Trujillo Hernández, *El Grito del Baobab* (Havana: Editorial de Ciências Sociales, 2008), pp. 95, 223.

56 Marinho, p. 142. However, a group of 20 African commandos assigned to assault the airfield deserted during the assault and voluntarily surrendered to Republic of Guinea forces.

57 Spínola was promoted from *Brigadeiro* to *General* on 4 July 1969.

58 'Guinea Seeks Planes to Fight Raiders,' in *The Times*, 26 November 1970, p. 6; 'Guinea Again Asks Arms to Fight Foe: Touré Appeals for Planes – U.N. Mission Arrives,' in *The New York Times*, 26 November 1970, p. 14.; 'Letter Dated 22 November 1970 addressed to the President of the Security Council from the Chargé d'Affairs of Portugal,' S/9989, 22 November 1970.

59 Gabinete do Governador, Provincia da Guiné, Memorando, 25 November 1970, GABMIN/007/0029/004, ADN; COMCHEFGUINÉ telegram to DEFNAC, 271843Z, 27 November 1970, GABMIN/007/0029/005, ADN; 'Token Force En Route,' in *The New York Times*, 28 November 1970, p. 3.

60 William Borders, 'Fighting in Guinea Spurs African Unity,' in *The New York Times*, 28 November 1970, p. 3; Thomas H. Henriksen, 'Portugal's Changing Fortunes in Africa,' in *Current History* 64, no.379 (March 1973), p. 108.

61 Gerhard Seibert, 'São Tomé and the Biafran War (1967–1970),' in *The International Journal of African Historical Studies* 51, no.2 (October 2018), p. 269; Tad Szulc, 'Craft from Lisbon Fly Men and Arms to African Rebels,' in *The New York Times*, 5 November 1967, p. 24.

62 These reportedly included FAP reserve pilots, but not active-duty military personnel.

63 Michael I. Draper, *Shadows: Airlift and Airwar in Biafra and Nigeria, 1967–1970* (Aldershot: Hikoki Publications, 2002), pp. 239–241; Arua Oko Omaka, 'Through the Imperial Lens: The Role of Portugal in the Nigeria-Biafra War,' in *Journal of Global South Studies* 36, no.1 (Spring 2019), p. 200; Szulc, p. 24; Seibert, p. 271.

64 Ben Dunnell and José Matos, 'Meteor Down,' in *Aeroplane* 48, no.11 (November 2020), pp. 88–89; Seibert, p. 270.

65 'The Biafran Airlift,' in *Flight International*, 21 March 1968, p. 430; Szulc, p. 24; Seibert, pp. 269–270.

66 UNSC Resolution 290, S/RES/290, 8 December 1970. The resolution 'Appeal[ed] to all States to render moral and material assistance to the Republic of Guinea to strengthen and defend its independence and territorial integrity.' It was adopted 11-0, with four abstentions (U.S., UK, France, and Spain).

67 COMCHEFGUINÉ telegram to RPFW/DEFNAC, 272138ZNOV70, 27 November 1970, GABMIN/007/0029/005, ADN; SGDN/1REP, 'Campos de aviação,' 18 March 1971, SGDN/1REP/105/0345/003, ADN.

68 COMCHEFGUINÉ telegram to DEFNAC, 271843ZNOV70, 27 November 1970, GABMIN/007/0029/005, ADN.

69 Yefim Gordon and Dmitriy Komissarov, *The Il-28 Beagle Light Attack Bomber* (Shrewsbury: Airlife, 2002), p. 124.

70 COMCHEFEGUINÉ telegramto GERALDEFNAC, 141132ZFEV71, 14 February 1971, GABMIN/007/0029/005, ADN; Director do Gabinete dos Negócios Políticos, letter, to Chefe do Gabinete de MDN, 14 February 1971, GABMIN/007/0029/005, ADN.

71 Letter dated 17 February 1971 from the Permanent Representative of Guinea to the United Nations addressed to the President of the Security Council, S/10125, 18 February 1971.

72 Nico, *A Batalha do Quitafine*, pp. 151–152. Effective Nigerian participation seemed unlikely, however. During the recently concluded Biafran War, the competence and capabilities of the Nigerian Air Force were reportedly 'a cause for some embarrassment' for the central regime. As a result, no Nigerian pilots saw combat during the conflict, and the Lagos government relied on Egyptian crews to fly their MiG-17s and Il-28s. Davis et al, pp. 101–102.

73 Gabinete do Governador, letter, to MDN, 14 February 1971, GABMIN/007/0029/004, ADN.

74 Gabinete do Governador, letter, to MDN, 14 February 1971, GABMIN/007/0029/004, ADN.

75 *Jane's Fighting Ships 1980–81* (London: Jane's Publishing, 1980), p. 256; Afonso and Gomes, *Os anos da Guerra Colonial*, p. 256.

76 CEMGFA, 'Relatório Sobre a Situação na Guiné,' 1971, CEMGFA/017/0037/060, ADN.

77 'Testemunho do Coronel Art Pereira da Costa,' pp. 108–110. The deployed units were *Bateria de Artilharia Antiaérea* (*Btr AAA*) 3371, *Btr AAA* 3434, and *Btr AAA* (Heavy) 3382.

78 'Testemunho do Coronel Art Pereira da Costa,' pp. 109–110.

79 CEMGFA, 'Relatório sobre a situação na Guiné,' 1971, CEMGFA/017/0037/060, ADN.

80 State Secretary for Aeronautics.

81 SEA letter to MDN, 19 April 1971, GABMIN/007/0035/050, ADN.

82 SEA letter to MDN, 19 April 1971, GABMIN/007/0035/050, ADN.

83 *Jane's All the World's Aircraft 1965–1966*, p. 93; Apostolo, p. 11.

84 Marcelle Size Knaack, *Encyclopedia of U.S. Air Force Aircraft and Missile Systems, volume II: Post-World War II Fighters 1945–1973* (Washington, DC: Office of Air Force History, 1978), p. 80; 'Standard Aircraft Characteristics: F-86F -25 thru -40 Sabre' (U.S. Air Force and North American Aviation, 1 October 1956), p. 5.

85 Mira, p. 9.

86 Designs initially considered included the U.S. F-104 'Starfighter,' F-4 'Phantom II,' and F-5 'Freedom Fighter,' as well as the UK-French SEPECAT 'Jaguar.'

87 In 1972, Amílcar Cabral reportedly scolded East German officials that 'Sweden is giving us more than a number of socialist countries put together.' Gleijeses, *Conflicting Missions*, p. 212.

88 SEA letter to MDN, 19 April 1971, GABMIN/007/0035/050, ADN.

89 For a full account of Portugal's attempts to acquire French fighter aircraft, see José Matos, 'A História Secreta dos Mirage Portugueses, 1a Parte,' in *Mais Alto* 50, no.400 (November-December 2012), pp. 37–42, and 'A

História Secreta dos Mirage Portugueses, 2a Parte,' in *Mais Alto* 51, no.401 (January-February 2013), pp. 25–29.

90 COMCHEFGUINÉ, 'Análise sumária à situação militar,' 15 June 1971, GABMIN/007/0029/005, ADN.

91 CEMGFA, 'Relatório sobre a situação na Guiné,' 17 July 1971, CEMGFA/017/0037/060, ADN.

92 'Exposição do Governador e Comandante Chefe das Forças Armadas da Guiné ao Conselho Superior da Defesa Nacional em 7-5-1971,' 7 May 1971, GB/GB0205/1729/057, AHPR.

93 Spínola, p. 32.

94 Spínola, *País sem Rumo*, pp. 25–26.

95 J. Silva Cunha, *Ainda o 25 de Abril* (Lisbon: Centro do Livro Brasileiro, 1984), p. 95. Joaquim Moreira da Silva Cunha was Portugal's Overseas Minister from 1965 to 1973, and then Defence Minister from 1973 to 1974.

96 Portuguese officials concluded the murders resulted either from divisions within the PAIGC, or deliberate treachery on the insurgents' part. Luís Cabral, 'Prender Spínola,' pp. 545–546; Felícia Cabrita, *Massacres em África*, 3rd edition (Lisbon: A Esfera dos Livros, 2011), pp. 181–210.

97 Gabinete do Governador, letter, to MDN, 21 April 1970, GABMIN/007/0029/004, ADN.

98 Matos, *Mar Verde*, p. 16.

99 SGDN, 'Nota sobre as Conversação entre o Presidente da República do Senegal e o Governador da Guiné, em 18 de Maio de 1972,' 8 June 1972, CEMGFA/017/0035/012, ADN.

100 Manuel Catarino, *As Grandes Operações da Guerra Colonial, 1961–1974, VII: Pára-Quedistas Encurralados em Cassebeche, Guiné 1969* (Lisbon: Correio da Manhã, 2009), p. 14; Catarino, *As Grandes Operações da Guerra Colonial, 1961–1974*, XIII, p. 9.

101 Presidência da República, 'Decreto no.48597, '*Diário do Governo , I Série*, no 229 (27 September 1968), pp. 1509–1510. Salazar died on 27 July 1970.

102 Marcello Caetano, *Depoimento* (Rio de Janeiro: Distribuidora Record, 1974), pp. 191–192.

103 Spínola, *País sem Rumo*, pp. 28, 42.

104 Afonso and Gomes, *Os anos da Guerra Colonial*, p. 690; Amílcar Cabral, 'Para a reorganização dos Exércitos Nacionais Populares,' 1970, Pasta 04602.052, FMS.

105 CCFAG, 'SUPINTREP no.35 – Aditamento no. 1 (evolução da actividade e da situação do IN no TO referente a 1970),' 20 April 1971, SGDN/2REP/088/0364/024, ADN; PAIGC, 'Para a Reorganização dos Exércitos Nacionais Populares,' 1970, Pasta 04602.052, FMS.

106 José Lemos Ferreira, 'No céu da Guiné,' p. 591.

107 COMZAVERDEGUINÉ, 'SITREP circunstanciadono. 22/72, Período Abrangido 210801MAI72 – 280800MAI 72,' 28 May 1972, SGDN/2REP/096, ADN.

108 COMZAVERDEGUINÉ, 'SITREP circunstanciadono. 09/72, Período Abrangido 200801FEV72 – 270800FEV72,' 1 March 1972, and 'SITREP circunstanciadono. 32/72, Período Abrangido 300801JUL72 – 060800AGO72,' 9 August 1972, ADN/SGDN/2REP/096. Both incidents occurred IVO the 'corredor da Missirá,' the PAIGC's primary infiltration route into northeastern Guinea from the Republic of Guinea.

109 COMZAVERDEGUINÉ, SITREPs circunstanciados Nos. 09/72, 11/72, 12/72, 48/72, and 52/72, 1 March – 28 December 1972, ADN/SGDN/2REP/096.

110 *PAIGC Actualités*nos. 3 (March 1969), 12 (December 1969), 15 (March 1970), 19 (July) 1970, and 23 (November 1970); *PAIGC Libertação*nos. 113 (April 1971) and 121 (December 1971); PAIGC, 'Sur la situation de notre lutte armée de libération nationale,' October 1970, Pasta 04344.001.002, FMS; PAIGC, 'Communiqué special: un helicoptere et un avion sont abattus par nos combattants,' 5 June 1972, Guinea-Bissau Collection, (The Hoover Institution, Stanford University, CA); Amílcar Cabral, *Unity and Struggle*, p. 197; Amílcar Cabral, *Our People Are Our Mountains*, p. 39.

111 Brochado de Miranda, *Acidentes Mortais em Aeronaves*, pp. 28–48.

112 Brochado de Miranda, *Acidentes Mortais em Aeronaves*, pp. 28–48.

113 Amílcar Cabral, 'A Brief Report on the Situation of the Struggle (January-August 1971),' in *Ufahamu: A Journal of African Studies* 2, no.3 (1972), p. 15.

114 Amílcar Cabral, letter to Pedro Pires, 9 July 1972, Pasta 07166.008, Fundação Mário Soares.

115 COMZAVERDEGUINÉ, SITREP circunstanciados nos.01/70 through 53/72, 5 January 1970 to 31 December 1972, ADN/SGDN/2REP/096.

116 COMZAVERDEGUINÉ, SITREP circunstanciados nos.01/69 through 53/72, 8 January 1969 to 31 December 1972, ADN/SGDN/2REP/096.

117 Catarino, *As Grandes Operações da Guerra Colonial, 1961–1974, VIII*, p. 7.

118 CECA, *Resenha Histórico-Militar das Campanhas de África*, 6-II-III, pp. 225–226; Catarino, *As Grandes Operações da Guerra Colonial, 1961–1974, VIII*, pp. 7 & 10.

119 COMZAVERDEGUINÉ, SITREP circunstanciadono. 51/72, Período Abrangido 100801DEC72 – 170800DEC72, 21 December 1972, ADN/SGDN/2REP/096; Catarino, *As Grandes Operações da Guerra Colonial, 1961–1974, VIII*, pp. 7–12.

120 Catarino, *As Grandes Operações da Guerra Colonial, 1961–1974, VIII*, p. 16.

121 CCFAG/2REP, 'Colaboração de Rep.Info. do Comando Chefe das Forças Armadas da Guiné no 'Briefing' a Sua Exo. O General Cem General das Forças Armadas,' 4 January 1973, CEMGFA/017/0037/061, ADN.

122 CCFAG/2REP, 'Colaboração de Rep.Info. do Comando Chefe das Forças Armadas da Guiné no 'Briefing' a Sua Exo. O General Cem General das Forças Armadas,' 4 January 1973, CEMGFA/017/0037/061, ADN; Filipe Meneses, *Salazar: A Political Biography* (New York: Enigma Books, 2009), p. 522.

123 'Guinea to Declare Independence' (interview with Amílcar Cabral), in *Pakistan Forum* 3, no.4 (January 1973), pp. 4–6.

124 Amílcar Cabral, 'A sua última mensagem ao povo da Guiné e Cabo Verde,' January 1973, Ronald H. Chilcote Collection, University of California, Riverside CA.

Appendix I

1 Data for 1963–1966 compiled from Comando da 1a Região Aérea, 'Missão do CEM do Comando da 1a RA à Zona Aérea de Cabo Verde e Guiné entre 5 e 23 Agosto 1963: Relatório,' 14 September 1963, SGDN/1REP/077/0270/002, ADN; SGDN/2REP, 'Exposição da situação operacional na Provincia da Guiné (Jan 61 / Mar 64),' SGDN/1REP/92/307/7, and Fraga, p. 122.Values for 1967–1972 derived from ZACVG SITREPs circunstanciados nos. 01/67 through to 53/72, 10 May 1967 to 31 December 1972, SGDN/2REP/096, ADN.

2 Diniz and Proença, 'P2V-5 Neptune No.4711,' pp. 39–40.

3 COMZAVERDEGUINÉ, SITREPs circunstanciados nos. 10/71 through 25/71, 10 March – 26 June 1971, SGDN/2REP/096, ADN.

Appendix II

1 COMZAVERDEGUINÉ SITREPs Circunstanciados Nos. 01/68 through 01/72, 2 January 1969 – 31 December 1972, ADN/SGDN/2REP/096.

Appendix III

1 Mensagems 8991, 9045, 9396, and 9777, COMCHEFGUINÉ to DEFNAC, 21 July to 9 August 1966, GABMIN/007/0029/004, ADN; Miranda, *Acidentes Mortais em Aeronaves*, pp. 29, 34; José Brandão, *Cronologia da Guerra Colonial: Angola-Guiné-Moçambique 1961–1974* (Lisbon: Prefácio, 2008); José Manuel Correia, "Rotina' de Guerra: Os F-86F Sabre' na Guiné – 2a Parte,' *Mais Alto* no. 358 (November-December 2005), p. 35; 'Avião militar incendiado na Guiné,'*Diário de Lisboa* 44, no. 14953 (1 August 1964), . 2; COMZAVERDEGUINÉ, 'SITREP Circunstanciado no. 25/68, Período Abrangido 120000JUN68 – 190000JUN68,' 19 June 1968, SGDN/2REP/096, ADN; 'ASN WikibaseOccurrence # 63149,' AviationSafety Network, 3 July 2018, https: //aviation-safety.net/wikibase/63149.

2 For PAIGC claims, see *PAIGC Libertação* nos. Nos 29 (March 1963), 30 (May 1963), 35 (October 1963), 44 (July 1964), 63 (February 1966), 72 (November 1966), 74 (January 1967), 75 (February 1967), and 91 (June 1968); PAIGC communiqués dated 28 November 1965, 22 March 1966, 6 November 1967, and 28 November 1965; 'Africans Report Forcing Withdrawal of Portuguese,' *New York Times*, 21 April 1964, p. 12; 'L'an deux de la guerre de Guinee, Janvier – Decembre 1964' (Paris: Comite de soutien a l'Angola et aux peuples des colonies portugaises, 1965), p. 3;

Amílcar Cabral, 'Sur la situation de notre lutte de libération nationale,' March 1968, www.tchiweka.org/documento-textual/0103000023; 'Deux faits décisifs sont inscrits dans l'histoire de notre lutte,' *PAIGC Actualités* no.3 (March 1969), p. 4.

3 Amílcar Cabral, *Unity and Struggle: Speeches and Writings* (New York: MonthlyReview Press, 1979), p. 233; PAIGC, 'Comunicados,' 5 October 1965, Pasta 07065.068.024, FMS; PAIGC, 'Comunicados,' 28 November 1965, Pasta 07065.068.023, FMS; *PAIGC Libertação* no. 72 (November 1966), p. 3; PAIGC, 'Comunicado do Bureau Político,' March 1968, FMS; SGDN to Director Geral dos Negócios Políticos do Ministério dos Negócios Estrangeiros, 'Acção dos Terroristas Contra a Base Aérea 12 (Bissalanca),' 19 April 1968, SGDN/2REP/106/0413/017, ADN; Norberto Tavares de Carvalho, *De campo em campo: Conversas com o Comandante do PAIGC Bobo Keita*, 2nd Edition (Porto: Edição de Autor, 2020), pp. 197–199; Amílcar Cabral, 'Sur la situation de notre lutte de libération nationale;' PAIGC, Relatório das operações militares na Frente Sul, December 1969, FMS; '44 attaques contre les positions ennemies,' *PAIGC Actualités* no.23 (November 1970): p. 6; Amílcar Cabral, 'A Report to Our Friends,' *Africa Today* 20, no.1 (Winter 1973), p. 11; PAIGC, 'Aucune manoeuvre ou crime des colonialistes portugais ne sera a même d'eviter la victoire ineluctable de notre peuple africain,' January 1972, FMS; 'Importantes acções das nossas forças armadas contra Mansoa, Catió e Gabu,' *PAIGC Libertação* no.113 (April 1971), p. 1; PAIGC, 'Communiqué,' 16 May 1972, Pasta 07197.160.012, FMS; 'War Communiqué,' *PAIGC Actualités Quarterly English Edition*, September-December 1972, p. 5.

4 Mustafah Dhada, *Warriors at Work: How Guinea-Bissau Was Really Set Free* (Boulder: University Press of Colorado, 1993), p. 171; Robert D.S. Higham, *100 Years of Air Power and Aviation* (College Station: Texas A&M University Press, 2003), p. 292.

Appendix IV

1 COMZAVERDEGUINÉ SITREPs Circunstanciados Nos. 01/67through 01/72, 10 May 1967 – 31 December 1972, ADN/SGDN/2REP/096; CECA, *Resenha Histórico-Militar das Campanhas de África (1961–1974)*, 6-II-IIand *Livro III*, passim; Afonso and Gomes, *Os Anos da Guerra Colonial*, passim.

Appendix V

1 Serviço de Instrução da Força Aérea, 'Manual do Apoio Aéreo na Contra-Guerrilha,' 17 February 1972, 2a Região Aérea Manuais Collection, AHFA.

About the Authors

Matthew M. Hurley is a military historian (PhD, The Ohio State University, 2009) and retired U.S. Air Force colonel. His 24-year military career included intelligence assignments worldwide as well as instructor tours at the NATO Tactical Leadership Programme and USAF Air Command and Staff College, and he left active service in 2014 as the outgoing Chief of USAF Intelligence Doctrine and Policy. Since 1989 he has published and presented numerous studies regarding military history and aerospace developments, including works for the Air Force Research Institute and the Mitchell Institute for Aerospace Studies. This is his second book for Helion.

José Augusto Matos is an independent researcher in military history in Portugal with primary interest in operations of the Portuguese Air Force during the colonial wars in Africa, especially in Guinea. He is a regular contributor to numerous European magazines on military aviation and naval subjects, and collaborated in the major project *The Air Force at the End of the Empire*, published in 2018. He recently co-authored *Rumo à Revolução*, a history of Portugal leading up to the April 1974 overthrow of the *Estado Novo* regime. This is his seventh book for Helion.